VICTOR
An Unfinished Song

VICTOR
An Unfinished Song

JOAN JARA

BLOOMSBURY

This edition published 1998

First published in Great Britain 1983 by Jonathan Cape Ltd

Copyright © Joan Jara 1983
Epilogue copyright © Joan Jara 1998

The moral right of the author has been asserted

Bloomsbury Publishing Plc, 38 Soho Square, London W1V 5DF

A CIP catalogue record for this book
is available from the British Library

ISBN 0 7475 3994 4

10 9 8 7 6 5 4 3 2 1

Typeset by Palimpsest Book Production Limited,
Polmont, Stirlingshire
Printed in Great Britain by Clays Ltd, St Ives plc

CONTENTS

PREFACE

It is a relief, at last, to tell this story quietly, in my own way, instead of responding to sudden questions which allow me to tell only the parts of it which interest the person who is interviewing me.

During the years since the military coup in Chile, I have received so much love, friendship and support from so many people all over the world, that I feel sufficiently insulated now from the pain to remember the happiness.

Life has taught me that most of us are victims of our prejudices, of preconceived ideas, of false concepts of who is our 'enemy' or what is 'alien' to us, caused by our environment and, above all, by the mass media to which we are subject. But it has also taught me that these barriers are artificial ones and can be swept away.

The lesson began when I went to live in post-war Germany and found suffering and friends; it was continued when I went to Chile and that far-off country became my home; and in the last nine years, because of the strength of the world-wide movement of solidarity with the people of Chile, I have been lucky enough to talk to and to exchange friendship with so many apparently diverse people: with women factory-workers in Japan, with miners and aborigines in Australia, with singers and students in the USA, with children in the GDR, with artists in France and Spain, with veteran fighters against fascism in Italy, with poets and young people in the USSR, with dancers in Cuba – to say nothing of the old and new friends I found in Britain when I returned as a refugee after almost twenty years.

It is to these people that I humbly dedicate this attempt to put memories into words, together with all the Chilean and Latin American friends whose experiences I have partly shared, and to my own daughters, with hope for the future.

My deepest thanks to all the people who have helped me with this book, with their memories and their suggestions: Fernando Bordeu, Patricio Bunster, Eduardo Carrasco, Bélgica Castro, Atahualpa del Cioppo, Maruja Espinoza, Jan Fairley, Ricardo Figueroa, Francisco Gazitua, Inti-Illimani, Georgina Jara, Julio Morgado, Enrique Noiswander, César Olhagaray, Raquel Parot, Angel Parra, Isabel Parra, Roberto Peralta, Omar Pulgar, Alejandro Reyes, Claire de Robilant, Alejandro Sieveking, and Nelson Villagra, for allowing me to use his article about his friendship with Victor. My special gratitude goes to María Eugenia Bravo without whom this book might never have been started, to Frances Brown, who has accompanied and helped me all along, to Mike Gatehouse without whom it might never have been finished and to Liz Calder for her constant encouragement and inexplicable confidence in me.

London, April 1983   J.J.

VICTOR

An Unfinished Song

AN END AND A BEGINNING

As I stepped on to the plane at Pudahuel Airport, Santiago, escorted by the British consul, on 15 October 1973, I was a person with no identity. Whoever I had been – dancer? choreographer? teacher? wife? – I was no longer. I looked at my two small daughters scrambling into their seats ahead of me, both of them pale and subdued, not even quarrelling about who should have the window seat, and I was only too aware that they depended entirely on me now. Indeed, I needed them to go on living. I knew that a part of me was dead, had died with a man whose body was now lying in a coffin, in a concrete niche, high up on the back wall of the General Cemetery of Santiago.

I had left the niche covered with a rough-hewn stone which said simply:

VICTOR JARA
14 de Septiembre 1973

The date was wrong. At the time there was no way of knowing exactly which day my husband had been murdered. I had left no space for flowers. The usual little troughs in front of the niches look bare and sad when they are empty. I could not know that Victor's grave would never be without flowers, that unknown people would go to any lengths to climb up and tie tins and pots with bits of wire and string in order to leave their offerings, even though in doing so they risked arrest.

I was in a state of shock, but Victor's pain and his agony were inside me, haunted me in a very real sense. I could not close my eyes without seeing his dead body, the morgue, horrifying images of the events of the last four weeks, the result of military violence used ruthlessly against unarmed civilians, a violence so out of proportion, so annihilating that it seemed impossible to believe that such a plan had been conceived in Chile.

I was filled with the sense of an unfinished struggle, the struggle of a people who were peacefully trying to change their society, obeying the rules that their enemies preached but did not keep. I felt as though I were not one person, but a thousand, a million . . . the agony was not only a personal one, it was a shared agony that linked so many of us, even though we were forced to separate, some staying in Chile, others escaping to every corner of the world.

I was one of those who were leaving. I had a British passport, but after almost twenty years in Chile, I was returning to England as a for-eigner. Even now, I was thinking in Spanish rather than English. I had no job, no money, all our possessions were packed into three suitcases, and rather than clothes we had taken photos, letters, records.

The plane was almost empty. The flood of refugees had scarcely begun, most still waiting for visas, crowded into the foreign embassies in Santiago. The air hostesses in their neat tartan suits and brisk smiles seemed unreal, made of cardboard. As I looked down on Santiago disappearing beneath me, looking grey and undistinguished on the flat plain of the central valley, I wondered when I should return, when I should see my friends again . . . then came the rising foothills with their scrubby vegetation – was that the Maipo valley where we had spent so many holidays? – then the cordillera, the great mass of the high peaks, a lonely desert of snow and ice and jagged rocks which is always overwhelming however many times you cross it . . . and finally good-bye to Chile . . . Victor's country . . . my daughters' home . . . and mine.

The mountains dropped away, and the alien monotony of the Argentine pampa stretched ahead, all the way to the Atlantic Ocean. I had no idea of what the future might hold for me. I only knew that I had an urgent need to communicate, although the medium of dance, which had always been my own, no longer seemed relevant or possible. I had to learn to speak, to tell the outside world, on behalf of those who couldn't, about the suffering of so many people in the country which for so many years had been my home.

The children settled down to doze in their seats. Awake and alone, I felt that Victor was with us, as though I could reach out my hand and touch him. I knew that I had to come to terms with life without him. But at the same time, I knew that he would always be part of me, as though in dying he had come to inhabit me in a way that I had been less aware of when he was beside me. It gave me courage and the knowledge that I should never be lonely. I would do everything in my power to allow Victor, through his music and his recordings, to continue to work for the cause he had made his own. His murderers had misjudged the power of song.

There was no hope of sleep. I found that I was clutching my handbag in a grip of iron. Trying to relax, I opened it and took out the papers inside. There was my Chilean identity card with my fingerprints and photograph and the formal description of the stranger who had travelled to Chile nineteen years before: JOAN ALISON TURNER ROBERTS. Next to it I felt my British passport. I took it out and opened it: 'Name of Bearer: Mrs Joan Alison Jara.' I was glad it bore Victor's name. With pride and defiance I would use it through the years ahead.

Manuela and Amanda were sleeping peacefully now. I wondered where their lives would take them: when I was a child, I could never have imagined that one day I would find myself fleeing from a distant country as a refugee.

1

JOAN

My own childhood during the Second World War was dominated by the imminence of death. Living as we did in the middle of London, for several years we automatically went to bed every night in an air raid shelter in the garden, even before the siren sounded. There were long periods when every night the German bombers droned overhead and I lay listening to the whine of falling bombs, and shattering explosions which broke all the windows in the house, and saw the sky turn red with the reflection of fires. I always went to sleep wondering if we should survive the night.

The shape of my life was decided one day in July 1944, at the height of the flying bomb attacks on London, when my mother took me to the Haymarket Theatre to see a modern dance company called Ballets Jooss. That experience not only convinced me that I wanted to become a professional dancer, but also, in an indirect way, provided my link with Chile. The ballet that made such an impact on me was a choreography by Kurt Jooss called *The Green Table*. A powerful message about the horror that war brings to human beings, it acquired a special urgency when first seen at a time when death could fall at any moment from the sky.

The green table symbolised the conference table at a summit meeting, any summit meeting of world leaders. The curtain went up to a tinkling, satirical tango played on two pianos, while politicians around the table flattered one another, made rhetorical speeches, argued, applauded, took sides and confronted one another, all with precise, well-timed gestures. Ceremoniously they brought out their weapons and gave the signal for war. Death appeared, seemed to grow out of the floor, a monstrous figure part skeleton, part machine, part God, which from that moment dominated the action. Six scenes followed in which different characters met death, sometimes violently, sometimes willingly, because there was no alternative. In one, a woman saw her husband go off to war and decided against her own nature to fight in the guerrilla resistance. The dance of this woman had nothing of the conventions of other ballets I had seen. It was vital, dramatic, impulsive. I felt that she was a real woman, maybe a peasant, dancing with her whole being. I decided then and there that one day I would dance that role.

I had danced by myself since I was a small child, improvising for hours to a variety of old records that I found at home. Then, later, I had made long journeys across London during the air raids to attend classes, coming home late when people were already dossing down for the night in the Underground stations. But it had never occurred to me to become a professional dancer. The North London Collegiate School, in comfortable, middle-class Canons Park, where I had been educated since the age of nine, prepared us to go to university, and supposedly I was bound for an academic career. The other girls all seemed to live in pretty villas with gardens. Their fathers were clergymen or colonels. My family was very different.

I can remember my father only as an old man, but even then he had intense blue eyes and a way of charging around like a bull, full of tension and energy. He was the son of a bootmaker and had had no formal education, but he had read widely and become a free thinker. Proud of his working-class origin and the ability to work with his hands, he was too egocentric to be a real socialist, although he had read Karl Marx and thought of himself as one. Even at his most prosperous he did nothing to hide the fact that he was a working man. His hands were the hands of a labourer and he dressed and spoke like one.

My mother, twenty years younger than he, had been involved with the suffragette movement. She also was a socialist and had worked for Fenner Brockway as a volunteer secretary, taking notes at meetings. But after she went to live with my father, she gave up her political activities and lost touch with her own friends. She dedicated the rest of her life to bringing up her large family, sometimes regretting what she felt to be an imprisonment, not wanting her daughters to fall into the same trap.

At the peak of a successful career as manager of a large typewriter company, my father had resigned in order to go into business on his own. He bought two large, dilapidated houses in Highbury Place in north London, at that time a distinctly seedy area, and tried to make a living from his hobby – buying and selling antiques. He would buy up the contents of entire houses, and the residue – what he found difficult to sell or couldn't bear to part with – came to rest in our home, filling it ever fuller, until every space was invaded, room after room impossible to enter.

As the youngest of the family, by a large gap, I was brought up almost as an only child. Before I went to school, afraid of being left alone in what I felt to be a hostile place, I used to stick close to my mother as she worked about the house. She made journeys down to the damp, stone cellars to fetch coal for the old-fashioned boiler. From those dark sinister cells, packed with strange objects covered in cobwebs, she hauled the coal up the narrow steps to the wash-house, a place of antediluvian washing and ironing machines. Every task meant trekking through endless dark areas, with dusty pictures and maps covering the walls, lines of bookcases on stairs and landings, strange Buddhas, coats of Samurai armour sneering out of dark corners, chests full of rotting lace and embroidery, birds' eggs and butterflies, porcelain figures . . . everything you could possibly imagine, but all in a state of neglect and decay.

Worst was the bathroom, the only inhabited room on the third floor. It was large – too large, because the single lightbulb left creepy dark patches and shadows. An ancient gas boiler, coated with verdigris, exploded when it was lit, and then let out a meagre stream of tepid water accompanied by a strong smell of gas. The bath stood alone on taloned legs in the middle of the room, so that there was no protection once you were inside it. I always felt very vulnerable in the cooling water, thinking of the dark chaos in the surrounding rooms and mother so far away on the floor below.

The stories that she used to tell me were not fairy tales, but rather about her own childhood and the struggle of her family to survive in the slums of London. Her grandmother, long dead, had migrated from rural Essex to Clerkenwell to seek better fortune, but found that slaving in a laundry was the only alternative to the workhouse. She had lost a leg in an accident, and I have always retained a vision of her limping along the road to London on her wooden leg, with no money, and several children tagging along behind. Decades later, my mother had still been working in a laundry and then later as a secretary, in a struggle to keep her younger sisters from the workhouse.

The anxieties of my childhood were not helped by the fact that my parents rarely spoke to one another. My elder brothers and sisters had left home, called up into the services, so there was little to break the atmosphere of brooding silence, almost like a physical presence. At school, my home life was a guilty secret which I couldn't share, even with my closest friends. I tried to pretend that I was like them, to speak without a cockney accent, hiding my real self all the time. Only when I was dancing did I really feel happy and free, and on equal terms.

The deep impression which *The Green Table* made on me was a lasting one. A year later, Ballets Jooss came back to London. I found that if I crept up the gallery stairs after the first interval, I could get in without paying and in that way, as it always came at the end of the programme, I managed to see *The Green Table* about thirty times. On the last day of the season, an extreme sense of urgency made me overcome my shyness and be daring enough to ask at the stage door to speak to Kurt Jooss.

He came out into the narrow passageway, still in the costume of Death, his kind eyes twinkling at me out of the skull-like mask of paint. He told me that Ballets Jooss had no school at present – their school at Dartington Hall in Devon had had to close at the beginning of the war – but that I could go to their Cambridge headquarters where he would see me dance.

After my audition there a week later, at which I was almost paralysed with nerves, Jooss miraculously said that it was certainly worthwhile my having a full professional training and that he could see me as a future member of the company. So when Sigurd Leeder opened his school in London in 1947, I rather guiltily backed out of a scholarship to read history at University College so that I could continue my dance education in earnest.

Jooss and Leeder were both pupils of Rudolf von Laban. Reacting against the formality and stylistic limitations of classical ballet, they were pioneers in fusing a much wider range of dance movement into a contemporary expression that could extend from extreme lightness, elevation and fluidity, to real heaviness, fall and percussiveness. We were taught not only to dance, but to relate dance to an analysis of human movement in its widest sense and were challenged to find new forms for what we wanted to express.

In January 1951, after three years studying with Leeder, I at last achieved my ambition of becoming a member of the Jooss company, and left England to join them. Forced to flee from Nazi persecution in 1933, they had made their home for many years in Dartington Hall. Now, after the war, Kurt Jooss had returned to Germany at the petition of the new authorities of the City of Essen, who were anxious to re-create some of the cultural life which had been destroyed by the Nazis.

Joining Ballets Jooss meant going to live among people whom I had been taught to consider as my enemies. I had never attempted to make any distinction between the people of Germany and the Nazis, so to find myself among a cosmopolitan group, in which at least half my colleagues were German and had fought as conscripts in the war, was a good lesson in human relationships. In all, among the twenty-four dancers, there were ten different nationalities, speaking seven or eight languages between us. Among them were two Chileans whom Jooss had engaged as a result of a visit to Chile in 1948. In that incredibly distant country three former soloists of Ballets Jooss, Ernst Uthoff, Lola Botka and Rudolf Pescht, had created a school and ballet company when they were stranded in South America at the beginning of the war. I remember well my first sight of one of the Chileans, who later became my lifelong friend. Alfonso Unanue was sitting on the wide window-sill of the large studio in the Folkwangschule where we rehearsed, his long legs doubled up beneath him. He was tall and extremely thin and could pack his bones into amazingly small spaces. His face was a thin and exaggerated version of Fernandel and he was the most gifted clown I have ever known.

The other Chilean was a mystery man who had not yet arrived. Jooss had cast Patricio Bunster as my partner in several of the ballets. I therefore spent a month dancing with him in theory, cursing him for not arriving on time and nourishing all sorts of romantic visions of him. My first impression of Patricio when he eventually did arrive was one of shock. After three weeks of sunbathing on a ship, he was dark copper-coloured, black-haired, with large brown eyes and a face something like a Peruvian Indian pot, with wide cheek bones and a hooky nose.

At 26, Patricio was more mature than I was, full of ideas for his own choreographies, and determined to learn as much as possible during his stay in Europe. He was the first person I ever knew who professed to be a communist and he was also an extremely talented dancer. It wasn't long before I was madly in love with him. Our relationship revolved very much around our profession. The soft, liquid sounds I heard when he and Alfonso conversed together in Spanish meant nothing to me, but luckily he spoke English. We had much in common. His life, too, had been changed by seeing *The Green Table* in Santiago. It had inspired him so much that he had left the university, where he was on his way to becoming an architect, to become one of the first young men to study dance in Chile.

The next two years we spent constantly on tour around Europe, mostly in buses and rarely staying more than one night in any one spot. There was a strange contrast between the dignity of the performance and the sordidness of our daily lives. Long stretches of one-night stands probably make any group of people slightly hysterical. We were always tired, and every day had the same pattern: bus journey, theatre, performance, hotel. The days of the long tours were distinguished from one another by certain basic factors: theatres with or without showers; hotels with or without eggs for breakfast; short journeys (maybe two hours) or long journeys (anything up to eight); and the occasional dramatic interruption to the routine – such as when the bus fell into an ice-covered canal in Holland. It was a luxury to stay more than one night in one place, and it meant that we could catch up on sleep or maybe do our washing, which was a constant problem.

In 1952, when I had been with the company just over a year, I fulfilled my ambition to dance the part of the Woman, the *guerrillera*, in *The Green Table*. To perform it in the ruins of cities that had been devastated by British and American bombing was a moving and unforgettable experience. I saw what fascism had brought to Europe. In Rotterdam, Kassel and, above all, Berlin, I saw acres of rubble where before had been city centres, and audiences who had lived through the horror of it. Wherever we danced it, *The Green Table* had the same universal impact, and as the curtain went up on the first scene, an electric atmosphere was produced in the whole theatre as with no other ballet, among audience and performers alike.

In the spring of 1953, after a seven-week tour of Britain – exciting for me because it was the first time I had danced professionally in London – the company disbanded. The City of Essen had withdrawn its financial support. Patricio decided to stay on in London for a year to study with Sigurd Leeder, while I, to earn some money, auditioned for a part in *The King and I* which was being put on at Drury Lane. I was chosen to dance the 'baddie' – Simon Legree – which according to American-Siamese tradition had to be danced by a woman. It was quite a positive experience, apart from the fact that during one of the last dress rehearsals I was dropped and injured my back – an accident which was to have serious consequences later. Also, sitting through eight performances a week of *The King and I* relayed over the dressing-room intercom was rather hard to bear.

Patricio and I were married in October 1953. Even on my wedding day I had a performance, though to make it more special Patricio sat through it in the stalls rather than the gallery.

Patricio left England in March 1954 to return to Chile, leaving me to follow four months later, to a country of which I knew little except that it was his home, and that it had a ballet company with some of the same repertory as Ballets Jooss. That strange country, a long, thin ribbon on the world atlas, had become my future.

It was not surprising, therefore, that I was feeling slightly panic-stricken when on a gloomy day in July 1954 I said good-bye to my mother and boarded the S.S. *Cuzco* at Liverpool. The long sea journey, lasting six weeks, gave me time to think, while I tried to study Spanish from a Teach Yourself book. Every day, in a rather futile attempt to keep myself in training, I did a drunken barre, hanging on to the ship's rail, ignoring the curious stares of my fellow passengers. Most of the rest of the time I spent by myself, right up on the prow of the ship, looking down on the porpoises and sea-birds, enjoying the sun and the swell of the great Atlantic waves.

The glimpses that I caught of Latin America as the ship reached the Panama Canal and began the long journey down the Pacific coast were not at all reassuring: Panama itself, so full of American Marines that I thought I had arrived in the wrong country; the smell of sewage and poverty, the huge rats of Buenaventura in Colombia; in Callao, my first sight of Peruvian Indians, squatting in the streets with their babies on their backs, their costumes not in the bright colours of the tourist photos, but faded and dull with dust and the dirt of never washing, flies settling relentlessly around the babies' eyes; in the north of Chile, seemingly uninhabited ports in the middle of the desert.

Although I held on to the idea that I was going to see Patricio again,

I had bad attacks of homesickness. My whole life was centred round being a dancer, the need to belong to a company, to work under good teachers and choreographers, to have a theatre to work in, a studio to train in. Although theoretically I knew that these things existed in Chile, I couldn't connect them with the poverty and isolation I had seen on the journey.

We docked at last in Valparaiso – the 'pearl of the Pacific', the most beautiful bay along the coast and Chile's largest port – on 7 September 1954. But it was for Santiago, the capital city, eighty miles inland, that I was bound.

Arrival in Santiago meant coming face to face with the Andes mountains, massive snow-covered peaks, dominating the sky and the city, a great wall lying in wait for you around street corners, so close it seemed that surely you could reach out and touch it. Once you see it you understand immediately why Chilean children invariably paint landscapes with a line of mountains in the background.

Apart from the savage dignity of this setting, there was nothing especially pleasant about the centre of the city. The streets were set in monotonous, right-angled blocks, too narrow for the amount of impatient, noisy traffic. Everything seemed to be in a state of transition, either being pulled down, rebuilt or repaired, rather like Heathrow Airport. Frequent earth tremors had eliminated most of the older buildings, and only later would new techniques allow high-rise construction. There was a look of seediness and decadence; old-fashioned, but with no sense of the past as in a European city. Seen from above, from San Cristóbal Hill, the centre of the city seemed to jut out of an immense sea of low, dusty, flat roofs, overhung by a menacing pall of smog.

The *barrio alto*, or up-town part of Santiago, was the luxurious residential area nearest to the foothills of the Andes, where the air was clearer and fresher. Its wide shady avenues were lined with imposing mansions in a great profusion of architectural styles, set in enormous landscaped gardens complete with swimming pools. They were tended by butlers, footmen, house-maids and gardeners, while monstrous American limousines stood in the driveways. We lived in a small flat opposite Bustamente Park, on the dividing line between the centre and the barrio alto, in a neighbourhood with expensive blocks of flats and older houses.

One evening, soon after I arrived, I was walking home as it was getting cold and dark, when I saw what I thought was a bundle of rags on the pavement. A hungry-looking mongrel lying beside it snarled at me as I hurried past. When I looked closer, I saw that it was two little boys huddled together under a ragged blanket, trying to sleep and keep warm where the central heating boiler of the flats gave a little warmth to the pavement. These were *los pelusas*, stray children who had run away from their homes in the shanty towns and survived by begging, stealing and scavenging for odd scraps of food. The sight of them struck a spark of anger inside me which I suppose was the beginning of my political education.

But for the most part I was living on the other side of an abyss of inbuilt privilege. In the inbred society to which I now belonged, surnames defined class and identified the small group of families considered aristocratic. It surprised me that both father's and mother's surname were perpetuated and that a woman kept her own name after marriage. But it was less, I think, out of respect for women, than an obsessive means of pin-pointing identity and preserving a 'good' surname. I was now called Joan Turner Roberts de Bunster. Please note the 'de', which seemed to me to imply that a woman was her husband's property.

Chilean society had as many layers as puff pastry, with subtle distinctions between each layer, although at first I wasn't able to appreciate all the differences. I was invited to spend a holiday with a friend on her large estate in the south; they had extensive vineyards and wine-making plant. Her husband remarked casually at lunch one day that he would shoot outright any peasant who went on strike or made any gesture of rebellion – all communists should be killed, he said. Ridiculously, he later hurried out after me over the fields in his dressing gown, abandoning his siesta to apologise to me for what could be taken as an insult to my husband, Patricio. My host belonged to that small group of families who sent their children to Europe to be educated, went to the opera in Milan, the theatre in London, bought their clothes in Paris, and even spoke French or English at home. This was my introduction to the Chilean oligarchy, *los pitucos*.

Another expression I learned at this time was *roto*. According to my dictionary it meant broken, ragged, useless; but it was used colloquially to describe the poor and the dispossessed. Along with the term went certain expected physical attributes – Indian features, dark hair and skin, shortness of stature, and qualities like laziness, dishonesty and alcoholism, supposed to be inherent in the poor. At the same time, *el roto chileno* was supposed to be a great patriot, something of a buffoon, with an unfailing sense of humour in adversity. It was a kind of identikit character invented by the establishment so that the lower classes would recognise themselves and know their place.

For my part, although I was settling down in Chile, I was still a *gringa*: a nickname that was used for foreigners, sometimes with affection, but more often as an insult – as in 'Gringo, go home!'. It conveyed the idea of a person with little sense of humour, rather rigid and *deslavado* – faded or drab, as though the colour had come out in the wash. But being a gringa could have a certain snob value, too. My class status rose automatically because people seemed to believe that anything imported had to be superior, from culture to paraffin stoves, and to be British in particular was to be somehow pituco, as though one were related to the Queen.

I found the ballet company in Santiago very different from Ballets Jooss. Here dancers were civil servants with steady salaries and the prospect of a pension. The intensity, the speed as well as the insecurity of Ballets Jooss were missing. There were too few performances and too much rehearsal time. At midday everyone would go off home for lunch and work would start again at about four o'clock after a long siesta.

The ballet rarely went on tour – most performances were in the red plush and gilt atmosphere of the Municipal Theatre in Santiago – and when it did it was a major enterprise involving a full symphony orchestra, forty or so dancers, heavy scenery and trunks full of elaborate costumes. Some productions, like *Carmina Burana*, which also involved a large choir, could only be performed in Santiago.

This staid atmosphere was perhaps partly due to the fact that the ballet company, as well as the orchestra, was part of a great national institution, the University of Chile. In the early forties the Popular Front government had been anxious to stimulate cultural activity, and an *Instituto de Extensión Musical* was established within the Faculty of Music at the University. The Institute, in turn, founded a symphony orchestra, the ballet company and a large amateur choir. A theatre company and drama school were also added to the Faculty.

University autonomy was jealously guarded in Chile, so that these new ventures had a kind of protective buffer against the whims of changing governments. Although the predominant influences were still European and, later, North American, a kind of home-grown cultural movement grew up within which many Chilean artists were able to work and develop. Protection had its disadvantages, too. It tended to produce a stable, ideal vacuum within which work proceeded with no relation at all to people and events outside. In the fifties the university was like an ivory tower. It was a closed, élitist world controlled by members of the oligarchy. The Popular Front's dream of creating a grass-roots cultural movement had not yet been realised.

The Chilean National Ballet, as the company came to be called, had been founded and was still directed by Ernst Uthoff. He was a tall, handsome man, very nervous and excitable, whom most of the dancers respected very highly, but were afraid of because of his rather violent temper in rehearsals if he were not pleased with the results. He could be very charming or cruel in his comments. In spite of having lived in Chile for many years, he was still very German and spoke Spanish with a strong accent. 'Maestro' Uthoff had a great sense of theatre and his ballets were extremely successful, though thoroughly European in both theme and style.

On their return from Europe Patricio and Alfonso rejoined the company not only as dancers but as directors. They tried to speed up the rhythm of work and above all insisted that it was better to tour in a more mobile way, to use recorded music in order to become independent of the orchestra when necessary, and to be prepared to dance in theatres which were not ideal but were the only ones that existed outside Santiago. We had all learned from our experience with Ballets Jooss that much can be done with very simple means.

When I arrived there was some natural ill-feeling that yet another foreigner had come to compete for the very limited opportunities, but it didn't last long and soon I was accepted with apparent affection. I immediately set to work and had a stack of roles to dance: ones that I had danced with Ballets Jooss like the Woman in *The Green Table* and curiously, considering that I was a gringa, a succession of fiery, temperamental parts. One of the ones I most enjoyed was the Woman in Red in the tavern scene of Uthoff's *Carmina Burana*, where I did dervish turns on a round table and got thrown around by a lot of drunken he-men.

As I had time on my hands, I also allowed myself to be persuaded to start teaching, first of all in the school attached to the Faculty which trained dancers for the company, and later also in the theatre school, giving movement classes for actors. I had never especially wanted to teach, but faced with a class of expectant and enthusiastic pupils, I found my tongue in Spanish and began to have more contact with people. I also found that I had something worth teaching. The great quality of Sigurd Leeder's method was that he didn't impose his own style on his pupils like a fixed ideal or corset, as so many dance teachers do, both classical and modern, but rather gave each one the means to develop her or his own talents.

Meanwhile Patricio and Alfonso won their battle and in 1956 the Ballet set off on its first tour to the south without the orchestra. Now we could visit smaller towns and dance in theatres which didn't have the luxury of an orchestra pit. This was before the great earthquake of 1960 which destroyed all these buildings. Some, like the one in Concepción, were quite large, but they were all in very bad condition, cold, very dirty and infested by rats because they were so seldom used.

It was exciting to take the night train to the south – which for me was unknown country. When we woke up in the morning the train was already nearing the region called La Frontera, a reminder of the resistance of the Araucanian Indians to the Spanish conquest. I remember staring frowstily out of the window of the train and then suddenly waking up with a jerk because not only was I seeing my first volcano, an unmistakably perfect snow-covered cone among the other mountain peaks, but the green rolling countryside, with huge spreading trees the like of which I hadn't seen since I left England, was dotted with *rucas*, wigwams built from mud and branches. We were passing a settlement of Mapuche Indians.

All the way southwards the mountains kept us company, sometimes quite close by, sometimes further away, but always present. We passed forests, lakes like inland seas, and crossed wide rivers. At every halt, peasants came up to the train selling hand-woven blankets, ponchos of natural wool, thick and heavy to keep out the rain of the south; the women sold sandwiches of home-made bread with spicy pork and chili.

The first performance took place in a gymnasium in Puerto Montt – a draughty place where the wind from the South Pole whistled through the broken windows and the local population of dogs joined in the rehearsal. But the audience was warm and enthusiastic. Our visit was a great event because any sort of theatrical performance was a rarity. However, even to me our essentially European repertoire seemed very out of place in these surroundings.

Next day a *curanto* was organised in our honour – that sounds like some sort of abracadabra, but is actually a traditional meal of that region where fish and seafood abound. All sorts of things, abalones, mussels, oysters, clams, *picorocos, piures* (no English names for these), are assembled in a sort of bucket, together with pieces of pork, unpeeled potatoes and other oddments and are then buried in a hole in the ground with some hot stones. The mixture cooks slowly for hours and is then dug up and eaten. It takes a strong stomach, but when washed down with abundant wine, a curanto tastes like nothing else on earth. Although supposed to be very stimulating, it wasn't the best preparation for the next day's performance.

On a later tour we went north. Here the landscapes were different, the moist green of the south replaced by endless deserts of sand, coloured rock formations, and low, greyish scrub. The great breakers of the Pacific Ocean crashed down on to huge beaches inhabited only by sea-birds, but further north again the sea became gentler and warmer, the climate a year-round monotony where no rain ever fell.

In Iquique we danced in a beautiful miniature theatre made entirely of wood, with hand-carved seats and balconies. There Sarah Bernhardt and other European artists had performed for the millionaire, mostly British, colony, owners and managers of the nitrate mines. There were other, less graceful memories in the place. In 1907, in front of the school of Santa Maria de Iquique, three thousand striking miners with their wives and children were killed by troops sent by the mine-owners.

To reach Chuquicamata, the second-largest open-cast copper mine in the world, high up and distant in the Atacama desert, we had to travel for hours in a rickety old bus through a moonscape of rocks and stones, with mirages of lakes in the distance, until we reached the gigantic crater of the mine. It was odd to find the place full of Americans and to be shown around by them.

These early experiences in Chile seemed to me like going backwar͟
fifty years in time as well as travelling so many thousands of kilometres,
while the extraordinary beauty of the landscapes, the ocean and the
mountains made the poverty and misery much harder to see. I was
wrapped in a kind of cocoon – the egocentric life of the professional
dancer, bounded by the disciplines of training and rehearsal, as strict
as the routine in a convent. We might find ourselves in the middle of
the Atacama desert or in the land of the Mapuches, but we travelled
in our own micro-climate.

But I would have had to be really stupid not to realise what
tremendous contradictions existed between the 'official' university
cultural movement, at the service of a 'cosmopolitan aristocracy', as
the great Chilean poet Pablo Neruda put it, and the reality in which
the majority of the Chilean people lived. Neruda himself, more than
anyone else, writing when he was a political fugitive and then in
exile, sparked off the search for a way of changing this situation.
One of the few books that Patricio had brought to Europe with
him in 1951 had been a fat little red volume, already shabby with
much reading although it had only been published the previous year.
It was Neruda's *Canto General*. While I had no Spanish at the time, I
could sense that this book had a significance for Patricio which went
far deeper than the mere enjoyment of poetry. It was providing him
with the basis for what he wanted to express as a choreographer.

At this period, in the late fifties, Neruda's home in Avenida
Lynch in Santiago, where he lived with his second wife, Delia (*'La
Hormiguita'*), was in itself a sort of cultural centre where people
congregated to listen and to discuss ideas. Many activities were
launched there, because Neruda was a poet of action. I went there
with Patricio for the first time one Sunday in the autumn of the
year I arrived in Chile. We had lunch in the garden under a vine
heavy with ripe grapes and afterwards Neruda took us to some
outbuildings to show us his collection: shells gathered by him on
beaches all over the world, bottles of every shape and size, some
with ships imprisoned inside them. He showed us his collection
of quaint or vulgar picture postcards and other objects of 'kitsch',
including a porcelain hand made into a pipe holder, of which he
was particularly fond. Patricio, knowing Neruda's love of objects
with a history behind them, presented him with a policeman's cosh
which had been captured by English suffragettes in one of their

and which we had salvaged from the cellar of my

naive as I was, I was amazed at the influence of a poet –
stood in awe of him, and everyone hung on his words. His
latest was always awaited with impatience, and it was considered
an enormous honour to be invited to 'Pablo's house'. He was very
kind to me, although I must have seemed very much a gringa. 'She
looks like a dove,' he said to Patricio in his nasal voice, looking at
me across the garden. I felt like a fool, as usual.

So my first awareness of the cultural influence of Neruda was
only a superficial one. Only gradually did I begin to realise why,
especially since the publication of *Canto General*, it was so important,
affecting every cultural field, including my own of dance. Neruda
himself described how the idea of writing *Canto General* came to
him in 1938, the horror of the Spanish Civil War and the death
of García Lorca still fresh in his mind and his emotions. He had
been invited to read his poetry to the workers of the main vegetable
market in Santiago and found himself unprepared, not knowing
what to read to them. Inevitably he began to read his latest poem,
'España en el corazón', and then, he writes, 'The most important
event of my literary career took place. Some applauded, others
lowered their heads. Then all of them looked towards one man,
maybe a trade union leader. He stood up, dressed exactly like the
others with a sack round his waist, his great hands clutching the
back of the chair, and looking straight at me he said, "Compañero
Pablo, we are people who have been forgotten. I must tell you,
we have never been so moved . . ." and then he broke into tears,
heartbreaking sobs . . .'* It was after this experience that Neruda
decided that his poetry must contain the history, the geography
and, above all, the real people of his own country and his continent.
This example was followed by a whole generation of artists, in a
change which, for the Latin America of those times, was a profound
revolution.

Canto General was written in the next decade while Neruda was
on the run, in hiding, at a time of repression directed against the
Communist Party. It had begun as a poem dedicated to Chile, but
after a visit to the ruins of Macchu Picchu in Peru, Neruda converted

---

* 'Algo sobre mi poesia y mi vida', *Aurora*, July 1954.

it into a work which represented the common roots of the whole continent of Latin America.

In 1959, five years after my arrival in Chile, Patricio choreographed one of his most important ballets, and one which made dance history in Latin America. *Calaucán* was based on three verses from *Canto General*, with percussion music by the Mexican composer Carlos Chávez. To compose it, Patricio steeped himself in poetic images from Neruda's work; he studied reproductions of pre-Colombian art, Mayan and Aztec sculpture, Incaic pottery, the forms used by the Araucanian Indians in their jewellery and weaving. In spite of the grandeur of the theme, it was a short ballet, essentially a visual and kinetic synthesis. In the design of the costumes and décor, Patricio worked with Julio Escamez, a Chilean painter who had studied with the Mexican muralists.

Even the name was a synthesis. *Calaucán* is a mixture of Araucanian and Aymara words: *Callán*, which means bud, and *aucán* which means rebellious. The ballet had three parts: it began in silence, the symbolic figure of the Mother of indigenous America giving birth. Rooted to the spot, like a tree growing out of the earth, a single figure in the light, with the pulsating movements of the labour of childbirth in slow crescendo like a moving pre-Colombian sculpture. At the moment of birth, the percussion music explodes and a great stylised sun is illuminated on the backcloth. There follows a development of work, growing, fertility and sex, culminating in a great earthquake. The second scene, which grows out of the first, is the representation of a hierarchical society, the ceremonial surrounding a tyrannical god, a human sacrifice, the empire of the Aztecs. The third scene shows the arrival of the Spanish conquest, the bloody and unequal struggle where mother and son become warriors, and the eventual massacre of the indigenous people – although a repetition, now decisive and conscious, of the labour of childbirth, suggests a continuation of indigenous America.

It was exciting to be involved in the creation of *Calaucán* and to bring to life the part of the Mother. Interest was aroused in the ballet even before the première, and many people used to ask permission to come and watch rehearsals. We all felt that a great step forward had been taken and that something which was important for the future was happening – and the public and critics on the first night shared that view. Among the crowds that came backstage afterwards was

Pablo Neruda, who told Patricio he should be proud of what he had created.

But Patricio's and my fruitful professional relationship did not extend to our marriage. We were so immersed in our work that we forgot about living. I was very immature when we married. My emotional dependence was then accentuated by the fact of living in a country that was strange to me, with my profession as my only point of reference. In that field, too, Patricio had the dominant role – as choreographer. Although he was naturally a very considerate person, I found my dependent roles as listener or performer in contradiction with my potentially bossy temperament. I think it was a sort of symbol of our relationship that if we went out together, Patricio always walked tensely and hurriedly about two paces ahead of me, in the Indian tradition, while I drifted along behind, resenting it but saying nothing.

Although professionally there was great understanding between us, our marriage just dried up and I was suddenly presented with the fact that Patricio had fallen for a younger dancer in the company, an ex-candidate for Miss Chile who whizzed around on a mauve motor scooter. I couldn't cope with it. To make matters worse, I was expecting my first baby. It was an agonising time, which I won't dwell on, but it brought upon me a physical and nervous breakdown. Our marriage had ended before Manuela was born.

In May 1960, before Manuela was four weeks old, the southern region of Chile, from Santiago to the island of Chiloe, was shaken by a cataclysm which changed its whole geography: earthquakes too great to be registered on the seismograph; volcanic eruptions from six volcanoes at a time. Mountains moved, rivers changed their courses, and in Chiloe ships were swept inshore and the coastal town of Puerto Saavedra disappeared under tidal waves which were felt as far away as New Zealand and Japan. Even after the main cataclysm on 22 May, the earth continued to tremble constantly for a long period. Although Santiago suffered relatively little, the continuing earthquakes, combined with the horrifying news of the disasters in the southern part of the country, produced in me a sense of doom. Living in Chile, you get used to mild earth tremors, but this was different. It had a prehistoric dimension. You were reminded of how precariously Chile was perched between the Andes and the Pacific Ocean.

For me, memories of the horror of that time are mingled with my own personal nightmares. Lying ill in bed, looking up at the swaying lamp, hearing the furniture rattling, in a state of deep depression, my mood was completely in tune with the disasters that were taking place. I had come to an end, a full stop, and wouldn't have cared if the building had fallen on top of me. Only the thought of Manuela, my wrinkled, wizened little baby, forced me to hold on to a thread of responsibility and not give up completely. When I came round from the anaesthetic after she was born, she was lying in a cot beside me, her large, intense eyes wide open in her congested little face. She seemed to look at me accusingly, demanding to know what I had got her into. I didn't know myself, I had no way out of the mess we were in. For the first time in my life my body wouldn't respond. It had gone on strike. My mind went round in obsessive circles, chained to a hopeless situation, to the past, which was all over. I was full of desperation, fury and even hatred.

Patricio's leaving me had made me feel a completely useless and unwanted outsider in Chile. At the same time I had already spent too long there not to have cut many of my links with Britain. I couldn't face the idea of coming 'home'. I hardly remember the details of that long winter, but I spent most of it ill in bed, my body refusing to get better. I tried on several occasions to get back into training, although it was impossible for me even to think of going back to work with Patricio. However, each time, my efforts were frustrated by ill-health and by the condition of my spine, which needed extensive treatment and perhaps, they told me, an operation. Maybe it was foolish even to contemplate continuing my career, which seemed to be all that was left to me.

While I was still in this frame of mind, on a dull afternoon during my long convalescence, I heard a rather timid knock on the front door of the flat. Wondering who it might be, I opened the door and found myself looking at a white-toothed smile which gleamed at me out of the dark passageway. It was one of my pupils from the theatre school, Victor Jara, standing with a small bunch of flowers held in front of him like a shield, a stocky figure with black, curly hair. I asked him in for a few minutes and thanked him for the flowers. I believe he asked me if I knew of a book about Japanese Noh theatre in which he was interested. It was a brief conversation, but it made me feel just a little bit less desperate for a moment. It was good to feel that my students remembered me.

2

VICTOR

Under a brilliant starry sky at the end of a long, hot summer, flames from a huge bonfire lit up the group of men, women and children squatting on the dry ground. They were peeling the husks off the golden maize cobs, piling them into great heaps, ready for spreading out to dry on the low, tiled roofs of the adobe houses. In the tiny village of Lonquen the peasants were gathered in a traditional *trilla* (threshing). Less than fifty miles from Santiago, but completely remote from it, Lonquen was tucked away in the hills near Talagante, with only an unmade track connecting it to the main road. It was a region where folklore and superstition were a part of everyday life, where furniture was made out of local rushes and where, although there were no shops, clay cooking ware could be bought from the nearby potters' village of Pomaire.

When the maize was ripe, the families of the peasants who were *inquilinos*, or labourers on the great estates, took it in turns to help each other harvest the modest crops that they grew for themselves, working late into the night in the only time that was their own. With a drink of *chicha* (a potent, semi-fermented grape juice), story-telling and, above all, guitar music and the singing of traditional songs, they converted a long night of collective work into a celebration. Most of the older children worked side-by-side with the adults, but the smaller ones played around the heaps of corn, keeping within the circle of light from the bonfire, scared of the flickering shadows and the surrounding darkness.

This was Victor's earliest childhood memory. He told me how he would lie on the ground, looking up at the stars, and see his mother sitting on one of the piles of maize, singing and playing her guitar, talking and joking with the people around her. He would fall asleep to the sound of her singing.

Lonquen belonged almost entirely to the Ruiz-Tagle family. The surrounding land was their estate and their great mansion dominated the village, which consisted only of a church, a school and a straggling unpaved street lined with the houses of the labourers. As the owners of a *latifundio*, the Ruiz-Tagle family, powerful and immensely rich, belonged to the Chilean oligarchy. Like other members of their class, they organised their domain on almost feudal lines. Each inquilino received a tied cottage with a small patch of land surrounding it which, together with another strip some distance away, had to suffice to grow the family's food – principally maize, beans and potatoes. The inquilinos were allotted the poorest land, and it wasn't easy to harvest good crops from it. Actual wages were minimal, and were usually spent in advance on flour, sugar, *mate* and perhaps, once a year, some material to make clothes.

In return, long hours of labour were expected by the *patrón*. Each household had to provide a workforce of at least two men, while the women too had their own special duties. If the children were too small to work, then the inquilino had to 'employ' someone worse off than himself, who, in exchange for board and lodging, would make up the necessary quota of work.

In Lonquen, the inquilinos' houses were all identical – made of adobe, with a heavy roof of curled clay tiles jutting out to cover a narrow veranda at front and back. There were just three small, dark rooms, with shuttered windows; no electricity, only oil lamps or candles; water from a well or the nearby stream; cooking done outside in a round earthen oven with a grid for boiling.

On the outskirts of Lonquen, where the land of the Ruiz-Tagle family ended and the estate of Fernando Prieto began, lived Manuel Jara and his wife Amanda, with their children Maria, Georgina (Coca), Eduardo (Lalo), and the youngest at that time, Victor. Manuel was slight, dark, with weather-beaten, aquiline features. He was embittered with the heavy toil of being an inquilino and saw his children more as additional labour than as independent human beings. When he was 6 or 7 years old, Victor used to accompany his father to work in the fields. Sometimes, as a great treat, he would get a ride on the harrow, but mostly he remembered trudging along the line of the furrow, helping to guide the heavy oxen, as his father plunged the primitive wooden plough into the earth, backwards and forwards the whole day long.

> I tighten my grip
> and plunge the plough into the earth,
> for years and years I have worked . . .
> no wonder I am worn out.
>
> Butterflies are flying, crickets singing,
> my skin gets darker and darker,
> and the sun glares, glares and glares.
> Sweat furrows me, I make furrows in the earth,
> on and on.
>
> ('El arado')

Amanda was a short, thick-set woman with a wonderful smile that lit up her whole face. She came from a tiny hamlet called Quiriquina in the province of Ñuble in the south of Chile and obviously had a strong strain of Mapuche Indian blood in her. She never spoke about her mother, nor knew who her father was, but as a child she had learned the folk music of the countryside, the songs which are sung at weddings, funerals and harvest-time. She had a sweet, strong voice and was very much in demand as an entertainer, as well as being respected as a hard-working woman.

Victor used to go with his mother to other houses in the village when, as happened all too often, a baby died. Strangely enough, the all-night wake was a festive occasion. People believed, or tried to believe, that the dead baby had been converted into an *angelito* or little angel who would await his parents in heaven, perhaps putting in a good word for them with God in the meanwhile. By tradition, the baby's body was propped up in a sitting position, made-up, dressed in white paper and surrounded by home-made paper flowers – real ones would have been too expensive.

The singing went on all night. For the first few hours it was *canto a lo divino* – solemn religious songs, to console the parents for their loss, very often as though the child itself were singing. But towards morning they changed to *canto a lo humano* – songs with a more earthy content. Although the musical form and the style of singing were traditional – a sort of strange chanting, with a slurred lowering of the voice at the end of each phrase – the verses were improvised endlessly by the singers. Half asleep and half awake, Victor curled up on the floor beside his mother as she sang, mesmerised by the long ceremony in the candlelight, hearing the wailing and sobbing of the dead child's mother and the drunken laughter as dawn broke.

Like so many Chilean peasant women, Amanda was the mainstay of the household. Every night she kneaded dough and left flat lumps of it, *tortillas*, buried in the ashes of the dying fire so that next morning, after scraping off the charred bits from the outside, the bread was ready for breakfast. To hungry children it tasted very good. Amanda grew vegetables and kept chickens as well as a pig on the small plot of land behind the house. She also made cheese from goat's milk, so although meat was a luxury kept for very special occasions, the family diet was healthy enough.

It was the children's job to collect firewood every evening before it got dark, so Lalo and Coca, with Victor trailing along, would go off into the walnut woods armed with a large knife and an axe, to come back, dragging bundles bigger than themselves, with armfuls of grass for the pig. Amanda did her best to supplement the family budget and mobilised the children to help her, gathering herbs on the hillside, and tying them into small bundles to sell with the big basket of eggs she would take once a week to the neighbouring town of Talagante. Sometimes, too, they helped her make sausage-shaped curd cheeses, when there was milk left over from the round she had on the next-door estate.

To earn a little extra money, Amanda also took in a lodger, the teacher from the village school. She provided a room and meals, as well as doing his washing, together with that of the rest of the family, in a cauldron over the fire. Victor was happy with this arrangement because the young man played the guitar, which gave him the chance not only to listen, but also to hold the instrument and to learn to play his first chords. His mother was always too busy to teach him.

Victor and Lalo slept together in the same bed, in their parents' bedroom. It was very cold in winter, but early every morning Amanda hauled them out of bed to go and wash in the nearby stream before breakfast. Shoes were an unknown luxury. At best they had *ojotas*, rough home-made sandals with leather thongs and thick soles cut from an old motor tyre. Clothes were scarce, too, so they shivered with cold in the early-morning frost as they ran down the road to the school.

The relationship between his parents was strained even when Victor was small. His father became more and more morose, seemingly unwilling to face the responsibility of supporting his family. He had already begun to drink heavily and would disappear from home for days on end, leaving all the work to Amanda. He used to return, drunk and aggressive, to quarrel with her and to beat her. After punishing his children, too, Manuel would sit down and expect to be waited on and fed. These scenes of violence at home filled Victor with a sense of resentment against his father which never left him.

> I remember the face of my father
> as a hole in the wall,
> mud-stained sheets,
> an earthen floor,
> my mother working day and night
> weeping and shouting.
>> ('La luna es muy linda')

Even as a small child he began to feel that it was his duty to help and support his mother. Her hard work, her optimism and discipline, kept the family together and, as Victor put it, 'made hardship bearable'.

When the house was full of shouting and quarrelling, Victor would escape up the hillside that loomed over the house, to find refuge in the quietness and space high above. The hill was crowned with a rough wooden cross to keep evil spirits away and there was a large slab with the imprint of a cloven hoof which people called the Devil's Footstep. It was an eerie place, but on a hot summer's day Victor loved to lie on the warm rock looking out over the wide spaces of the fertile plain, with the straight lines of willow and poplar marking the irrigation channels, towards the ranges of the coastal mountains in the far distance. Behind, the snow-covered peaks of the Andes; nearby, the tall, twisted cacti, dry gorse and bare rocks of the hillside. Lizards and crickets kept him company. He observed the life and relationships of the insects and always collected special stones or plants that drew his attention. He kept them afterwards under his bed. Coca commented to me later, 'Victor always noticed the form and texture of things.' However, when dusk began to fall, he would slide down the hillside on his behind and run home as though the Devil were really after him.

The Devil haunted Victor's childhood – as a real and menacing figure who would take him away to eternal punishment in Hell if he were a bad boy. There was no radio in the house, and on summer evenings the grown-ups used to sit out in the fresh air on the veranda, talking and telling stories. Victor, in bed with the other children, could hear the murmur of voices through the open shutters. He listened to the tales they told about evil spirits, about La Calchona, half woman half goat, who was supposed to haunt the surrounding countryside, frightening people who walked alone into giving up their possessions. He heard of fugitive lights which would lure you away for ever if you followed them, and he heard above all about visitations of the Devil.

Even though the family didn't go regularly to mass, certain religious rites were an essential part of their lives. More from superstition than a truly religious feeling, they paid money to the Virgin to ward off bad luck, money that was badly needed to buy food and clothes . . .

> Candles always burning,
> one must take refuge in something.
> Where will the money come from
> to pay for faith?
> They frighten the poor so much
> so that they will swallow their suffering,
> so that they will cover their misery
> with the images of saints.
> > ('La luna es muy linda')

Traces of this background of superstition and a feeling for magic were to remain with Victor all his life, whether in small things, like an inexplicable, but always successful, cure he had for warts, or in more important ones, like an eerie sense of premonition, almost like 'second sight'.

The children were very different in temperament. Maria, the eldest, was grown up for her age. Coca was a tomboy and didn't like 'girl's' work. She preferred to run wild with Lalo and was good at fighting. Together they teased Victor, who was not only younger and quieter, but annoyed them because he was independent and seemed to have a life of his own.

Manuel was illiterate. All he wanted was for his children to be ready to help him with his work on the land. Amanda, however, had different ideas. She herself could read and write – very unusual for someone in her position – and she was determined that the children should receive the best education possible. All of them were sent to school and attended very regularly.

Victor was a very good student. He was interested in everything, pestering the teachers with questions, absorbing information and ideas like a sponge. He loved taking part in end-of-term performances with sketches improvised and invented by the children themselves, and had great success as an actor. Two years running he was voted *El mejor compañero* by the children of his class, a term which meant not just most popular classmate, but the person most likely to stand up for them.

Later, the children were to remember the time in Lonquen as a happy one. In spite of Manuel's absences and their spartan life, there was usually food to eat and some peace and continuity.

All of it came dramatically to an end one day when Amanda was out, as usual, doing the milk round and the children were at home alone. Maria, now 13 years old, was doing the family washing. She had a cauldron of boiling water on the stove and tried to push a large log into the fire below to stoke up the flames. Almost in slow motion, the other children saw the cauldron overturn on top of her. She screamed and screamed, but they didn't know how to help her. In desperation, she ran out of the house and threw herself into the stream to try to stop the pain. Coca rushed to get help, and when Amanda came back she managed to organise transport to get her to a hospital in Santiago – there was no medical attention in Lonquen.

Maria had to stay in hospital for almost a year. At the time, Amanda was pregnant with the youngest son of the family, Roberto. Maria's help in caring for her younger brothers and sisters had been indispensable, allowing her mother the freedom to go out to earn extra money. Manuel could not be relied upon, and with the new baby coming, Amanda took the decision to move to Santiago, in the hope of finding work which she could undertake without abandoning her children.

*   *   *

The Central Station of Santiago, a cast-iron structure designed by Eiffel, lay in the heart of a neighbourhood which seemed to have enduring links with the far south of Chile and also with the nearer surrounding countryside. Around seven o'clock every morning the slow trains from Puerto Montt and Temuco arrived, bringing Mapuche Indians armed with ponchos, blankets and bunches of red copihue flowers to sell. The wooden carriages were full of peasant families migrating to the city, laden with packages of food, live chickens and spiced sausages from Chillan. They seemed to get no further from the station than their legs would carry them, mixing with the peasants in the nearby bus station who had arrived from Talagante, the Isla de Maipo and the provinces closer to Santiago. Some had relatives already settled in the city. Others had to start from scratch.

Surrounding the station was a busy commercial centre, with small shops selling cheap working clothes, haberdashery and electrical goods. There were all-night chemists', dubious restaurants and bars on the ground floors of decaying buildings whose upper storeys were converted into tenements. Narrow, dark staircases disappeared upwards between peeling walls. It was the district of prostitutes. The brothels were concentrated in Maipu Street, just opposite the station, and it was a dangerous place to walk at night.

Just a couple of blocks away, behind the shops in the Alameda, the main thoroughfare, was a large, shabby, oblong building. This was a covered stadium, the Estadio Chile, a local centre of entertainment used regularly for boxing tournaments, bouts of 'Catch' or all-in wrestling, and sometimes for song festivals or seasons of operetta. Holding about five thousand people, it was a place that was to figure largely in Victor's life. But close to all this and mostly along the western side of the railway line to the south, were block upon block of low, flat-roofed houses in sordid streets. The further you walked from the Alameda, the seedier and more poverty-stricken the streets became; there were more dirty, barefoot children; more drunks hanging around the street corners; hungry stray dogs investigating the rubbish strewn in rutted, unmade roads; crumbling stucco giving way to a patchwork of wood, corrugated iron, tin and cardboard. Passing the gasometers, where the air became heavy with the smell of gas, you came to a piece of waste land where Población Nogales had grown up. It was a grey, depressing place; hot and dusty in summer, it became knee-deep in mud when the winter rain-storms came. Through it ran an open sewage canal, a playground for children who poked around among the debris on its rat-infested banks and even bathed in it in hot weather.

This was Victor's first experience of the city. Huddled into one room, sleeping together on mattresses on an earthen floor, the children found themselves in a hostile environment. After the quietness of the countryside, the noise, the filth and the lack of privacy were unbearable. The gangs of other children seemed aggressive, knowing and self-sufficient. Amanda did her best to protect her children by maintaining strict rules and discipline, trying to keep the same standards of cleanliness and order as before, but it wasn't easy.

Victor was sent, with Lalo, to a nearby Catholic school, called Liceo Ruiz-Tagle, after the same family that owned Lonquen. Julio Morgado, a friend from Población Nogales and a classmate of Victor's, told me that both Victor and Lalo were very diligent students who always gave in their homework on time. 'They arrived together, very early every day,' he told me, 'and they were always clean and tidy. They weren't allowed to stay out in the street after school like the rest of us.' This must have been Amanda's discipline in action.

Victor finished his primary education in this school, receiving the highest marks in every subject except handicraft – which is odd, because he was clever with his hands. Being a Catholic school, religious instruction was obligatory. The obligation of confessing his sins seems to have made the Devil of Victor's childhood nightmares reappear. Later he said, 'I was frightened . . . They made me learn the catechism by heart in order to take communion . . . but when it came to confessing I felt a terrible pressure on me . . . I felt that I was a very bad person and that I wasn't telling the truth about myself . . . that I was only confessing to some of all the wicked things I had done.'

Through a friend, Amanda had got a job as a cook in a small restaurant opposite the station, and the family were able to move into living quarters on the floor above. After a couple of years of slaving away there, she had saved enough money to be able to buy a stall in the market and set up her own *pensión* where market-workers paid by the week for their daily meals. There was no lack of clients and the family were a little better off, but Amanda was rarely at home and the children missed her companionship. Victor used to lie in bed at nights worrying about his mother working herself to death, resenting his father for his long absences and his sudden brutal reappearances.

Soon, they all moved to a small house in Jotabeche, a street to the south of Alameda. It was an improvement on the lodgings over the restaurant, if only because it had a small patio with fruit trees at the back. It was quite a walk to the market, and every day at two o'clock in the morning Amanda would set out, with only her dog to protect her, to cross the iron footbridge over the railway and thence to the deserted market. She had to prepare the soup and stew and bake the bread to be ready for the first workers who began to arrive at around four o'clock and liked to begin the day with a proper meal.

At dawn the market-workers would be joined by men who had spent the night in the brothels in Maipu Street or in the bars around the station. They came to guzzle hot, oniony shell-fish or pig's-head soup to clear their heads before going home to face their wives. Amanda worked all day long until six o'clock in the evening, cooking, serving, washing-up, and was exhausted when she got home at night. During the week, after school, and on Saturday mornings, Victor used to help her in the restaurant or earn a few pesos carrying sacks or baskets for the buyers in the market.

Amanda didn't sing now, partly because she had no time, but also because nobody asked her to. In the city most families had radios and the music to which they listened was that of the commercial groups singing boleros, mambos, tangos, Peruvian waltzes and Mexican corridos. The musical invasion from the United States had not yet begun.

His mother's guitar stood abandoned in a corner and Victor tried to play it, discovering chords and melodies by ear, making his own music, inventing the words of songs, but desperately wanting to learn to play properly. Next door to the house was a wine-shop with an illegal bar in the back patio, but from the house beyond it Victor used to hear someone playing the guitar very beautifully. One day the front door of this house was open and he leant against the doorpost to listen.

The player was a young man called Omar Pulgar. He was about eighteen, and had had some musical education. His family had come down in the world when they came to live in Jotabeche and tried not to mix with their neighbours, feeling themselves to be superior. However, when Omar looked up from his playing and saw this boy whom he had seen occasionally passing in the street, listening so quietly and attentively, he realised that he must have a real understanding for music.

Omar invited Victor into the house and offered to teach him what he knew. He was surprised by Victor's capacity for absorbing everything he could teach him and also by his ability to invent melodies and songs. Omar didn't know that Amanda was a folksinger – he knew her only as a hard-working stall-holder in the market – but one day he took a recording of a very beautiful folk-song to play in Victor's house and he noticed that Amanda was crying as she listened to it.

At home, Amanda was very quiet and hid her feelings from her children. Outwardly stern and strong, she seemed inaccessible to them, although at work she was very sociable and easy-going. Her continuous efforts had improved the family fortune, but Manuel no longer lived with them. He was growing melons on a small plot of land to the south of Santiago, bought by Amanda with profits from the restaurant. Sometimes by chance Victor would see him with his horse and cart when he brought his produce to market.

When Maria, who had become a nurse, got married, she and her husband remained in the house in Jotabeche, while the rest of the family moved to a district nearer the market, behind the Central Station, which had the expressive name of Little Chicago because of the concentration of small-time gangsters, thieves and criminals of all sorts who lived there.

The only escape from this atmosphere of organised crime, and the only source of cultural activity in the neighbourhood, was the church. On the wide avenue called Blanco Encalada was a cultural centre for young people belonging to Acción Católica. An early symptom of the outward-turning that was to sweep through the church in Latin America as a whole, Acción Católica aimed to involve young people and workers both in church affairs and in the community. Later many of these young people became activists in the Christian Democrat Party when it was formed.

Victor joined this community group in his adolescence, meeting other young people from the same kind of background as his own. They sang, listened to classical music, formed a choir, went on excursions and played football. It also involved going to mass regularly, studying the lives of the saints and the defence of religion against heresy.

Meanwhile, in obedience to his mother's wishes, and with the idea of being able to help her with the family business, Victor was studying at a commercial institute where the secondary education was oriented towards accountancy. But he hated it and got only very mediocre marks for his work. His secret dream was to become a priest. That seemed to him to be the highest ideal to which he could aspire. He was concerned about his brother and his sister Coca, both of whom had long ago abandoned their studies. Lalo had become a father at sixteen. Coca had become pregnant and had tried to commit suicide, while in spite of Amanda's efforts, they had become involved with local gangs. Then, one day in March 1950, a normal day at the beginning of the school year, Victor was called out of the classroom to learn that Amanda had collapsed and died from a stroke while she was serving in the market. It was the end of an epoch.

Victor was 15 years old when Amanda died. It was a profound shock for him. He loved her deeply and had always felt that one day he would be able to help her more, to relieve her of the need to work so hard. Now he was left with a sense of desolation and emptiness, almost of guilt.

It was in Población Nogales that he found real friends to help him. Julio and Humberto Morgado had been classmates of Victor's in primary school, and their father 'Don' Pedro Morgado was a generous man who had been a friend of Amanda. Almost six feet tall, a giant in a Chilean shanty-town, he was the owner of a lorry which looked as if it would fall to pieces if the engine were started. He earned his living doing *fletes y mudanzas* – removals. He and his wife Lydia gave Victor a bed and a meal when he needed it, and their house became the nearest to a home that he was to have for many years. Victor did not go back to the Commercial Institute, but took a job instead at a furniture-maker's, helped Don Pedro on the lorry and tried to manage on his own.

He sought help from one of the priests in the church in Blanco Encalada with whom he was friendly. Padre Rodriguez knew something of Victor's problems, understood his sense of loneliness and even let him stay in his own house for some weeks. He thought he detected in Victor a real religious vocation and on his advice, in the winter of 1950, Victor entered the seminary belonging to the Redemptorist order in San Bernardo, a small town to the south of Santiago.

In 1973 Victor recalled, 'It was a very serious decision for me to enter the seminary. Looking back now, from a more mature point of view, I think that it was for very intimate and emotional reasons; it was loneliness and the disappearance of a world which until then had been solid and enduring, with a home and maternal love. I already had a relationship with the church and at that moment I found refuge in it. At the time I thought that that refuge would guide me to other values and to find a different and more profound love which perhaps would compensate for the lack of human love. I thought that I would find that love in religion, dedicating myself to becoming a priest.'

Victor entered the seminary full of idealism and a sense of mysticism, to find himself part of a community which had no links with the outside world. It was an enclosed religious order with a life of strict discipline in the framework of a rigid hierarchy.

The most enduring and positive parts of this experience for Victor were the sacred music, Gregorian chant in particular, and the theatrical elements of the mass itself. But he found unbearable the obligation to deny his body. The prime, the cardinal sin was fornication or the mere temptation to it. It had to be met with self-inflicted punishment – by beating one's own naked body under the shower. Victor found it sick and deforming. 'During those two years,' he later commented, 'everything healthy, that implied a state of physical well-being, had to be put aside. Your body became a sort of burden that you were forced to bear.'

He himself realised that the studies, the rigour and discipline of the seminary demanded a profound and authentic vocation which he did not have. He discussed his problems with his superiors and in March 1952 it was agreed that he should leave.

Ten days later he was called up for military service. This was obligatory for all men at the age of eighteen, but apart from those who chose to go to the military school as officer cadets, the majority of middle-class youth successfully avoided it. Victor, however, accepted it as inevitable and even convenient, because it postponed any decision about the future. The conditions, which were spartan in the extreme, were no hardship to him and meant that he did not have to worry about clothing, food and lodging. The contrast with the seminary couldn't have been greater. For Victor it was a sort of liberation and he began to grow up at last. He enjoyed the weekend leaves, going out with a gang of fellow-conscripts to the local bars and brothels.

When questioned many years later, in August 1973, about his military service, Victor said, 'I think that the professional soldier, from the fact of wearing uniform and having power over the rest of the contingent, loses the sense of his own class. I think the exercise of command makes him, consciously or unconsciously, put himself on a different plane and see life from a different point of view. He believes himself to be superior. As a shaven-headed private, I remember having to polish an officer's boots or do the cleaning in his house and I thought it very natural . . . indeed, I thought it almost a privilege to be called upon to do it, because it meant that I was a very disciplined bloke who could be trusted to do the job properly. But looking at it now, without that innocence, I think it was a conditioning – it conditions the servility of the private, just as it conditions the superiority of the officer.'

But at the time, Victor didn't analyse the pros and cons. He just got on with the job in hand. The results can be seen in the comments on the certificate he received on leaving the service as a sergeant first class, with officer potential:

Military conduct:	Excellent
Preparation for superior grade:	Accomplished
Military aptitudes:	He has military spirit and leadership quality
Personal aptitudes:	Very hard-working, polite, co-operative, good habits
Military arrests:	None
Has he military value?	Yes

On 12 March 1953, at the same time that I was dancing with Ballets Jooss at Sadler's Wells, Victor left the Infantry School in San Bernardo. He came back to Población Nogales with no idea of what he wanted to do. He had no training, no prospects, no money, no real family, no girl friend. The future was a blank.

After leaving the seminary, Victor never again went to mass, and on his return from military service he cut all his links with Acción Católica. He never returned to Little Chicago either. He had no home there now. Indeed he had no real home anywhere. His sister Maria's husband disapproved of his abandoning his career in the church and refused to have him in the house. Victor preferred to return to Población Nogales where the Morgado family and his group of friends welcomed him with casual hospitality, without much curiosity about what he had been doing in the three years he had been away. He began to study for his final exam as an accountant which he had abandoned when his mother died and at the same time he got a job as a porter in the casualty department of the local hospital.

The one aspect of life in the seminary that Victor missed was the music, so when he chanced to see an advertisement in the paper for an audition to enter the University Choir for the production of *Carmina Burana*, he decided to present himself for it. He was accepted as a tenor and took part in Uthoff's production in the Municipal Theatre, dressed as a monk in a brown habit. Here, about a year later, he saw me dancing the Woman in Red.

By the end of 1954, Victor had acquired a new awareness. He gave up his job, took out his meagre savings and travelled to the north of Chile with a group of new friends from the choir to collect and investigate the folk music of the zone. He was beginning to rediscover the musical heritage that had come to him from his mother.

His access to the Municipal Theatre enabled him to see a performance which impressed him deeply. It was a mime group, newly formed by Enrique Noiswander. Victor immediately went round to the dressing room to ask Noiswander how he could study the art of mime. Enrique answered by inviting him to come for an audition to the studio where the group rehearsed. There, Victor's sense of movement and expressivity were so evident that he was offered a chance to study.

At that time the mime group rehearsed in the evenings. They were enthusiastic, dedicated people who worked all day long in different professions – Enrique, for instance, was a qualified engineer – and then rehearsed until twelve o'clock every night. They worked in a large room in a very old house, colonial style, with several inner patios where many artists had their studios. There were painters, sculptors, poets, solo dancers – the 'bohemian' set, who worked individually outside the structures of the university. Many of them came from aristocratic or middle-class families, but had put aside the strict conventions of contemporary Chilean society.

For Victor it was all completely new and he observed rather as an outsider. He became friends with members of the group, but he never talked about himself, nobody knew where he lived, nor what his background was. It was evident that he was extremely poor and didn't have enough to eat, but he seemed to overcome everything by sheer enthusiasm.

In Noiswander's very successful season at the Talia Theatre in 1955, Victor had two important roles, one in a work set to Ravel's *Valses Nobles et Sentimentales*, and the other as a bored and over-worked bureaucrat in *Los Vecinos*, to music by the Chilean composer Leni Alexander. This was followed by a tour to the southern provinces, where Victor had his first experience of audiences outside Santiago. To the rest of the company he now revealed himself for the first time as a folksinger, because he sang to them for hours during the long train journeys. He must have been very happy.

One of his friends from the mime group was a young man from a very wealthy family, Fernando Bordeu. Fernando used to invite Victor for the odd meal, give him cast-off clothing and even invite him to stay in his father's very elegant flat off Ismael Valdés Vergara Street, while his family were away in Europe 'for the season'. To Fernando, Victor seemed very much alone. His broad smile was like a defence mechanism, almost a mask to prevent people from knowing about his intimate problems. Fernando said, 'If you saw him from a distance in the street, he might look preoccupied, worried, introverted, but when he saw you his face would light up into a broad and brilliant smile and he would inquire cheerfully how you were.'

In 1955, Fernando entered the Theatre School of the University of Chile, the only established drama school in Chile at that time. To Noiswander's great annoyance, when he found out, Fernando convinced Victor, too, to audition for a place there. Victor went along for his entrance exam in March 1956. He felt very nervous and inhibited in his handed-down clothes. His jacket was too short and, worst of all, his boots, heavy ones with thick soles, were a size too small and hurt his feet. He wasn't going to let that interfere with his improvisation, so he sat down on the floor and removed them before taking the floor in front of the commission of rather stern-looking people sitting behind a long table. He only hoped that he didn't have holes in his socks.

Conscious of his working-class accent, he didn't do too well in the reading exercise, but he came into his own when he had to show how he could move. He was admitted into the three-year acting course and as a student with economic difficulties was given a tiny stipend. As these difficulties were extreme he was also awarded a

Caritas scholarship – Catholic aid to the third world which came in the form of small quantities of processed cheese and dried milk once a month. There was no chance of finding part-time work.

As in all drama schools, the work was both practical and theoretical. Movement classes, vocal training, acting exercises went together with studies in the history of theatre and the method of Stanislavsky. There were student productions and sometimes tiny parts in the productions of the professional company.

It was a period when many especially gifted and talented students were in the school who were later to play an important part in the development of the theatre in Chile. Some came from very wealthy families and were pitucos; there were a fair number of young married women, with rich husbands, who were bored with staying at home all day; young men who enjoyed flirting with them and others who were politically active. A student with Victor's background was the exception.

Although as an actor Victor was by no means the most brilliant student of his year, he was respected for his hard work and his determination to overcome his difficulties. In movement, however, he was brilliant and at the end of his first year, in a festival organised by the students themselves, he was called upon to play the part of a bear, the hero of *The Ballad of Atatrol*. He took it so seriously that his friends in the población would see him setting out in the morning almost before it was light and when he got back late at night he would tell them how he had been studying the bears in the zoo for hours before going to class. He had to walk several miles to the zoo, and then back to the centre of the city to the school because he had no money for bus fares.

Meanwhile, I was giving movement classes in the school. I taught Victor's class in their second year. I remember them as a specially gifted lot and Victor as the best of them. The classes used to take place at eight-thirty in the morning in the rehearsal room of the Antonio Varas Theatre – a horrible basement room which never saw daylight and had a slippery, tiled floor. You might have expected a high degree of absenteeism but that particular group of students worked with great enthusiasm and creativity. Although they were always very respectful, they used to make fun of me in a nice way and at the end-of-term party did a lovely take-off of my teaching, organised, I suspect, by Victor. I was easy prey because I used to make rhythmic and atmospheric noises to inspire the students to further efforts, while I myself bounded around, steaming and sweating more than any of them.

With increasing confidence in himself and more and more integrated into the student movement, Victor entered his third year of studies. It was presidential election year, an election in which Salvador Allende, representing a broad alliance of the left, FRAP, was fighting against the candidate of the Chilean oligarchy, Jorge Alessandri.

Alessandri was heavily backed by the multi-nationals and it was the first time that US commercial advertising methods were used in political propaganda in Chile, a high-pressure campaign with millions of dollars spent on it. Meanwhile the left made up for its lack of economic power with people and staged massive demonstrations and marches. The economic polarisation of Chilean society had begun to be more truly reflected in the political life of the country. In that election, Allende won 28.8 per cent of the votes to Alessandri's 31.5 per cent.

The Chilean Communist Party was just coming out of hiding after being banned for almost a decade by a law known as the 'Ley Maldita' ('the Accursed Law'). To the mass of working people who made up its membership and support, it had a heroic image. But this respect was shared by many artists and intellectuals, particularly because of the awe-inspiring reputation of Pablo Neruda, whose Canto General had been printed secretly in Chile in 1950, thousands of copies being circulated from hand to hand. If Victor had never left the población, or if he had come from a middle-class family into an artistic career, his involvement with the young communists would have been probable – but the combination of his background and his participation in the cultural movement made it almost inevitable.

The growth of the left was reflected in the student movement and in the theatre school the students were demanding to have more connection with the outside world, to take initiatives in organising festivals where new dramatists, designers and producers could have their chance. There was interest in developing amateur theatre groups in trade unions, schools and colleges, especially in the provinces.

Against the background of the election campaign, Victor had his introduction to the work of Gorki, when his class produced The Lower Depths. In it he played the part of the dye-maker. It started him reading other works of Gorki, especially The Mother, which was always one of his favourite books. Then, perhaps because of their gift for improvisation in style, his class was given Peter Ustinov's *The Love of Four Colonels* for their final exam. Victor was the Russian colonel, which I remember he did very well. Indeed, the whole production was good. As their teacher of movement I was on the examining commission.

One of Victor's closest friends in the Theatre School was Nelson Villagra, who later became one of Chile's finest actors, famous for his role in the film *The Jackal of Nahueltoro*. Nelson was a dark, good-looking young man from a family of peasant farmers who had a small property near the city of Chillán in the south. Newly arrived from the provinces, he was attracted to Victor because of his obvious working-class background and also his exuberant way of laughing.

Victor at this time was living wherever he could kip down, but Nelson had the support of his family and stayed in a seedy boarding house in a working-class district. Both, however, were chronically broke, and at lunch-time would sit out in the park on the Santa Lucía Hill near the city centre, and try to stay their hunger with brown bread and a bottle of milk. Only when Nelson's family sent him a parcel of food could they really eat their fill and enjoy 'banquets' that included meat and cheese.

In their 'after-dinner' conversations they discussed the contrasts between city and peasant life and agreed that on the next long summer vacation they would go together to the farm of Nelson's parents in search of the 'authenticity of rural life'. But they also sensed that this exploration of the Chilean countryside and its people was important for their future work in the theatre. Victor proposed that they get hold of a couple of guitars and form a folk duet – an idea which didn't appeal very much to his partner, who only strummed a little – so that they could give performances and at the same time collect the folk-songs of Ñuble, a region with a great tradition of peasant music.

Victor, meanwhile, had passing relationships with girl friends in the Theatre School, none very serious, and one with an older woman who was very fond of him. He felt rather guilty about not being able to reciprocate her feelings. His most intimate and constant dream was to have his own guitar, and this woman – let's call her Margarita, because I never knew her name – was always offering to buy him one. He had conflicting feelings about accepting such a gift, but the temptation was very great.

He consulted his friend about the problem. Nelson understood immediately and threatened that if Victor did not tell Margarita straightforwardly that he needed a guitar, he, Nelson, would do so for him. So one hot afternoon found them in the city centre, Nelson, Victor and Margarita, approaching the Casa Amarilla, the best music shop in Santiago. Nelson made conversation about the guitar being necessary for their future investigations and Margarita pretended to listen, but really her attention was on Victor, moved by the way he was walking along, seeming to count every step like a well-behaved child on his way to the sweet shop.

They entered the music shop in the baking January heat and Margarita took charge, deciding that she would buy the best guitar available. This turned out to be one with a wide sound-box, like a woman with generous hips, and a veneer of walnut. Victor took it in his arms and blew gently across the strings which emitted the universal *Lá* . . . He tried it string by string, and the beautiful object was perfectly tuned. He began to play it in his own characteristic way, softly, lovingly and then demanding strength and harshness of it. It was obvious that the guitar already belonged to him . . . It was love at first sight. Victor smiled . . . placidly embracing that guitar with the wide hips.

Nelson played out his role as the cheeky young friend. 'Frankly,' he said, 'it seems to me that such a beautiful guitar deserves a case to protect it from being knocked about, and from getting dirty with the dust of country roads.' And so it was. With the guitar safely tucked away in a black case they emerged from the Casa Amarilla and said good-bye to Margarita. She even gave them the money for a taxi back to the boarding house.

A few days later they arrived at the little town of El Carmen in the province of Ñuble, which lies in the first foothills of the Andes. Here, in the gentle wheat-sown hills, began a chapter of experiences that were to strengthen Victor as a man and as a creative artist. It soon became obvious that Nelson would not be able to leave his parents' farm and travel around the region as they had hoped. There was too much work to do in preparation for the harvest. So Victor set out on the planned investigation without his friend, but not alone . . .

José 'Rat' (the nickname referred to his wry sense of humour and his ability to survive in the most adverse circumstances) was a

mechanic who was paid a wage to travel round the region with a
harvesting machine. The machine, pulled by a tractor, was rented
out to farm after farm during the harvest time. José 'Rat' was also a
troubadour, a popular poet and, if nobody prevented him, a confirmed
drunkard. This man was Victor's host and guide. A skilled mechanic
was a privileged person in those regions. He got the best and biggest
portion of meat at dinner-time and preferential treatment to meet all
his needs – all the wine he wanted, as long as he didn't get drunk during
working hours – what more could you ask? There was nothing better
than a haystack to sleep in at night, telling stories, counting the stars.

Between mid-January and the beginning of March a harvester was
rented out to an average of twenty-five to thirty farms and on every
farm, when the harvest was over there was a grand celebration. So
Victor helped José 'Rat' not only with his work, but also to eat,
drink and be merry. It was a rich basis for folk and sociological
investigation.

Occasionally, he returned to Nelson's farm to change his clothes
and then set off again to rejoin the harvester which was installed on
some farm many miles away. At first he did these journeys on foot,
but he soon learned to ride a horse and there was always some good
friend who would lend him one.

Nelson noticed the changes which were taking place in Victor
between one visit to the 'laundry' and the next. He had consciously
chosen to become friends only with the farm workers of the region
– he wanted nothing to do with the landowners – and he really did
merge himself with them, seeming to change both physically and
psychologically. After six weeks in the country there was nothing
left of the young man who had been incapable of shouldering an
eighty-kilo sack and who had been much teased for his inability to
ride a horse or bind a wheatsheaf.

After their first holidays together, the two friends returned to
Santiago transformed into a pair of peasants who viewed the people
and life of the city with suspicion. Victor's return to El Carmen during
the next two summers served to deepen his relationship with the
peasant way of life, but his vision also became more objective. He
stopped idealising the peasants and saw them as real men and women.
He also fell in love.

She was a dark, rather thin peasant girl, about 17 years old, with
features like a Mayan sculpture. She looked shyly out from under

her eyebrows and seemed to think it disrespectful or almost lewd to laugh. She blushed every time she did so, but Victor had her laughing very often. It was a fleeting relationship because after the third summer Victor never returned to El Carmen. Only the memory remained, and a collection of folk-songs which he had learned from his peasant friends in the region.

It was in 1957, while he was in his second year at the Theatre School, that Victor began frequenting the Café São Paulo in Calle Huérfanos in the centre of Santiago. It had become a meeting place for artists and intellectuals, who gathered there at midday over a cup of coffee. It was there that he met Violeta Parra. At that time she was known only to a smallish circle of people in Chile, but she had just returned from her first visit to Europe where she had travelled around making known the folklore of her country, possibly for the first time. Among other things, she had made extensive recordings of authentic Chilean folk-songs for the archive of the BBC.

A completely unconventional woman with no regard for ap-pearances, Violeta dressed as simply as a peasant, and at a time when other women of her class wore bouffant hairstyles or perms, she left her hair long and almost uncombed, rather as nature left it. She was a pioneer and had already spent years tramping throughout the country with her two children, Isabel and Angel, collecting folklore. She lived with the peasants or performed in the poor, ramshackle circuses that toured around during the summer months. She sang in the peasant tradition, almost monotonously, without artifice, but her guitar and her voice seemed to grow out of the earth.

Victor liked to join the crowd of people who always gathered round her table in the Café São Paulo. Sometimes they would all go off together to the studio of a friendly artist who lived nearby and Violeta would cook enormous saucepans full of Chilean beans for everyone. There would be wine and lots of discussion, interchange of songs, guitar-playing, story-telling, until it was time to go back to work.

Violeta was living at that time in La Reina, on the outskirts of Santiago near the mountains, where she had a small bungalow. Victor was a constant visitor to the house, passing into the back room to spend an afternoon with her, and she was interested in his way of playing the guitar and how he sang. She encouraged him to go on and even had the idea that he and her son Angel could perform together like the popular poets who improvise alternate verses, challenging and trying to outwit each other. This idea never materialised, but the two became lasting friends.

Younger than Victor and rebellious, Angel was an undernourished-looking adolescent. He tended to despise the studious people who made pilgrimages to the house in La Reina, equipped with notebooks and tape recorders, to listen to and learn from his mother. He had tramped around with her all his life and thought it all rather a bore, especially as it was always his job to lug the heavy tape recorder about on field expeditions. He had a passion for Argentinian folk music, especially the songs of Atahualpa Yupanki, whose songs at that time had a strong social content, and whose guitar playing was richer and more subtle than that of Chilean folk music.

At about the same time Victor met another group of people who occasionally frequented the Café São Paulo and who were taking movement classes with Patricio and Alfonso in the Theatre School. They had formed a folk group which was the first to use an indigenous name, Cuncumén, which in Mapuche means 'murmuring water'. Rather than become soloists, they had wanted to find a collective way of performing folklore.

Alejandro Reyes, one of the founders and leaders of the group, who became a close friend of Victor's, told me later, 'We were part of a massive movement of people who used to go out into the country surrounding Santiago at weekends or on holidays to look for and collect typical shapes and forms – not only in dance and music, it could be a clay pot or a lamp from colonial times, or maybe a saying, a turn of phrase, a manner of speaking or a way of life.'

Cuncumén performed at demonstrations, in May Day celebrations, at Neruda's home on his birthday. Their audiences were mainly ordinary working people. In 1957 they made their first album and although Victor was not officially a member of the group, he made a solo recording of a very beautiful love song which he had collected in Ñuble – 'Se me ha escapado un suspiro' – which was included on it. It was the first time that he was involved in the making of a record.

Violeta had a special understanding and appreciation of Victor, of his musicality and his artistic talent. 'He is Chile's number one folksinger,' she told her children later. The following year, in 1958, she composed two songs in the style of typical Chilean Christmas carols, especially for

Victor to sing. 'Doña María te ruego' and 'Décimas por el nacimiento' were recorded, together with other Christmas songs, and released on a Cuncumén album called *Villancicos Chilenos*.

That same year, Victor became a regular member of Cuncumén, which meant that he acquired the short-jacketed suit and coloured poncho of the *huaso*, the bailiff or farm-overseer who owned a horse and wore traditional high-heeled boots with the enormous, cruel-looking spurs which played an important part in the *zapateo* of the dances of the central zone of Chile. It wasn't until later and partly at Victor's insistence that when the group began to perform the dances of the poorer peasants, *gañan*, they abandoned their boots and used the ojotas or rough sandals of Victor's childhood. It produced a different way of dancing, a more down-to-earth, relaxed style, without the pride and posing of the macho cowboy, but annoyed people who believed that to depict poverty in any way was an offence to national dignity.

Victor now began to learn innumerable folk-dances from the different regions of Chile which expressed many facets of the character of the people and were far richer than the eternal *cueca* from the central zone which had become the cliché for the national dance. Even the cuecas changed from one region to another and this was something Cuncumén wished to make known when in 1959 they gave an important recital in the Antonio Varas Theatre. Alejandro had written a text which, in linking the songs and dances, put them in their historical and geographical perspective and showed how the differences of class and occupation modified their character. Victor both performed and directed the staging, and according to Alejandro his artistic sense and clear conception were important factors in its considerable success. It was something new.

I have an idea that the other members of Cuncumén were more conventional than Victor. They called him 'The Wild One' because he went around in a black leather jacket (presumably inherited from some friend) and jeans, which wasn't usual in those days. It used to rather annoy Victor, because although he may have been rather rebellious, he didn't intend to imitate an alienated North American teenager.

The only time of year when Chilean music came into its own was on 18 and 19 September, which were the days dedicated to the celebration of Chile's independence from the Spanish empire. In a wave of chauvinism which made even the wealthy and sophisticated prepared to listen to the traditional cueca, the radios continuously played strident versions of the national dance, while commercial groups plugged one or two sentimental Chilean songs. It was 'tourist folk' which gave the landowners' vision of the countryside: blue skies, loyal and elegant cowboys, pretty girls, no problems, in the most beautiful country in the world.

In the parks of Santiago, especially the Parque Cousiño, in outlying districts and in every town and village, *el Dieciocho* – the Eighteenth – was celebrated in *fondas* – primitive wooden structures roofed in with leafy branches from fragrant eucalyptus trees to give shade from the sun, row upon row of them, each with tables, chairs, a bar and loudspeakers blaring out cuecas, cumbias, tangos and boleros. Hundreds of paper flags hung in garlands from the roof; there was wine galore, dark beer mixed with toasted flour and raw egg, and *empanadas* – the Latin American version of a Cornish pasty.

Late into the night in the darkness outside, couples lay on the ground amid the left-overs of a hundred family picnics, while inside the fondas there was the waving of handkerchiefs, stamping and handclapping of the cueca – the woman timid or flirtatious, hiding behind her handkerchief, with not much chance to show off her prowess, the man dominating like a cock, shoulder forward, clashing his spurs, stamping, until he conquers her. This, at least, was the cueca of the central zone of Chile, of the rich huasos. Further south, among the poorer peasants and maybe where the indigenous influence was stronger, there seemed to be more equality between the sexes.

The first day of *Fiestas Patrias* everything was still quite orderly and it was a happy celebration, but on the 19th things usually began to degenerate and very often ended in knifings and violence. However, the afternoon was marked by the annual parade of the Armed Forces in the Parque Cousiño. All I remember about the only time I saw it was my astonishment at the marked difference in stature between the small, plebeian recruits and the tall officers and cadets – a visual demonstration of the contrasting results of malnutrition and very good feeding over several generations.

In 1958 and 1959 Violeta set up her own fonda in the Parque Cousiño and to it flocked all the people who were interested in real folklore. They had a wonderful celebration, all together. Violeta sang with her children, Victor solo and with Cuncumén, and many others.

They went on singing and dancing for two days until the small hours of the morning.

All these activities in folklore were subordinate to Victor's main interest in theatre. Music was an integral part of his life, but a personal pleasure, a relaxation rather than the main business of it. He had already achieved the first step in his career in the theatre, when he passed his final exams as an actor, but 1959 was to be an even more important year.

Among the close-knit group of students that made up his class was a young man to whom Victor was close for many years, both as a friend and as a professional colleague. This was Alejandro Sieveking, who was considered a promising young playwright, having had several plays performed already, although none as yet had been a sensational success. He looked rather like a gringo, tallish, bespectacled, intellectual, with a drawling way of speaking. He came from a very different sort of background from Victor's, but in spite of that there was great affinity between them. They seemed to share the same taste in many things.

By the time that Victor's group passed their final exams, they had reached a collective decision, together with Domingo Piga, the progressive-minded director of the school, that instead of being immediately absorbed as individuals into the professional theatre company, they should stay together for another year, working in a small company of their own, supported by the school. In this way they could continue to work together as a team, and get more practice as actors, dramatists, designers and directors in an experimental group, while also doing useful work by performing in small towns in the provinces where the larger and more cumbersome professional company couldn't go.

It was a good idea and a new one, but the year didn't begin too well. They spent a lot of time rehearsing what seemed to be a most unsuitable repertoire – *The Importance of Being Earnest* and a musical comedy, *A Sophisticated Affair*, written by Alejandro with the idea of preparing it for the student festival in September.

Unfortunately the rehearsals of the musical comedy didn't progress well. It called for a large cast of sixteen, and as their own group was reduced to eight, students from other courses had to be incorporated into the production. But with the rehearsals for the festival on a voluntary basis, it was difficult to get everyone together. It gradually became obvious that it wasn't going to be ready. It seemed that the fourth year would have nothing to show in the festival, which would have been unthinkable. It was Victor who said, 'Look, this is ridiculous. We must do something. Alejandro, why don't you write a short play with just four characters, which takes place in one room? I'll direct it. I have this idea . . .'

He suggested to Alejandro that he should write about something that had happened to some classmates of theirs: Miriam and Hernán were in love but had no freedom to be together. Hernán lived in a typical student's bedsit and one night Miriam stayed there . . . the next morning at breakfast her mother turned up. It was such a simple idea, but a very real situation with which all of them could identify. The play was written in a week and called *Parecido a la Felicidad* – 'Something Like Happiness'. Rehearsals began. Bélgica Castro, an actress from the professional company who was also a teacher in the school, was asked to play the part of the mother and she accepted with great enthusiasm. Thus a team was formed which worked together for many years, so much so that Bélgica later married Alejandro.

It was the first time that Victor had directed a play. There was no time for a great deal of intellectual analysis, but he used all his instincts and talent to make the play come to life on the stage with all the nuances and subtleties of the human relationships involved. It was a wonderful experience for all of them, even for Bélgica as a seasoned actress, because it was a new way of working which stimulated all the creativity of the actors.

They had one month of concentrated rehearsals, working morning and afternoon. Alejandro had a part in the play, so his main preoccupation was with his work as an actor. But he said, 'Victor co-ordinated everything, he got things out of you that you didn't even know were there. There was a sense of tranquillity which allowed the creativity of the actors to develop. He guided you without your feeling oppressed. You didn't feel that you were being pushed, but directed, orientated . . .'

Parecido a la Felicidad was ready in time for the festival and I saw its first performance in the tiny Teatro Lex. I was amazed by it. It was the first production I saw in Chile that didn't make me homesick for London. Everything, acting, decor, movement, rhythm, was delightful – with the human relationships treated with the utmost insight and sensitivity. Of course, it was an enormous success. So much so that when the leading actor of the Teatro Experimental became ill just before the première of *Macbeth*, *Parecido* was transferred in its place to the Antonio Varas Theatre for a week. The news spread that something new was happening in the theatre and people flocked to see the play.

It was after this that Victor decided that he wanted to study theatre direction. Although he had had some success as an actor, he never felt entirely comfortable and lacked a burning desire and ambition to perform. Perhaps he had felt more at home in mime. In any case he thought that as a director he would have more scope to use his creative abilities.

I think it was a heroic decision to take, because it involved practically going back to the beginning again. No allowances were made for the fact that he had already completed a three-year course as an actor, nor for his obvious talent. So in 1960 he enrolled as a student of direction. Luckily the course was more elastic in its timetable than the acting course and was rather a matter of completing projects, like an obstacle race, than actually learning much from the teachers.

In July 1959, a few months before *Parecido a la Felicidad* had made its impact in the theatre, *Calaucán* had had its première. Victor admired the work of Patricio and, since he had first seen me dance as the Woman in Red in *Carmina Burana*, had become my ardent fan. When he heard that the role of the Mother was being created for me, he asked permission to come to rehearsals to watch how we worked, to find out how dance language was created. In those rehearsals, where he sat quietly, absorbing, never speaking to me and hardly to Patricio, he couldn't help realising that, although we worked together with great understanding, there was tension in our personal relationship. A few months later our problems were public property and Victor became very concerned for me, always asking for news of me from my sister-in-law, Carmen, when he saw her in the theatre.

That summer, a long and unhappy one for me, awaiting my first baby, Victor visited El Carmen for the last time and then together with the rest of the company set off on tour to Buenos Aires and Montevideo. *Parecido a la Felicidad* made a tremendous impact in both cities, as it did also later in the year on a long tour throughout Latin America, in Mexico, Costa Rica, Guatemala, Venezuela, Colombia . . . and Cuba.

It was only a year after the overthrow of Batista and the new revolution in Cuba was a source of inspiration to people all over Latin America. You can imagine the excitement of being able to see what was going on at first hand. They stayed there for two or three weeks and saw the frenzied activity, the changes, the construction. Of the whole group, Victor was perhaps the most politically aware and he explored, asked questions, saw as much as he could, making friends, trying to understand everything that was going on.

As representatives of the group, Victor and Hernán, their stage manager, were given the chance of an interview with Fidel Castro, who had the best disposition in the world to meet people. They were told to wait in a small ante-room in some ministry until Fidel came out of a meeting. After an hour or so, they were giving up hope, when the door opened and a young man in uniform entered the room. He said in a friendly way, 'I just came to tell you that unfortunately Fidel won't be able to see you today because something has come up and he can't get away. However, if there is anything I can do or discuss with you, I should like to . . . my name is Guevara . . . they call me "Che".' Victor and Hernán were disappointed at not seeing Fidel, but they spent some time with this lesser-known comrade, who asked them many questions about Chile and their life and ambitions for the future.

One day at the end of April, when Victor had just arrived back from his first visit to Buenos Aires, backstage at the Antonio Varas Theatre he met Patricio wandering about nervously. He asked after the baby and Patricio almost pounced on him and said that at that very instant he was going to the clinic to see her for the first time and would like Victor to go with him. Victor liked the idea very much . . . so his first sight of Manuela was when she was only two or three days old. In spite of the tension of that moment I can remember him standing in the doorway, smiling shyly. As the year passed he heard that Patricio had definitely left me and that I was alone and rather ill.

3

OUR MEETING

On a bright spring morning towards the end of October 1960, I was walking along Calle Huérfanos in search of a new dress. I was beginning to recover from the physical and nervous breakdown which had beset me after my separation from Patricio, and this was part of a campaign to raise my morale. My women friends had tried to cheer me up and give me confidence in myself. I had been given a lot of well-intentioned advice: I should go out and buy new clothes, go to the hairdresser, give myself a 'New Look', have a manicure . . . all tips designed to make me look more attractive, or how-to-get-your-man in easy stages, according to the customs of the time.

I did try. I obediently cut off my long hair and had it set in the current fashion . . . I looked awful. My short, stubby nails were always breaking. In new clothes I felt dressed up and as though I were playing a part. I had never managed to fit into the mould that Chilean women employed to try to please their men – not through any consciously feminist principles on my part, but simply because I was incapable of doing so. Tight skirts, high heels, gloves and hats were not for me.

However, this morning I was determined to buy myself a very glamorous dress because, as part of a programme of would-be frivolous activities, one of the dancers of the company had invited me out for the evening with a group of her very sophisticated friends. I eventually bought a dress, but wasn't quite sure about it. Carrying the results of my shopping in a very elegant carrier bag, I passed the Café São Paulo about midday and decided that I would drop in for a coffee and to see if any of my friends were there, in the hope that they would approve my choice.

In the semi-darkness inside, I looked around and saw no familiar faces except that of Victor Jara, who was sitting alone at a table, reading a book. He looked up and smiled at me, beckoning me to come and sit with him, but I greeted him stiffly and sat down at another table, even looking over my shoulder to see if it were really me that he was waving at. When I had finished my coffee, I got up and went out into the heat of the street. Victor must have followed me out. He overtook me, greeted me warmly and asked me how I was and whether I had started working again. He found out that I had a new dress in the bag I was carrying and tried to persuade me to go out with him that evening instead of to this elegant dinner party. I laughed at the idea. The fact that I was newly unmarried made me feel somehow naked and defenceless, so I was very unforthcoming.

The famous dinner party that evening was a disaster from everyone's point of view. I went dancing in a night club for the first and last time in my life and ended up by defending myself vigorously on the sofa from the genuinely kind-hearted but rather tipsy person who had brought me home. He sent me flowers and an apology the next day. It was my last adventure in the 'high life' of Santiago.

Victor began to invade my thoughts a little. I remembered him smiling at me in the clinic, bringing flowers when I was ill, being so glad to see me when we met in the street. He seemed so kind and easy to talk to, but I didn't take him seriously. I knew nothing about him except that he was a very gifted student and that he seemed of a younger generation. I was an old woman of thirty with a failed marriage and a career behind her.

After that there were one or two 'chance' encounters which Victor managed to bring about, and then one evening in November we found ourselves together in the Open Air Art Exhibition along the banks of the Mapocho River. It had been initiated as an annual event the year before, but I had missed it, being too busy with my own problems. Now Victor, with his infectious enthusiasm, convinced me that it was too interesting to miss. The best professional painters and sculptors were exhibiting their work side by side with folk artists, peasant craftsmen and potters.

It was a warm spring night and crowds of people milled around the stands, struggling to see the good, bad and indifferent paintings, the photos, jewellery, sculptures, handicrafts and pottery. There were stalls with the brightly-coloured butterflies, angels and flowers made from woven horse-hair by the peasants of Rari; the fat, shiny black or terracotta pigs and guitar-players, pottery figurines from Quinchamali, decorated with fine-drawn white flowers; ponchos and woven blankets from the north and south. The air was full of charcoal smoke, the smell of fried onions from the food stalls selling empanadas and red wine; little home-made carts in the shape of steam-ships wobbled along on shaky pram wheels, their funnels belching smoke, selling roasted peanuts, plain or sugar-coated. The ground was uneven and dusty. In the patchy lighting I saw Violeta Parra sitting on an old deck-chair, surrounded by her work, her children and musical instruments. Illuminated by the light of naked electric bulbs hanging from the trees, Violeta's tapestries glowed with her own vision of the world. As we passed, Victor greeted her and they exchanged jokes. Nearby someone was singing and playing the guitar.

It was when we were walking away from the crowds and the noise, under the great trees of the Parque Forestal, that Victor took my hand, and his gentle touch, with its human warmth, marked a new stage in our relationship.

At first it was very unequal. We were both afraid of being hurt. Victor didn't want to be a passing rebound for me. He was genuinely in love for the first time in his life. With his sensitive perception of people he saw very well the state I was in and wanted our relationship to develop gently but truly. He tried to help me to relax, to thaw out, to free myself from a painful obsession with the past. I was like a hedgehog, full of bristles, variable, sometimes ready to throw myself at him, sometimes threatening to kick him out of my life. I was really immature in spite of my age . . . but I gradually began to feel younger than I had ever done in my life. I began to realise that life could be fun. I even started to enjoy myself.

There was so much to talk about; everyday things like food, trees, clouds . . . or human relationships; about the theatre; or about dance and how it is related to everyday life; about what is inherent in the way people touch, not only one another, but objects and the very air about them, and how this becomes a means of communication and an expression of their character – why do some people 'attack' their shoes and leave them misshapen and exhausted, while others barely alter their shape or wear them out? – about how in order to be light one must know how to relax; and how in movement nothing is absolute, but everything is relative.

Through our discussions, through Victor's questions and comment, I began to be able to relate many of the concepts which I had used as a dancer to my own life and character. I began to understand myself better and to have more confidence, at the same time learning to be less egocentric and to consider and to communicate with another person . . . perhaps I had never really done that before in my life.

Victor had admired me from afar for a long time, had fallen in love with me, according to him, when he saw me dance for the first time. It may seem contradictory that someone so passionately interested in things Chilean as Victor should have fallen in love with a gringa; or it might seem that he had fallen for the romantic ideal of me as a dancer rather than the real woman. But it wasn't so. It is often possible to perceive the essence of people when you see them dancing, without the barriers of language, of different customs and inhibitions; and for me dance was my only real form of expression.

Victor had never really opened out, even to his best friends such as Nelson, to whom he had told very little about his background and childhood. He had always hidden himself under layers of defences and at the time when I got to know him his student life had separated him further from his own roots. Although he kept in close touch with his friends in the población they could not really supply the support he needed in the new circles in which he was moving. Like me as a child and adolescent, Victor had two separate worlds in which he lived and I think that I was the first person who was able to help him bridge the gap between them.

He invited me to see the room that he had rented when he had returned from Cuba and the Latin American tour with a little money. He was very proud of it. It was in Calle Valdivia, in a bohemian district next to Santa Lucía Hill with narrow twisting streets instead of the ubiquitous right-angled blocks. Many of the old houses contained artists' studios and workshops. Victor's room was up a narrow winding staircase and was quite large, but completely bare of furniture apart from an old wooden bedstead. The rest of Victor's possessions were packed away in the cardboard boxes which had followed him around from one lodging to another, but by now were not only worn out but also half-burned from when an overturned paraffin stove had set fire to the house in the población where he had been living. He had managed to rescue his books, but most of them were charred at the edges.

What struck me most about the room was that in spite of its bareness, all Victor's possessions were scrupulously neat, clean and ordered. His few clothes were neatly hung on nails knocked into the wall, with his huaso suit in place of honour carefully covered in plastic, his shoes and spurred boots in a neat row beneath. On that visit I was introduced to his most precious possession, his '*compañera*' until that moment, the guitar that Margarita had bought him.

Victor was gentle and patient and funny . . . sometimes sulky and neurotic if I hurt him, but his bad moods didn't last long. At first, if we quarrelled he would disappear, sometimes for days on end, and I knew that he had gone off to Población Nogales to be with his friends. But on the whole he was very generous with himself. Although most other people describe him at this point in his life as very reserved, with me he wasn't like that. He hid nothing. I didn't feel that his smile was a defensive mask, but rather open, generous happiness, infectious happiness. When he wasn't about, or was late in arriving, I began to realise how much I was relying on him emotionally and even began to think that I was really falling in love with him, although I was too wary to use that term.

So the spring passed and summer began. It was New Year's Eve, and Victor was invited to a party. He asked me to go with him and this was the first time I met his friends of the theatre school, not as their teacher, but as Victor's compañera.

What I most remember about that party is Victor singing. He was asked insistently, and eventually allowed himself to be persuaded. He sang songs from Chilean folklore, most of which were new to me because he had collected them himself on his visits to Ñuble and other parts of the country, and from Argentina songs of Atahualpa Yupanki. If I wasn't already in love with Victor before then, his singing put an end to my resistance.

I can't say that he became another person, but he was transformed, he became himself with wings. He showed all his warmth, his tenderness, his passion, his capacity for fun. His voice expressed all these things, as well as strength. I looked at him embracing his guitar, bent over it, or looking up and out . . . seeing the pulsing of his throat, his eyes closed in concentration or looking at me across the room as he sang song after song. My defences collapsed, a great happiness welled out of me . . . I felt like shouting and singing, and when after midnight had sounded he embraced me and in English wished me very tenderly 'Happy New Years', I knew that the final 's' was not a mistake. It was a nice way of putting it.

Soon after this, Victor asked me to come with him to visit his sister Maria and to bring Manuela, who by now was a gorgeous fat baby of eight months, lively and happy in spite of all my anxieties. Victor was wonderful with her and loved to take her out. It was the first time that he had taken a friend from outside the población to meet a member of his family. So off we went to Jotabeche, choosing the time carefully so as not to run into Juan, Maria's husband, who had turned Victor out of the house after he left the seminary. The sordid street that had been Victor's home was deserted except for a couple of drunks lying on the pavement outside the bar, waiting for it to open, another propping up the lamp post. But Maria's children came running out of the house to hug Victor, and there was Maria behind them.

The little peasant girl who had looked after her brothers and sisters was now a typical Chilean woman, small and plump, with curly black hair and the same beautiful white teeth that Victor had. She was so warm and affectionate, obviously pleased that her brother was in love and happy at last. It was easy to talk to her. She had heard a lot about me from Victor already and asked me lots of questions about my work. She knew more than I would have imagined about Victor's activities in the theatre and with Cuncumén, although I don't think she had ever been to the theatre or to a concert in her life.

Meanwhile I had been attempting without success to get back into full training, but was still hindered by problems with my spine. In January, the doctor told me that my only hope was to spend the summer holidays 'hanging' myself – putting my body into traction, with sacks of flour or sand as weights, a home-made corset round my hips, and one end of the bed standing precariously on wooden blocks so that my head hung downwards. I was ordered to spend at least a month, day and night, in this contraption, getting up only to go to the loo and to wash myself scantily. It was extremely difficult to eat upside-down and I felt myself getting longer and longer, like chewing gum.

So, while most of my friends were going to the beach or to the mountains, I was immobilised in the summer heat, looking out at the old cedar tree and the funicular railway which crept up and down San Cristóbal Hill. Victor saw me through it, keeping me company for hours on end, entertaining me, cheering me up and generally making me feel that I was an interesting and worthwhile person whose opinions were worth listening to.

During the day he had quite a lot of time to spare because the Theatre School was closed for the summer holidays, but every evening he was working intensively with Cuncumén. He had been invited to join the group as their artistic director in preparation for a long European tour which was due to start in June and last four to five months.

It was horrible to think that Victor was going away for so long. The idea of such a long separation made us rather tense, but I think that we both had confidence that our relationship would survive.

Victor was leaving on 30 May and, a few days before, his friends in Población Nogales organised a farewell party to which I too was invited. I felt as shy or even shyer than when I had been to dine at some elegant mansion or to an evening at Neruda's house. We took the *liebre* or 'hare', a small bus usually driven at suicidal speed, to Pila de Ganso, and then a *micro*, a larger, more ancient and much slower bus, along General Velasquez, past the gasometers, the railway sidings and the warehouses.

It was a Saturday night, and it was already getting dark. The street lighting was very dim, with lampposts few and far between and many of those without their bulbs. We got off the micro next to the waste ground, just before the bridge over the canal, and here I clutched Victor's hand because it seemed such a sinister neighbourhood, the sort that I had always been warned never to enter, especially after dark. The only lights visible here were in the street-corner bars, or the gleam of an oil lamp shining from the doorway of a rough wooden house. The street was of large cobble stones, but with gaps of unmade road, deeply rutted.

Now we were really entering the población and Victor took my arm as we set off over the waste ground by the canal to a little house on the other side. But then everything was all right . . . The Morgados were waiting for us in the doorway, Julio, Humberto, their sisters and girl friends, and we were ushered inside. The living room was quite small, but two tables had been pushed together to make a large one. There was an old sewing machine, a sideboard, and on the wall above, in the place of honour, a large framed photograph of Don Pedro and

Doña Lydia on their wedding day. Don Pedro had died a few months previously, so I never knew him.

Very potent fruit punch was passed around, and *mistela*, a sweet wine home-made by Doña Lydia. Conversation was about friends, excited speculations about Victor's coming journey to far-off and exotic Europe, and reminiscences about the past which got more and more sentimental. Then the tables were cleared away to make room for dancing.

My memories of the party are rather blurred, but the house seemed very small for so many people and so many young children who played around until in the early hours of morning they dropped off to sleep exhausted in one of the two rooms which led off the living room. Julio had a sly sense of humour and the others made fun of him, but he was not well, and should have been in hospital. He couldn't take care of himself, now that he was responsible for the lorry which was their main source of income. Underlying all the joking and cheerfulness, you sensed the daily problems and the generosity that this party represented, with food and drink for so many people.

Victor showed his gratitude by singing and getting them all to sing with him. Then, slightly drunk now, everyone danced to cha-cha-cha, tangos . . . in that tiny room with the wooden chairs around the walls, illuminated by a single bare bulb. It was the only time I ever saw Victor drunk. To have refused their wine would have been to refuse their love and generosity. But it meant that he was rolling about the pavement on the way home.

I think that first visit to Población Nogales was significant for me, although at the time I wouldn't have been articulate about it. The fact that Victor took me there to share his world was a measure of his love for me. It introduced me to a new world where I was accepted with affection, almost like a sister. I no longer felt cut off from the majority of the people around me. Now I had a new family.

Two days later I was alone again. Victor had departed to Europe with Cuncumén and I had to face going back to the ballet and begin the uphill work of getting back into training after such a long leave of absence. Patricio was waiting for me to recover to begin a new choreography called *Surazo* or Southwind, with music by Ginastera, in which I was to dance the main role.

Victor was to spend the next four months travelling through Eastern

Europe. Although I sensed that his love went very deep, I spent some anxious moments before his letters began to arrive. But then they became so frequent, so loving and so entertaining that the separation was not so hard to bear. I think it strengthened our understanding of one another.

July 1st   *Prague*

. . . Our first performance was near some famous thermal springs called Bojnice, and afterwards they took us to have baths in a swimming pool with warm spring water, followed by a massage from a specialist. We felt like new afterwards, and accepted the invitation to eat and drink beer . . . then the singing began and we ended up by dancing typical Slovakian dances where you literally have to spin like a top . . . the Slavs are very like ourselves, festive, merry, rather exuberant and also very sentimental. They rather look down on the Czechs as cold and formal.

This region seems to be the richest in folk tradition. I've seen the most marvellous peasant costumes in the Slav cities. I have stopped peasant women in the street to examine their dresses more closely and to take photos of them. They get very nervous at first, but when they realise that you are friendly, they begin to relax and are very affectionate. When they shake hands, they caress you and you can feel their calluses and the hardness of their hands from the work they do in the country, just like the men. They move you with their simplicity and friendliness . . . I'm very sentimental, as you know, and sometimes I want to cry when I feel and see human kindness and understanding overcoming language barriers.

Lots of kisses for Manuelita. For you my love, all my life . . .

August 18th   *Leningrad*

. . . In every city we have performed in one theatre doing four or five performances in a row and generally we have two days' rest when we have time to go to the theatre and on sight-seeing excursions with visits to museums. Dearest, I am amazed at the Soviet Union. Everything I see, day by day, makes me anxious to study . . . it is much more impressive to see the results in person than to read about them . . .

The news of your progress as a dancer has filled me with happiness; to know that you are full of courage, patience and constancy makes me feel a profound admiration for you as well as immense love . . . I expect you will find a change in me when I get back, but one thing I am sure about is that I shall return loving you more than ever . . .

As far as life here is concerned, I try to understand everything and to make myself understood. The Russians teach you how to live together. They have in them a spiritual steadfastness which makes them serene, kind and firm at the same time. I should like to be like that, with convictions and objectives to lead me on. I know that it is difficult . . .

The Russians are fantastic; it's not that they are all over us immediately because we are foreigners; no, they feel a stimulus and react to it until everyone ends up by kissing one another. They are very straightforward and affectionate. Till now, I've not met one with a swollen head about the conquest of space. It seems to me that inside each person is a message of peace and friendship . . . and I'm talking about the people you meet in the street, passing by. If it were the people attending us you might be right in thinking that it was just diplomacy, but they are just as simple as the others.

Last night we left Moscow by sleeper train and after travelling all night we arrived at ten o'clock this morning in Leningrad. The journey was amusing because of a mix-up with the bunks and also because when we arrived at the station in Moscow I saw a multitude of Russians, men, women and children, waiting for the train to leave. Squatting and lying about all over the place, sleeping or eating black bread with tomatoes and salami; lying in the corridors one beside another, they looked like refugees from an air-raid. Our translator told us that we should soon get used to it, because in all the stations you saw the same scene. And we saw that this was true when we arrived in Leningrad. These Russians are very self-sacrificing and amazingly enthusiastic about travelling. They go to Moscow just to spend the afternoon seeing Lenin's tomb – and to do that they travel for two days. And they don't go alone, but with babies, baskets and all their relations, including Grandma. They're like us in this sense . . .

September 7th   *Odessa*

. . . Today something happened to me which I shall always remember. I went out for a walk at about nine o'clock in the evening and as I went along the sea front, I heard applause. On coming nearer, I found an open-air theatre where a variety performance was taking place. I tried to buy a ticket to go in, but it was sold out. I was curious to see what was going on and began to walk around the surrounding wall until I reached a group who were looking over the top with mirrors. I tried to join them, but it was impossible to see anything. As I turned away, I saw a tree with a group of people sitting on the branches. Just as I was about to climb up, the lights went on for the interval and the people began to climb hurriedly down. I wandered about to fill in time and when the performance began again I started to climb the tree, together with five Russians. Of course, once installed they started to talk to me as equal-to-equal in Russian and I had to tell them that I didn't understand. At first, they thought I was joking, but when they realised that I was telling the truth, they asked me where I came from. With the little Russian I know I told them that I came from Chile in South America and that I was here with a Chilean folk group. They were so surprised that they began to laugh and to congratulate me because, in spite of being a foreigner and an artist, I was up a tree just like them. Then they offered me the best place in the tree and took great care that I should see the performance in the best possible conditions, constantly asking me if I were comfortable and could see well and patting me on the back. When the performance was over, they helped me down and once on the ground, hugged me, laughing their heads off about my attitude. We were already great friends. Afterwards they asked me why, as a foreigner, I hadn't gone inside and been comfortable, insisting that as a visiting artist I had the right to preferential treatment. But I told them that I preferred to be like everyone else and buy my own ticket, and that as I hadn't managed to get one, I had climbed the tree. They laughed and embraced me and said 'What a good comrade.' I saw two of them, Vladimir and Piotr, again later, and then every day, becoming really good friends with them. They are both 35 years old, married, one with two and the other with three children, and they are workers in a tractor factory in Kharkov, a city in the north of the Soviet Union. They are here for the holidays. Of course I invited them to our performance and they liked it very much. The sensation of being able to communicate with them in spite of all the obstacles is wonderful. They are good men, so sure of themselves and yet so simple and healthy. They take you as you are and make you feel one of themselves. They were very concerned about the situation in Latin America and asked me about the conditions of Chilean working people . . .

September 28th   *Ashkhabad*

Dearest Love,

I am the happiest man in the world at this moment, because today, on my birthday, I have received the wonderful present of four letters and two beautiful photos of the two people whom I love so much – yours and Manuelita's . . . Now in the evening, I have read your letters more carefully and I feel rather disturbed and depressed.

First of all, you ask me not to idealise you, that you don't feel you have the human qualities that are necessary to be the compañera of a communist; that I ought to remember that you are not a sociable person; that you distrust people who live with very high ideals; and that you are also afraid of the intellectual position of communism.

How shall I answer so that you won't misunderstand me, my love? I never told you that I idealise you. I love you, and knowing you as you are with all your virtues and defects, I have learned to love you even more. Don't think that I am blind, that I have put you on a pedestal. I love you more with my heart than with my head, and if you are part of me it is because you, just as you are, are everything for me. I believe that love is that mutual comprehension that can exist between two human beings; that 'something' with which we can help each other to live. Also, I love you so much that my happiness consists in trying to make you happy whatever road we take.

And this is the second point: if I choose the road of communism, why should that be incompatible with my love for you? I don't demand that you too become a communist, my love. I can't ask that of you. You can never force anyone to think in a given way, however close to them you may be. I am glad, I must say, that you are not a Catholic, and that your sufferings have made you a great woman, capable of being a real friend and mother and capable, too, of loving me, in spite of your past disillusions. Please don't think that I despise people who aren't communists. We are all human beings and a communist should be aware of this above all else, because it is the very essence of his principles. The rest is fanaticism and snobbishness. Don't think that I shall turn into a sort of apostle – I have no gift for that – and no time, either, to turn into a fanatic. Don't think that being an active communist means shutting yourself away for twenty-four hours a day leaving everything else abandoned. No, my love, there is a lot of work to be done, but surely mine will be in relation to my work in the theatre.

What, then, are the terrible defects which would prevent you from being with me if we are both human beings? I am not Jesus Christ, and I shan't disappear up the mountains to meditate. My work begins in you and ends in you. That is all my desire . . .

You say that you are afraid of living with people who have very high ideals. I too fear that sort of person. But as far as I am concerned, I think that with the little you know about my family and the people among whom I was brought up, you can tell that I know what real poverty is like. I can't live in a dream world. And my ideal as a communist is nothing more than to support those who believe that in a regime of the people, the people will be happy. I shall try not to be obsessive and always to be aware that there is earth under my feet and that those who are walking beside me have two eyes and a mouth as I have.

Don't be afraid, my love. The only thing to be afraid of is not to be able to look deep into each other and to find simplicity. As far as being an intellectual is concerned, I must confess I'm not cold enough for that. You know me, and must realise how little I can intellectualise. I function with my heart, not my head. Something touches me inside and it begins to flourish there until it manages to find a way out. It is too much to say that I intellectualise about communism, because I don't even consider myself to be one.

But something has reached the inside of me and is beginning to take root. Also, I have a background which helps me to feel very strongly the hopes and problems of poor people and because I know their world so intimately, I couldn't intellectualise about it. If I did so, I should stop being myself. I couldn't even say hallo to the Morgados, Juanito and all the friends of my childhood, my brothers, my father, and I should be despising all that my mother gave me. I have to help them. I have to struggle for them, so that they can see for themselves and witness, I hope, a better world. I believe that in this you understand me and that you can help me as you have done already. My love, with you I am complete and if I go away from you, I feel that somehow I lose my wings . . .

Towards the end of October 1961, Victor arrived back in Santiago. He bounced off the plane, in a new green duffle coat, waving his guitar aloft, loaded with presents. He almost danced across the tarmac into the airport building in his excitement at seeing Manuela and me, waiting for him on the balcony above.

Although the tour had been so long and gruelling and he must have been physically very tired, his arrival was a great celebration in which even Manuela shared. Unpacking his suitcase was a ceremony in which Victor played Father Christmas. It was the first of many such occasions, because every time Victor went away he came back with the most beautiful and special presents for the people close to him. He took so much pleasure in being able at last to give something. This time it was folk art, pottery, hand embroidery, even musical instruments, from every corner of Europe (and Asia) that he had visited, from Bulgaria to Uzbekistan.

He never went back to live in his room in Calle Valdivia. From that moment we lived together. We had both achieved something during the long months of separation. I, nothing very spectacular, I suppose, but at least I was a whole person again; I could dance and teach with more confidence than ever and felt sure that I wished to continue my life in Chile and at Victor's side; that together we could make a home and that with Manuela we made a family.

Victor, as he had warned me in his letters, had changed. He was more mature and self-confident as a result of the widening of his horizons and because he had discovered his own powers of communication in song, both as a performer and as a composer.

During the tour, although his letters made little of this, he had sung for the first time as a soloist to audiences of thousands. He had also composed a very beautiful song, his first to be based upon his own personal experience in life. He had written it for me and was impatient to share it with me. Almost as soon as we arrived at my flat, he got his guitar out of its case and sat down to sing to me:

> My love I want to tell you
> that I am lonely and I love you.
> That my life is running out
> because you are so far from me . . .
> My love, I want to see you.
>   ('Paloma, quiero contarte')

And so began our life together. Our first year was overshadowed by the illness and death of the two people nearest us: my mother, having come to Chile on a long visit, suffered a stroke and died there in 1963 after an illness which lasted six months. Victor's sister Maria was discovered at about the same time to have incurable cancer and was sent home from hospital to die. Together we had to watch the physical disintegration of people we loved and at the same time the disappearance of the last links with our own families.

How lucky I was to have Victor beside me then – and I suppose that he was equally grateful to have me. He was a friend as well as a husband and with him I learned how important it was to be able to talk freely to someone, to express all those thoughts and feelings that, bottled up, are liable to ferment and poison human relationships and oneself.

He was very different from me. He was by nature a very peaceful, non-violent person, whereas I needed a good quarrel now and again. But he would somehow turn my blind outbreaks into reasoned, affectionate discussion of what lay behind them, and very often we would end up by laughing at the problem. However, he didn't take this approach from a feeling of superiority, but rather because he was deeply concerned that nothing should go wrong between us. He knew that a good relationship had to be worked at and he had a natural gift, which showed so clearly in his work in the theatre, for perceiving other human beings – I suppose that you could call it psychological insight.

It was due to his attitude more than to anything else that I was able to develop a reasonable and even friendly relationship with Patricio, which was so important for the happiness of Manuela, for ourselves, and also for the work which we could do together in the ballet, which Victor valued greatly.

When my mother had come to stay with us, we had rented a house rather above our means in order that she should be comfortable. Now that we found ourselves alone, we began hunting for a permanent home and eventually found a small house in a new complex which an architect friend of Victor's recommended as being more solidly built than most — quite an important consideration in a country prone to earthquakes. It was of whitewashed brick with green wooden shutters, and stood at the inner corner of a courtyard, surrounded by other houses. Once you were inside, however, you could be private and forget about the world outside. When we arrived, the land around the house was a rubbish dump, but we cleared it stone by stone, digging up rusty tins and old iron, until we could plant trees and grass.

Over the years, our semi-detached 'little box' gradually became defended by a jungle of high-growing bamboo, by bougainvillaea and wistaria which grew as fast as weeds, by a mimosa tree and shrubs from the south of Chile, honeysuckle, ivy and silver birches. Swallows nested under the eaves of the roof and on summer evenings the sky was filled with their swooping flight; humming birds hovered and darted, iridescent spots of colour, and the queltehue bird flapped and screeched, announcing the coming of rain when the mountain peaks became covered in cloud.

One of the first trees that we planted was a canelo, the tree looked upon as sacred by the Mapuches, which grows freely in the southern forests. The death of a canelo is a sign of impending ill-fortune and Victor was greatly upset when the first one that we planted dried up. Obstinately we replaced it and that one is flourishing today, converted into a multiple tree with many branches and roots.

Inside, the house began to take on a character which was rather a strange mixture of our different pasts. There were relics from my father's collection which I had brought with me when I first arrived in Chile — one or two pieces of antique furniture, Dutch marquetry, Chinese plates, an African drum, an Ashanti throne — but there was a dearth of ordinary furniture. We managed with bookcases made of old boxes or odd pieces of wood, a table and a mantelpiece made from old railway sleepers . . . and on the walls, the results of many journeys – masks from Brazil, embroidery from Tashkent, wooden spoons, pipes, musical instruments, ponchos.

During the first few years, before life began to accelerate, Sunday was often a day when we could enjoy being together. There was nothing that Victor liked better. He even appreciated my dubious cooking and celebrated my achievements in that field, contributing himself by making soups and other delicacies, recipes that he had learned while helping his mother in the market. He also helped with the cleaning – vigorously and efficiently – which was highly unusual for a husband in Chile, or thought up new ways of decorating the walls with all our treasures. He was always going round with a hammer and nails rearranging things.

In the summer we usually ate outside, in the shade of the mimosa tree. The sun was too hot to stand at midday, but the best time was at sunset and in the evening, when the heat still lingered in the stones of the terrace. Watering the garden was one of my favourite activities and I used to splash around, bare-footed, enjoying the way the parched plants soaked up the cool water, the smell of wet earth – so precious in a dry climate – and of wet foliage mixed with the scent of honeysuckle. Perhaps Victor would be playing the guitar somewhere in the background and I could just see him in the semi-darkness of the house. Then we might sit in the garden together, watching the stars appear in the darkening, translucent sky over the mountains, or we would swing under the trees in the hammock that I had brought back from Brazil. There was time to talk.

With this happiness in the background, it was wonderful to discover that I was pregnant. How different it was to be expecting a baby with a husband and family around me. I think I went on a real escapist trip, ignoring all the problems around me and revelling in swelling up like a balloon and still being loved. Manuela, a little girl of four and a half, was so impressed with Victor's happiness and excitement that she remembers to this day how he came to tell her the news that Amanda had been born. Victor's love for her seemed to strengthen rather than diminish with the birth of his own daughter. We seemed to make a good family.

Victor had adopted Manuela emotionally from the moment he first saw her when he came to see me in the hospital with Patricio, but he had grown closer to her as he had seen her growing into a lively, sensitive child. When, later, he was interviewed and asked about his family, it was always difficult for him not to say that he had two daughters. He couldn't disown Manuela. The first time he was asked, he was taken by surprise, but later he tried to avoid the issue in order not to hurt Patricio.

For Manuela it was quite natural to have two fathers – until she reached the age of five, when she was formally instructed in all the details by a little boy of the same age. For a few days afterwards she became very formal with Victor, calling him '*Tio*' or uncle, instead of '*Papi*'. When we realised what had happened we reassured her of Victor's love for her and that although Patricio was her real father there was no harm in her calling Victor '*Papi*', just as Amanda would.

Victor was a very good father. He learned how to change nappies and powder a small bottom, was good at doing things that needed a firm and gentle touch, like cleaning wounds on children's knees, extracting splinters or cutting babies' toe-nails. He was proud that Amanda seemed to look like both of us at once and loved her passionately, even though her voice was powerful in the small hours of the morning and deprived us of much-needed sleep.

Colleagues of Victor's, or people who knew him slightly in his professional world, tell me that they saw him as a solitary man, sympathetic and warm, but at the same time rather distant, as though he had an inner world, an inner happiness which didn't need to be accompanied by large groups of people all the time.

There is no doubt that Victor's home was vital to him, just as love and affection were, after the experiences of his childhood. He himself was capable of loving in a way that allowed me to breathe and grow. He never used me as a mirror, nor swamped me because I had to live up to his ideal of me. But as time went on, his happiness served only to strengthen his sense of responsibility, driving him on to work with increasing intensity for the things he believed were necessary to achieve. I think that he hoped, as I did, that one day there would be more time. He often said to me, 'Do you realise how lucky we are to love each other as we do?'

4

IN THEATRE AND SONG

For nine years after his return from the long European tour with Cuncumén, Victor worked as a member of the regular team of directors of ITUCH, the Theatre Institute of the University of Chile, and came to be recognised even by the establishment as one of the most creative and successful young theatre directors of the decade.

His productions ranged from the didactic works of Brecht to contemporary British and American drama, but also, and this was most important to him, new works by Chilean dramatists. He won prizes and invitations, was praised by critics, not only in Chile, but in other Latin American countries and even in the United States; he attended international theatre festivals and was invited by the British Council to observe British theatre; he came to direct for television both his own theatre productions and those of others; he became a teacher in the University Drama School, and was respected and liked by most of his pupils and colleagues, though some were jealous of his rapid progress.

It all began within days of his return. He had only two months – the remainder of the academic year – in which to prepare his final examination to graduate as a director. He had no hesitation in the selection of a play. Alejandro had presented him with a new work called *Animas de Dia Claro* which he had just written with Bélgica in mind for the main part. Victor fell in love with it on first reading. It had so many elements which attracted him and which would give him the chance to do something he had always wished to do: to re-create in the theatre the very spirit of Chilean folklore in its broadest sense.

Animas de Dia Claro, by a strange chance, was set in the region of Talagante, not very far from Lonquen. Based on the peasant's belief in magic as a part of everyday life, and on the widely-held superstition that the spirits of the dead can be bound to the earth by the strength of an unfulfilled wish, it was full of the supernatural atmosphere that had haunted Victor as a young child. He saw that he could use folk music, folk dance, the everyday customs and traditions of the peasants, to create an atmosphere part poetical, part comic, which would be authentic as well as having a magical, dreamlike quality.

Alejandro, himself a middle-class intellectual, had great interest in folklore, which his friendship with Victor had helped to develop. He trusted Victor to guide him in authenticity, with suggestions from his own intimate knowledge, and above all from him he learned to be respectful and to care deeply for these traditional ways of expression; to avoid at all costs the vulgar and patronising caricatures others resorted to – the typical peasant girl picking her nose, the typical peasant not simple but stupid.

The ghosts of five sisters inhabit a remote and decaying house, until a young peasant arrives who, taking them for ordinary human beings, sets off a train of events which fulfils each of their wishes. Victor wrote in the programme, 'It is a simple story about love, real love, which unexpectedly surges up from the depths of life and transforms everything, as simple as a peasant guitar, as a road, a poplar tree, a flower. It is a story of our people who use humour in all their forms of expression, even the most tragic ones . . .'

It had to be rehearsed at full speed. Victor worked essentially with the same method as he had done in *Parecido a la Felicidad*, inspiring and guiding the actors to be themselves creative. He fed them with many stimuli, product of his own knowledge of country life, took them on journeys of investigation to Talagante to speak with women of the region, especially those who worked in making the traditional painted pottery figures. Everyone worked with a deep sense of motivation and at the same time they all enjoyed themselves in re-creating this strange, tender and witty interweaving of reality and the supernatural. Victor himself composed, arranged and recorded the music with some of the members of Cuncumén.

The actual exam took place in the Camilo Henriquez Theatre in December 1961 and in spite of it being holiday time and midsummer, caused quite a lot of excitement. A large crowd of people, including the critics, turned up and the general verdict was that the production was too good to waste and should be incorporated into the next official season of ITUCH.

I shared Victor's happiness at the success of the production and there was a real celebration with the cast who had all worked with such enthusiasm. The whole result confirmed my belief that Victor was truly a person of exceptional talent and sensibility. It seemed to justify the long years of study against the odds and the 'handicap' of his background. It meant that he qualified with the highest possible honours and also, almost unheard of, was immediately offered a post as one of the resident directors of the Theatre Institute of the University – not only a job with a monthly salary, but a chance of working regularly with the professional company. He was to produce *Animas de Dia Claro* the following season.

Victor's professional association with Alejandro and Bélgica was important to him in his early years in the theatre, and they were also close friends. We spent many evenings at the Sievekings' flat discussing the theatre and also the latest gossip of the Institute. Victor admired Alejandro very much as a playwright and Alejandro in turn felt that no one understood or was capable of directing his work as Victor was. He had unfortunate experiences with other, more stereotyped and old-fashioned directors.

Animas was such a success that it became a kind of classic in the repertory of ITUCH. It was continually being revived, either for tours, television or international festivals – something unusual in the normal programme of the Institute. It was certainly popular with audiences and many people went to see it several times because it was a play with a fresh approach, and was very Chilean. Even the theatre critic of *El Mercurio*, the 'establishment' newspaper, praised it:

ITUCH has found itself an unusual play and Victor Jara has shown his understanding of it in giving the production a rhythm which is simultaneously happy, spontaneous and relaxed. It gives the impression that within the main idea of a given structure and style, he has given the actors complete liberty, allowing an absolute identification between the actor and the character. The enjoyment of the cast with their own work is noticeable and that enjoyment is communicated to the audience. There is much laughter.

Of course, Victor hadn't given the actors 'complete liberty'. He knew exactly what he wanted. But his method was such that he allowed them to feel that they had discovered everything for themselves, and in that he was an excellent pedagogue.

One of these revivals was for the International Theatre Festival in Atlantida in Uruguay in 1964. It was an important occasion for Victor because it gave him his first chance to see the work of other Latin American directors – people like Enrique Buenaventura of Colombia, Augusto Boal of the Teatro Arena of São Paulo, and Atahualpa del Cioppo of the famous El Galpón Theatre of Montevideo.

Strangely enough it was on this visit to Uruguay that Victor first met Salvador Allende and his wife Hortensia Bussi, both of whom were interested in the theatre and had been invited to attend the first night of the Chilean theatre company's season. In his speech at the reception afterwards, Allende made special mention of Victor as a gifted representative of a new generation of directors.

If Allende's praise was important for Victor, Atahualpa's, as perhaps the best known and most respected director in Latin America at the time, was even more so. He was already a man of over 60, tall, thin, white-haired, with a beaky nose and a personality which made it impossible not to love him. He had already been impressed by *Parecido a la Felicidad* which he had chanced to see in Buenos Aires. Of Victor's direction of *Animas de Dia Claro* he wrote, '. . . he was no longer a promising element, but a true director, mature and demanding, capable of welding reality and poetry.'

The cultural isolation of Latin American countries from each other was gradually being broken down. In Chile it was still easier to see European or American theatre companies than the progressive theatre of Brazil or the work of El Galpón, but in 1963 ITUCH took the initiative of inviting, for the first time, a director from another Latin American country to work with the company. An obvious choice was Atahualpa del Cioppo, whose production of Brecht's *The Caucasian Chalk Circle* had already made a very great impact in Montevideo and Buenos Aires.

Atahualpa made it a condition of his visit to Chile that Victor should be appointed his assistant. He appreciated Victor's insight into the temperament and talent of the members of the company. For Victor it was a chance to learn by working with the director whom he most admired, as well as fulfilling a desire to study the work of Brecht.

The political situation in Chile made the choice of a 'Marxist' play, which criticised bourgeois society and values, a controversial one. Ever since the triumph of the revolution in Cuba, the Latin American ruling classes had seen that there was a real danger of losing their power and privilege and all over the continent they had closed ranks, combining with the multi-nationals and the US government, to try to prevent the spread of Marxist ideas. The Alliance for Progress was one of these initiatives, which was combined with an anti-left campaign sustained in the mass media which they controlled.

So the production of *The Caucasian Chalk Circle* by the principal theatre company in the country was a stab in the back or a break through the blanket of political censorship, according to your point of view. Allende, already the candidate of FRAP – the left-wing alliance in the forthcoming presidential elections of 1964 – contacted Atahualpa on his arrival and offered his moral support in the tense and polarised atmosphere which surrounded the production of the play.

Allende himself was the object of a highly orchestrated campaign calculated to brainwash the population into believing that, if he were elected, Chilean children would be snatched from their parents and sent to Cuba to be indoctrinated, while Chile would become part of the Soviet 'empire'. Santiago suddenly became papered with posters showing Russian tanks entering the presidential palace, with pathetic images of crying children. There seemed to be so much money behind the campaign that everyone on the left went around saying that it must be being financed by the CIA. Perhaps at the time we didn't really believe it. Many years later William Colby was to declare to the US Senate that the CIA had given Eduardo Frei three million dollars for his election campaign in order to prevent Allende from gaining power.

Such was the furore caused by *The Caucasian Chalk Circle* that the Federation of Students organised an exhibition and a debate about the production to which Atahualpa, Victor and other members of the cast were invited. It was a very stormy political meeting and it was this atmosphere which prevailed on the first night, when according to Atahualpa there was no doubt that half the audience was fervently praying for a failure and the other half for a success, for reasons which had nothing to do with the production itself. However, the final applause was endless, and again Salvador Allende and his wife were among the mass of people who struggled backstage to congratulate the team of people who had been responsible for an historic event in the Chilean theatre.

It was impossible to get away from politics in Chile that year. In this same rather ugly political atmosphere, Victor was given the task of directing a play which touched directly on the middle classes' fear of revolution. *Los Invasores* was written by Egon Wolf, an engineer by profession, German by descent, and it was chosen in accordance with the ITUCH policy of producing plays by Chilean authors.

The play itself was ambiguous: the nightmare of a bourgeois family whose mansion is invaded by beggars and ragamuffins, very charming ones, who threaten their comfort and security by implementing plans which include digging up the garden to grow potatoes, melting down silver candlesticks to make spoons and converting museums into hospitals – rather an infantile revolutionary programme.

Within the production a class conflict was inevitable: Victor was bound to direct the play so that the sympathy of the audience would be with the beggars, while Egon would want the emphasis to be on the fears and insecurity of the middle-class inhabitants of the mansion with whom he himself felt identified. A short circuit was produced between Victor and Egon. Victor was worried that the play would fuel the campaign of fear among the well-dressed audiences which frequented the Antonio Varas Theatre. Egon privately accused Victor of having distorted his play. I know that in the discussions about this production one point was brought home very clearly to Victor: for him aesthetic values could not be separated from the realities of the Chilean political situation. He was incapable of doing something which betrayed or was contrary to his political position. Perhaps he should have refused to direct the play.

In 1965 Victor was awarded the two main prizes as the best director of the year – the Caupolican and the coveted Critics' Prize. They were for the direction of two very contrasting comedies, one, *La Remolienda* by Alejandro Sieveking, more of a robust farce, less delicate and poetic than *Animas de Dia Claro*; the other Ann Jellicoe's *The Knack* ('*La Maña*'), which he was invited to direct by the independent theatre company ICTUS.

We had collected visual material for *La Remolienda* on an expedition to the south the previous year. Victor had come back loaded with ideas and photographs. He was determined that in spite of being broad comedy, there should be nothing patronising or cliché-ridden about the vision of the peasants. If I hadn't actually experienced that journey I might have found far-fetched the idea of peasants being amazed the first time they encountered a made-up road or an electric lightbulb.

The production was great fun and the play was enriched during the rehearsal period by the addition of many details which made it a more authentic vision of peasant life. Victor also wrote the music, taught the cast to dance the cueca and other folk-dances and to understand the special sense of humour of the peasants, full of riddles and double meanings.

In spite of his success in the theatre, Victor had not lost touch with his roots. Folk music continued to be an intrinsic part of his life, his guitar a constant companion. In these crowded years he was developing powers as a composer and performer which were later to become a major part of his life and work, a means of communicating immediately with hundreds of thousands of people whom through the theatre alone he could never hope to reach.

As I grew closer to him, I realised how profound was Victor's necessity for music and how important his guitar was to him. I could have been jealous of it, because it was almost as though it were another person with whom he conversed. He played when he was depressed or especially happy, when he was relaxed or to help him relax when he was nervous.

Victor had never studied musical theory, and he couldn't write down the scores of his own songs. He had learned as the peasants do, by ear, and his style of playing was reminiscent of the region of Ñuble, his mother's birthplace and where he had spent his summers while at theatre school. When he composed, too, it was instinctively, with only his own creativity to guide him.

He always seemed to have two or three songs inside him. As he had said to me in one of his letters, 'Something seems to take root in me and then has to find a way of getting out . . .' His pockets were always full of scraps of paper with notes and verses scribbled on them. He would have ideas riding on a bus, walking in the street, at lunch or while reading the newspaper.

Because his work was so instinctive, it was important for him to try it out on an audience. I was the nearest person, so as soon as he had something ready, or had worked out an idea, he would play or sing it to me, asking for my opinions and comments. I was a built-in listening post. Because of this, I could see what he was looking for – a development of authentic folk music which would enhance rather than disguise its fundamental character, which would enrich its expressive possibilities so that the music could complement and underline the meaning of the text.

His first songs were very personal ones, almost autobiographical. His new-found happiness gave him the possibility of untying some of the knots inside him and expressing his feelings, his thoughts about his father and mother and their poverty, the anxiety of his childhood. He wrote of the priests who had frightened him so much and had seemed to hold the peasants to ransom with fear of Hell and of the Devil; he emphasised his belief that love between human beings was more important than religion: 'I believe only in the warmth of your hand in mine.'

In 1962, almost immediately after returning from his European tour, Victor directed the recording of an album of folk-songs with Cuncumén. It contained songs from every region of Chile from the far north to the island of Chiloe in the south and was called *Una Geografía Musical de Chile*. The innovation on this album was the inclusion of two of Victor's own songs – 'Paloma, quiero contarte' and 'Canción del minero'.

Cuncumén had always been a group dedicated exclusively to the investigation and performance of traditional folk-songs and -dances collected in the country. In Chile, as elsewhere, there were two prevailing schools of thought about folklore: one school saw folk as something static, already petrified, to be investigated only in an anthropological way and preserved for museums; the other, to which Victor belonged and which was only just beginning to make itself felt, saw it more as a living expression which could be contemporary and was capable of transformation providing it was firmly attached to its original roots.

This discussion continued throughout the first few years of the sixties, causing controversy and sometimes bitterness. Although Victor left Cuncumén at the end of 1962, he always maintained contact with them and supported them during the years that followed in their particular field of research into authentic folklore, even when to many people they seemed old-fashioned and out of touch with the times. Victor felt that although it was wrong to be dogmatic about folklore, it was also of great importance to investigate and to know as much as possible of the old traditions and the people who created them.

He himself had the opportunity to develop this side of his work when, in 1963, he was approached by Gregorio de la Fuente, then director of the Casa de la Cultura de Ñuñoa – a cultural institute in a suburb of Santiago – and asked to set up a school of folklore. With the help of one of the members of Cuncumén, Maruja Espinoza, Victor set about organising the classes, teaching the folk-dances which he especially enjoyed, while Maruja concentrated on teaching guitar. A large and enthusiastic group of students made it possible within a couple of years to form a very lively performing group from which several soloists later emerged.

It was still possible at that time to find peasant singers settled in the outlying districts of Santiago and the surrounding countryside. Victor encouraged the students to get out into the country at weekends to collect and record local folk-songs, and he himself did the same whenever he had the time. He also took a group on a field-trip to the north of Chile where the music and dances were completely different.

Victor's methods were probably very unscientific. He did not ask his students to use a written questionnaire as some of the academic investigators did, which often produced a barrier of incomprehension. Rather he encouraged both respect and friendship. With a bottle of wine and a guitar, an investigation session was converted into a real exchange of experiences. It was urgent and important to carry out this work. The global expansion of the music industry and the multi-national record companies was rapidly swamping Latin America, a secondary market which could be used as a dumping ground for the remainders of the international record industry.

The age of the disc-jockey had come to Chile. In order to 'make it', Chilean singers had to Americanise their names, so that Patricio Henriquez became 'Pat Henry', Los Hermanos Carrasco 'The Carr Twins', and so on. Pop stars from the United States arrived to be promoted by their record companies, and so long as they were blonde and Yankee-looking they were assured of instant success. The great majority of the radios, from the powerful networks to the local provincial stations, were owned by commercial corporations or large landowners. Only a handful were open to the influence of the labour movement or the left-wing political parties. That meant that anything of which the establishment did not approve had virtually no access to the mass media.

In neighbouring Argentina, however, President Perón had passed a law which made it obligatory for radio stations to devote a minimum of 50 per cent of their music time to Argentinian composers or traditional folklore. This provided an enormous stimulus for a musical movement based on folk, on typical dance rhythms, and led to the creation of many groups like Los Fronterizos, Los Chalchaleros . . . a whole range of music from authentic folklore to commercial pop, but all of it with a recognisably Argentinian character.

This wave of Argentinian music had also invaded Chile and provided the only massive alternative to the imported pop sung in English. Some of it was commercial and trite, but at least it was Latin American. It found fertile ground, not least because it fitted in with the political programme of the Christian Democrats. It was folk dressed up, without the smell of poverty and revolution. Folk for the comfortable middle classes.

Many imitative groups were formed in Chile, the most famous and successful being Los Cuatro Cuartos, smooth young men in evening suits, and their feminine equivalents Las Cuatro Brujas, slinky women, red-taloned and bejewelled, singing songs with patriotic or sentimental themes, rococo arrangements and a lot of 'boop-a-doop-a-doop'. Against this rather grotesque travesty, real songs of the people, folk-songs, had little chance of being heard.

But the taste for them was growing. They had become part of left-wing demonstrations and were heard at the rallies during Allende's election campaigns. In this uncommercial field there was plenty of work to do. Angel Parra had returned to Chile from Europe specifically to take part in the 1964 presidential campaign, so Angel and Victor renewed their friendship singing for Allende and began to work together with other singers like Rolando Alarcon, Patricio Manns, Hector Pavez and others who were campaigning for the same cause.

Angel and Isabel had both been earning their living in Europe as Chilean folksingers, together with Violeta, but on returning to their own country they found that they were too authentic to be accepted on the radio, in restaurants or night clubs, which were the only places available for professionals to perform. Angel found himself forced to acquire a dress suit, Isabel an evening dress. They sang between one commercial ditty and another on a show sponsored by a well-known brand of liver salts which had the improbable name of *Show Efervescente Yasta*. Perhaps the strangest thing was that they were there at all, considering that they didn't make the same concessions in their repertoire as in their dress.

In 1965, after the euphoria and activity of the presidential election, a rather general state of depression set in among Allende's supporters and it seemed a good idea to take advantage of the new contacts which had been made among artists during the campaign to try to create an alternative to the established mass media which were now largely dominated by the victorious Christian Democrats.

Just at this moment, Angel, together with his sister Isabel, opened the Peña de los Parra in Carmen 340 – an old house in a rather seedy street only a few blocks away from the city centre. Even Angel couldn't have envisaged the important role it was going to play in the development of the song movement, but immediately it became evident that it was the answer to a real need. The idea was simple – to create an informal atmosphere, without the usual censorship and commercial trappings, where folksingers could come in their everyday clothes to sing and exchange songs and ideas, a sort of artists' co-operative where people could eat simple food and listen to Chilean and Latin American folk music.

Victor and I were invited along by Angel, and we turned up one night at Carmen 340 soon after the Peña was opened. The entrance was dark and unprepossessing. If you weren't in the know you would have thought that it was a shabby private house. We went through a dark passageway past a couple of small rooms full of low wooden benches and rickety tables. Nothing seemed to be happening. We had made the mistake of arriving at the scheduled opening time of ten o'clock.

But out at the back, in the kitchen, we found a cluster of people busily heating up empanadas and pouring wine into rows of glasses. Angel's wife Marta, a tall, striking-looking woman, was directing operations, assisted by Frida, who was a close friend of mine. I felt very much at home and began to help with the preparations. A little later more friends and the public began to arrive and by about eleven o'clock the place was packed. There were many well-known faces – writers, intellectuals, other artists, people from the university, politicians – even some Christian Democrats from the more progressive wing of the party – with lots of young people, mostly students.

Although it had only been open for a few weeks, it was obvious that it already had a regular audience.

Squashed up on one of those uncomfortable wooden benches, in the dim and smoky atmosphere, you had to be really dedicated to last out the three to four hours of music. The performers sat on a tiny wooden platform in the division between two rooms where the wall had been knocked down, illuminated by a tiny spotlight. It was quite a dramatic effect and produced respect and concentration in spite of the informal atmosphere and wine.

The regular team at the Peña consisted at that time of Angel and Isabel, Rolando Alarcón, the ex-musical director of Cuncumén, who had recently started to make a name for himself as a composer in the 'neo-folk' movement, and Patricio Manns, a romantic-looking young man of German extraction from the south of Chile who was a writer and poet as well as a composer. Only recently a very beautiful song of his, 'Arriba en la cordillera', had 'made it' in the charts, so he was a great attraction for the Peña.

Sitting there that first time with Victor, the great impression for both of us, and we commented on it, was Isabel. We had known her for years, I only slightly because for a short time she had been a student at the dance school, but Victor had been close friends with her before she went to Europe. He knew that she had always been unsure of herself and her talent, and she had even been grateful to Victor for his encouragement to go on singing and to try herself as a soloist. She suffered, perhaps, from being labelled 'Violeta's daughter', and it was a struggle for her to find her own way. But there in the Peña, tiny in stature, she dominated the audience with her presence and her strong, passionate voice.

Angel was a masterly guitarist. When he sang he tied himself into knots around his guitar, and his deep, rather harsh voice seemed to struggle against its own strength. He seemed too small and frail for such explosions of emotion. But when brother and sister sang together in duet, they were all vitality, their voices mingling in perfect co-ordination, complementing each other exuberantly.

From the experience of their travels and the friendships they had made abroad, Isabel and Angel began to introduce Chilean audiences to songs of other Latin American countries – the counterpoint of the traditional songs of Venezuela, the political songs of Daniel Viglietti of Uruguay, the early songs of Atahualpa Yupanki. In another sense, too, the music being played in the Peña was new, because the Parras had brought back with them many Latin American instruments which enriched the accompaniment of the songs – the *cuatro* from Venezuela, the *tiple* from Colombia, *quenas, charangos, zampoñas, bombos* from the north which were almost unknown in Santiago, belonging as they do to the culture of the *altiplano*.

Angel was acting as host that evening in the Peña, and suddenly, in one of the pauses in the scheduled programme, he announced the presence in the audience of 'my friend, the well-known theatre director, Victor Jara', and thrust his guitar into Victor's hands, inviting him to sing. That first session marked a milestone in Victor's life. Singing a mixture of his own songs and little-known folk-songs which he himself had collected, he was received with electrifying silence and thunderous applause. For the next five years he was to be part of the Peña.

Victor accepted Angel's proposition as a challenge, knowing that it would be difficult to combine with his work in the theatre, that going to bed at three or four o'clock in the morning three times a week would be exhausting, but he thought that it would be worth the sacrifice. He felt that he had found a kind of workshop which would stimulate him to compose, a critical and sensitive audience that would really listen, a place where he could say what he wanted and exchange ideas with people who were interested in making songs which had some meaning. He knew that he had something to give as well as much to learn.

The commercial boom of folklore had reached its peak by now. By the following year it was already collapsing. A representative of one of the most successful groups, Los Paulos, declared in an interview that as the boom was over, they were changing to an international style; the director of Los Cuatro Cuartos made the even stranger statement that folklore should become 'international' in order to survive. Victor, Angel and Patricio all affirmed that the passing of the commercial boom did not affect real folklore in the least, since getting into the charts was not its main objective. A musical polarisation was beginning to take place.

One of the most immediate results of being in the Peña was that Victor had a chance to record his first 'single' record, with a lively traditional song from the north of Argentina on one side, 'La cocinerita', and on the other 'El cigarrito', with Victor's music, based on verses he had collected from a popular poet on one of his field expeditions. It was a strange experience for Victor to have a hit record, played on all the radios. He immediately became well-known outside the confines of the Peña and we even had to go to a big showbusiness festival in Viña del Mar for Victor to receive a prize for one of the most popular records of the year.

This record was quickly followed by another, with 'Paloma, quiero contarte' and one of Victor's repertoire of comic folk-songs with typically Chilean double meanings which poked fun at the passion of 'La beata' – an excessively pious lady – for the priest to whom she confesses her sins. It had a Chaucerian kind of humour. Victor had been singing it for months in the Peña and it had been appreciated by the audiences as light relief, but now, on record, some rather mischievous person played it on the radio at a time when there was a link-up of the whole national network.

It caused an uproar. Victor found himself at the centre of a scandal. Many radios banned the record. Then the Information Office of the Presidency requested its withdrawal from the shops and the destruction of the master. Father Espinoza, head of the monastery of San Francisco, made a statement to the press: 'I do not wish either to hear or to read that song, but I know what it is about. If they have censored it they have acted correctly because it is scandalous. I quote the words of Christ, "He who commits scandal would be better not to have been born".'

Victor was both amused and annoyed at such a reaction. Also interviewed extensively in the press, he said, 'I never imagined that an absolutely authentic and ancient folk-song, collected in the region of Concepción, could cause such a reaction. People who consider a picaresque and witty folk-song like this one to be insolent and irreverent are denying the decency of the people's creativity which is the very basis of our tradition . . . What do these same critics of 'La beata' think of the songs of Carl Orff, who took elements of mediaeval games for *Carmina Burana*? They are using an out-of-date morality which doesn't fit our century. The church itself is evolving. All over the world, folklore mixes religious and pagan themes because that is the human spirit. It is not for me to deform this material, especially when it is studied in a scientific way.'

Poor Victor, he had deeply offended the tight and prudish morality of the establishment without even meaning to. Our house was bombarded with telephone calls from people who insulted Victor and from others who supported him. The Peña was, of course, overwhelmed with people who wanted to hear 'La beata'. Only one disc-jockey supported Victor, and that was Ricardo García, perhaps the most popular of them all, who some years before had introduced Violeta Parra on his programme with a similar kind of song, 'El sacristán'.

During these first years together, I might easily have become immersed in our rather idyllic home life, and lost all touch with reality. But this didn't happen. On the contrary, my horizons were widened, and I got a closer view of the Chilean people and their lives, both in the city and the countryside, than I had had in all the years that went before.

After the death of his sister Maria, Victor had practically lost touch with his family, apart from an occasional glimpse of Coca, or a visit to more distant relatives, peasants in El Monte. But we maintained contact with many of his friends from Población Nogales and Barrio Pila. As they gradually married and started families, we went to their weddings and became 'godparents' to their children – more a sentimental than a religious relationship. But their horrendous problems – lack of work or miserable wages, scarcely enough to survive on, illness, nowhere to live – were a constant reminder, if one were needed, of the urgency of changing the structures and priorities of Chilean society.

This constant contact with deprivation, which concerned him in a very direct and personal way, motivated Victor to write several songs which had one common thread running through them: the dire consequences of poverty on human relationships, its capacity to destroy even the fundamental love of parents for their children, and the necessity of ending, once and for all, 'this dark and bitter sea'. Perhaps Victor's first song for children, 'Canción de cuna para un niño vago', had something to do with the emotion of becoming a father, because it was a lullaby. But it was not for his own daughter . . .

The River Mapocho runs through Santiago from the mountains to the sea. It is a dirty rush of water finding its way along a wide stony bed, scattered with rubbish. When the snows melt in spring it swells to a muddy torrent, but gradually dries to a trickle during the long, rainless summer months. Groups of children, 6 to 12 years old perhaps, but with the faces of old men and women, used to make their homes underneath the bridges, particularly near the Central Market, where the stall-holders threw rotten fruit and rubbish over the embankment. At night they slept huddled together with a collection of stray dogs who kept them company.

> The moon in the water
> flows through the city,
> underneath the bridge
> a child dreams of flying.
>
> The city shuts him in,
> a cage of metal,
> the child grows old
> without knowing how to play.
>
> How many, like you,
> will wander homeless?
> With money it is easy
> for love to exist,
> bitter the days
> when there is none.
>   ('Canción de cuna para un niño vago')

The majority of Victor's friends in the población were instinctive supporters of the Communist or Socialist Parties, and voted for Allende, but in those early years of the sixties few of them were politically active. As far as I could see, the average shanty-town dweller had an almost passive acceptance of suffering. The activists seemed to be those who were slightly better off, and at this period many of them were Christian Democrats. Victor had heated discussions with his friend David, whom he had known since his time with Acción Católica. David had meanwhile become an active supporter of Eduardo Frei and campaigned for him in the 1964 presidential election. He really believed that a Christian Democrat government would bring about fundamental changes which would give everyone a better chance.

Many of the women, too, believed that the Christian Democrats were going to change their lives, because they were 'good' people. Christian Democrat activists were moving into the poblaciones at this time, forming Neighbourhood Councils and Mothers' Centres. To my perhaps prejudiced view it seemed that the women were being taught to make too many pretty lampshades and felt toys, appearing in clean aprons to receive prizes or to be greeted by the mayoress . . . empty gestures when their children were begging in the streets.

Victor used to get very angry, and argue with the wives of his friends, 'You don't need charity! You have the *right* to somewhere decent to live, to a doctor within reach when you are ill, to a good education for your children! What's the use of a lampshade if you have no house to put it in?'

It wasn't only in Santiago that I began to have a different perspective. A new element in our lives, the acquisition of a *citroneta*, a Citroën Deux Chevaux car, gave us the freedom to explore the country together, as a family. These journeys, sometimes of hundreds of miles, meeting people who were very different from those who attended performances of the ballet when we went on tour, getting to know remote towns and villages where time seemed to have stopped a hundred years ago, gave me the feeling that I was growing roots in Chile.

On Sundays we would go out with Manuela and Amanda, up into the mountains or across the flat plain of the central valley. Victor's songs became populated with the people that we met on these journeys, songs which were human portraits of peasant men and women in their environment – their work, their problems, their hopes.

Several times we visited Lonquen, which had changed little since Victor had lived there. A peasant family, inquilinos of the Ruiz-Tagle family, still occupied the house he had known as a child, with pigs and hens rooting around the littered earth of the kitchen floor. He took us up to see the Devil's Footstep, and to visit some of the people he had known as a child. One of these was a very old man who sat outside his wooden shack, still plaiting the leather-thonged whips and lassos for which he was famous for many miles around. From this meeting came a song:

His hands although so old
were strong in their plaiting,
they were rough and they were tender
working the animal hide.

The plaited lasso, like a snake,
curled around the walnut tree,
and in every whip the imprint
of his life and bread.
How much time is contained in his hands,
and in his patient gaze?
Nobody has said 'That's enough,
no need to work any more!'

('El lazo')

We made many longer expeditions to the south, down the longitudinal Panamericana, which was so vital to Chile's communications. Starting off heroically as a highway, it soon degenerated into the equivalent of a bumpy B-road, full of potholes and sudden detours. South of Chillán the landscape began to change. Instead of the typical regimented rows of poplars and willows, growing along the irrigation canals, there were pines, oaks and other lusher vegetation. The rivers grew deeper and broader, and even the sky changed, with streaks of cloud which might rapidly turn to rain.

On one such journey we travelled into the wheat-growing zone of Traigen and then on until we reached Temuco. Turning off the main road on to a stony track, full of potholes, we set out eastwards, towards the cordillera. We drove for miles without seeing a single human being, through lush pasture-land and cornfields, occasionally passing the high wrought-iron gates of a latifundio, or a wooden ox-cart with a peasant sitting patiently behind the yoked oxen, deep in his own thoughts. This, too, became one of Victor's songs, 'El carretero'.

Late in the afternoon we came to Cunco, a market centre for the region. It was a typical conglomeration of wooden shacks, faced with rounded tiles of seasoned wood, with tiny windows and roofs steep-pitched against the torrential rains of the south. Many of them stood on stilts, to avoid the thick mud which accumulated on the unpaved, grass-grown streets. The pensión for travellers was a three-roomed shack with hitching-posts for horses outside the door. The sagging bed had clean sheets and old hand-woven blankets, but the floors were thick with dried mud, and a smell of damp pervaded everything. But perhaps the strongest impression was of silence. No footsteps, no traffic, a smell of rain-soaked vegetation, silent people who looked at you but did not greet you. Men and women with weatherbeaten faces and heavy clothes, whose feet made no sound on the earth of the road.

It was just before the presidential elections in 1964. We had seen occasional posters along the road for Alessandri or Frei, and more rarely a rough hand-painted sign for Allende. But as outsiders, we had the impression of a long unexpressed resentment, of too many years of silence, rather than of any organised political movement among the peasants. The landowners and their supporters were more aggressively organised and even armed, feeling themselves threatened by Frei's promises of land reform. Groups of men on horseback gathered outside the store in Cunco, overseers from the neighbouring latifundios, hostile, and with the air of owning the place. In that remote, silent place, a peasant would have to be very brave to campaign against the landlord.

We continued to Lake Calafquén, further south, and still almost unknown to tourists. We decided to try to reach Coñaripe at the head of it, driving round the shore on a road which was supposed to be passable in summer. It was, just, but had the peculiarity that it was interrupted at intervals by rivers of dried lava. On our left was the perfect, snow-covered cone of the great volcano of Villarica, slumbering.

The track seemed endless and the day was hot and sultry. It felt as though a storm was coming. We met no one on the road and there were no signs of human habitation, until, just as we crossed one of the more dramatic banks of lava, which had brought down great boulders with it, we saw a little wooden house. Children were playing outside, a woman was washing in a wooden trough, and a few goats were climbing the black rocks. We stopped to ask how far it was to Coñaripe, and the woman gave us some water to drink. We took a photo of the whole family standing in front of their wooden shack beside the lava trail. Most of them were dark, black-haired and Indian-looking, but there was one barefooted girl in a ragged pink dress whose father must have been a German settler, because she was blonde and blue-eyed. Her name was Prosperina.

Coñaripe was a tiny place, hemmed in on all sides by the lake, the slopes of the volcano, and an impenetrable forest on which it depended for its livelihood. A primitive saw-mill cut up the trunks of trees hundreds of years old. Most of the population were Mapuches, and on the outskirts of the village many still lived in rucas. Hungry by now, we at last found at the end of the village a woman who cooked lunch for the men working in the saw-mill. As we ate, she told us about her son who had gone off to the city to find work. She hadn't heard from him since he left two years ago, but she was very proud of him and showed us his paintings of birds and plants, some of them on wooden panels. We stayed talking to her for a long time – or rather Victor talked and I listened – and it was almost dark when we got up to go. Suddenly she took one of the paintings from the wall and thrust it into Victor's hands. It was impossible to refuse it. Embracing her, we thanked her and said good-bye.

We returned to stay the night at Lican Ray, a little village at the other end of the lake, planning to start our long journey home next day. During the night the expected storm broke and it began to rain as only it can in the south. By nine o'clock next morning the track out towards the main road, which wound up a precipitous hill, had become a waterfall. We knew that in winter the whole area became cut off except by boat, so we decided that we must try to get out before it became worse. Enlisting some help, we pushed the citroneta diagonally, zig-zagging up the hill, wet to the marrow of our bones, the rain streaming off our faces. We thought we should never make it.

It was lucky for us that we did, because only a few days later, before the road was open, the great volcano erupted in the middle of the night, and a huge wall of boiling lava and rocks surged down the mountainside, sweeping the little town of Coñaripe into the lake. It was never really known how many people lost their lives, although it was declared a disaster area and international aid was brought in. We never found out what happened to Prosperina and her family, nor whether the generous woman who gave us the painting had survived.

On another journey, we stayed by Lake Lanalhue, in the province of Arauco. In the last century, the region around the lake had been colonised by German settlers. Their descendants still farmed the green and sparsely inhabited countryside, and the pensión where we were staying was owned by a German couple – simple hospitable people who had made a quiet retreat without spoiling the wilderness of plants and trees along the lake-shore.

However, during the war, Lanalhue, like other areas of the south of Chile, had been a centre for the activity of the local Nazi party, as some of the original families showed where their sympathies lay. And still, every summer, fascist youth camps which specialised in paramilitary training were held in a remote inlet of the lake. Always, beneath the apparent calm, violence was present.

We made friends with some local people who owned a jeep, and they suggested that we should make an expedition around the lake, skirting the high hills which ran down to the shore, to the territory behind, where there were Indian settlements. It was there that we found Angelita Huenumán. I suppose for me she became a symbol, for Victor a friend whom he met again as the years passed and historic events drew people together. Her wooden hut stood in the midst of otherwise uninhabited countryside. As we approached on foot, because the jeep couldn't get very close, with Victor carrying Amanda on his back, a dog ran out barking fiercely. Victor was scared of strange dogs, having been bitten in the backside when a child, so there was a moment of panic, but then we saw a small upright woman, with long black hair, coming out of the hut and walking towards us. She was dressed in a dark-blue woven tunic, fastened with an ornate metal brooch, and had an air of dignity and calm. Her face, with its high cheekbones, seemed ageless, but I suppose she must have been around 40. She greeted us and offered Amanda a small, rather wizened apple which she took out of the depths of her pocket.

I think even Victor was made nervous by her extraordinary presence, but he overcame his inhibition and began to talk to her in a very natural way. She offered to show us round, and we found that she lived with her son, not much older than Amanda, and that alone she cultivated her small plot of land and took care of her pigs, hens and sheep. Victor asked her if she spun the wool and wove it herself. In answer she smiled and beckoned us towards the hut. As she opened the door, it was dark inside, but then she reached out to push open some wooden shutters and a shaft of sunlight fell on vivid purple, green, pink and yellow, a half-finished blanket stretched on a rough wooden loom, whose colours lit up the tiny space. We both gasped and asked her how long it took her to make such a beautiful blanket. She told us that she had time only during the winter months when the harvest was safely gathered. Only then could she spin the wool, dye and weave it. Once the blanket was finished, she would walk with it on her back across the hillside to the nearest town, and stand in the market-place to sell it to the highest bidder. Victor told her that he would pay her whatever she wished for the blanket when it was finished, if she would take it to our friends.

As we walked away we looked back and saw her standing there watching us depart. She lifted her hand in greeting, a lonely figure in the space and quietness of the deserted countryside. During the next few days Victor sat for hours on end on the shores of Lake Lanalhue, silently looking out over the water . . . a song for Angelita was the result:

In the valley of Pocuno
ruffled by the sea wind
where the rain feeds the moss
lives Angelita Huenumán.

Taken care of by five dogs
and a son left over from love,
as simple as her little farm
the world revolves around her.

The red blood of the copihue flower
runs in her Huenumán veins,
by the light of the window
Angelita weaves her life.

Her hands dance in the hemp
like the wings of a little bird,
she weaves a flower so miraculously
that you can smell its perfume.

Angelita, in your weaving
there is time and tears and sweat,
there are the anonymous hands
of my own creative people.

After months of work
the extraordinary blanket looks for a buyer,
and like a bird in a cage,
sings for the highest bidder.

Between the oak trees and the reeds,
between the hazel-woods and the gorse,
in the aroma of wild fuchsias,
lives Angelita Huenumán.

('Angelita Huenumán')

There were two sequels to this encounter. One, that when the blanket
was finished, Angelita remembered us, and in the spring it arrived at
our house in Santiago; the second, that when Victor met Angelita
again, it was in Santiago, taking part in a women's meeting . . . she
was happy with the song that Victor had written for her . . . but that
was in 1972.

5

THE MID-SIXTIES

The mid-sixties was a bad time for people on the left in Chile. A large proportion of working people, especially women, had voted for Eduardo Frei. His election campaign, with its slogan 'Revolution in Liberty', had promised many popular reforms, among other things more and better housing, anti-inflationary measures, economic and agrarian reform. He had also promised the 'Chilenisation' of the copper mines, a scheme which in practice involved the payment of many millions of dollars to the American mining companies in return for 51 per cent of the shares, but little effective control. The US government saw Frei as a dyke against a real revolution. To many ordinary people he appeared to offer a real alternative to the discredited right-wing oligarchy that had ruled for so many years.

The promise of a better standard of living for working people soon proved to be empty. In 1965, after the police were sent in to break a strike in the northern town of El Salvador, killing miners and their wives who were sheltering in a trade-union building, it became obvious whose interests Frei was serving. His other promised measures and reforms were bogged down in the face of right-wing opposition which was firmly entrenched and very powerful.

It was at about this time that I became aware of a new word to add to my growing glossary of Chilean terms – pituco, roto, gringo, etc. This was the word 'momio' or, strictly translated, 'mummy' – in the Egyptian sense. In my mind I always associated the term with a character in a play by Raul Ruiz which Victor had directed some time before . . . an ancient landowner who appeared to be disintegrating in his wheelchair, attended by a servant as decrepit as himself. He would call querulously for his binoculars and peer out over the audience, as though over the vast expanses of his estates, a symbol of the decaying yet petrified oligarchy, jealously protecting their lands and privileges. *Momio* was becoming the popular term for anyone with a reactionary position.

By this time, Victor's motives for singing and composing were gradually becoming less intimate and personal. The mainspring of his songs was a profound sense of identification with and love for the underprivileged people of Chile, in both the cities and the countryside; a very deep awareness of the injustices of society and their causes and a determination to denounce those injustices in the face of indifference and censorship . . . and also to try to do something to change them. In that sense Victor's songs were 'political', but in these early years only indirectly so. When he was asked by a journalist why he was devoting so much time to singing, perhaps at the expense of his work in the theatre, he answered:

I am moved more and more by what I see around me . . . the poverty of my own country, of Latin America and other countries of the world; I have seen with my own eyes memorials to the Jews in Warsaw, the panic caused by the Bomb, the disintegration that war causes to human beings and all that is born of them . . . But I have also seen what love can do, what real liberty can do, what the strength of a man who is happy can achieve. Because of all this, and because above all I desire peace, I need the wood and strings of my guitar to give vent to sadness or happiness, some verse which opens up the heart like a wound, some line which helps us all to turn from inside ourselves to look out and see the world with new eyes.

I myself was no longer a raw gringa. With my gradual Chilenisation came also the shedding of many feelings and prejudices which I had had when I first arrived in the country. I no longer felt an unbridgeable abyss between myself and the extremely poor who lived in the shanty-towns and urban slums. I had many friends and acquaintances among them. Not only did I understand much more intimately what their lives were really like, but, without idealising them, I felt much more comfortable in their company than in that of our middle-class neighbours.

When Victor and I began living together, I was at first wary of his political commitment. I had already been married to one communist. I could not understand why so many artists in Chile, so many of my friends, insisted on becoming members of 'The Party'. Now I was increasingly sure of where my sympathies lay, although I never felt I could become a *militante*, a member of any party. The dedication which Victor demanded of himself was something that I knew I wasn't capable of, and my full-time work was about as much as I could manage. My political development, such as it was, was reflected as the years passed in my professional career.

I had gradually become so much a part of what was going on that most of my colleagues had forgotten, I think, that I was a foreigner. European names abound in Chile, anyway. I spoke fluent Spanish with a Chilean accent and my English had become rusty through disuse – so much so that it was difficult and unnatural for me to speak it to Manuela and Amanda. There was no way that Victor and I were going to make conversation in English in the scant amount of time we could all spend together, although to allay my slightly guilty conscience I used to take both girls to extra English classes at the British Institute. Neither of them was especially aware of her British connection, nor had I any friends among the British community in Santiago, who for the most part frequented the Country Club and played golf.

Before Amanda's birth in 1964, I had taken the decision to resign from the National Ballet. The work of the company had become increasingly all-absorbing as its international fame grew. We spent a lot of time abroad in other Latin American countries and a long tour to the United States was being planned. I decided that the moment had come to spend more time with my family.

The decision was made easier, not only because I was happy in my private life, but also because I was in disagreement with the artistic direction of the Ballet. In my view, the strength of the company had always been its modern repertoire to which the work of Patricio was giving an increasingly Latin American focus. It was a homogeneous group, not an hierarchical one, with all its members having a chance to create roles in keeping with their own particular talents. Uthoff had guided the Chilean National Ballet along these lines with great ability, developing it from nothing into a company which was welcomed in other Latin American countries as an example. When we danced in the enormous Teatro Colón in Buenos Aires – an opera house even larger and more imposing than Covent Garden – queues for tickets formed around the building days in advance.

But within the company there was a group of dancers whose one ambition was to dance a classical repertoire – *Swan Lake, Nutcracker,* the lot – and to become classical dancers, even if it meant being third-rate ones. With the arrival of a new ballet master from the United States, the situation became even more acute and eventually Uthoff was forced to resign – by which time, happily, I had already left the company. But I stayed on as a full-time teacher in the university dance school.

Somehow, as in all things in Chile during these years, there were political undertones even to these apparently professional problems. In our rarified world, the polarisation existing in the country seemed to be reflected in two opposing camps: those who felt the company should be transformed into a classical one tended to be momios, while those who wished to continue to develop a modern focus, with new, home-grown choreographers and a truly Latin American dance movement, were all politically on the left. In the *coup d'état* which took place in the Ballet, Patricio also was forced to resign as deputy director, for purely political reasons.

My friend Alfonso had left the Ballet some time before and he now convinced me to join him in setting up an amateur dance centre at the Casa de la Cultura de Ñuñoa. The idea was the more attractive to me because Victor had just started to work there in folklore. It was a relief, like a breath of fresh air, to get away from the enclosed world of the university. The Faculty had become an unpleasant place, full of intrigues and internal tension. The flood of applicants for the new school in Ñuñoa was an indication of the untapped talent and enthusiasm that abounded.

I enjoyed working with amateur students and it opened my eyes to the potential of dance as recreation, which was almost completely undeveloped in Chile. I spent a lot of energy in Ñuñoa. Together with Alfonso, who had a genius for teaching children, we created an amateur group, capable of giving simple performances in the open air. If I had any talent as a choreographer, it was in creating dances which didn't present too many technical difficulties, but gave the students the pleasure of performing without the audience suffering too much.

Two years later, I found myself forced to make yet another choice – this time between my work in the professional dance school in

the university and the flourishing little group in Ñuñoa. If I chose
to concentrate on the latter, it was because I was bored with being
part of a kind of factory which put young children into ready-made
moulds. Since the resignation of Uthoff, increasing emphasis had been
put on trying to convert children into classical ballerinas, and my work
as a teacher was reduced to pouring a kind of modern sauce over
them, trying to keep open their rapidly narrowing horizons. It wasn't
a situation in which I could feel comfortable.

To resign from the university, to give up its motherly embrace, a
secure monthly salary and a pension when I retired, seemed a rash
step to take. However, Victor and I discussed it and he supported
my decision. We should manage somehow. Financial considerations
never seemed to be the main factor in our lives. Victor, of course,
had great sympathy with any effort to make dance accessible to wider
groups of people. He loved to dance himself and sometimes came to
my classes.

In 1967 Alfonso and I transferred our group to the Cultural Institute
of Las Condes, which had more facilities and even a small theatre.
Neither there, nor in Ñuñoa before, did we have any real claim to say
that we were working in the local community, and even less 'bringing
dance to the masses'. In those days there were no organisations which
made such a project possible. Both suburbs were in the heart of the
barrio alto and although we did give a few open-air performances
in some nearby working-class districts, our pupils came from all
over Santiago and they were mostly from fairly well-off families.
Our merit, I think, was that in having escaped from the rather
stultifying atmosphere of the Faculty, Alfonso and I had gradually
formed not only an amateur group but also a dance workshop where
new choreographers could have the chance to experiment.

It was gratifying to see how many of our ex-colleagues from the
National Ballet offered their co-operation, both as choreographers
and guest performers, until by 1969 we had an established group
with our own repertoire, the Taller de Danza de Las Condes – a very
mixed group perhaps, but bound together by great enthusiasm. Many
distinguished musicians, composers and designers co-operated with us,
among them Sergio Ortega, an important composer of symphonic
music and teacher in the Faculty, who wrote the music especially for
a ballet of mine called *Orbita*, while five or six budding choreographers
had their first chance with us, most of them going on to produce larger

works with the National Ballet. It was heartening to see what could be done in an informal atmosphere with the good will and enjoyment of many people working together.

The fact that I was able to work at all during these years was owing to the presence at home of Monica, who shared with me the responsibility of the housework and looking after the children. Almost all middle-class women in Chile owed their 'emancipation' to others less fortunate who carried out the typical 'women's tasks' of cleaning, cooking, washing, sewing and even caring for their children, while we, their employers, went out to our professional work. Often their lives were those of slaves, with little free time, living in tiny rooms in other people's homes and continually at the mercy of the *patrona* from early morning to late at night.

I hope that my relationship with Monica was not the typical one of employer and maid. A handsome girl from a large peasant family, she came to live with us soon after Amanda was born, and stayed with us for nine years. She was more a friend than a servant, a person on whom I could rely in an emergency. Most of the women who took jobs as domestic servants were illiterate or nearly so, but Monica had reached secondary school level and we encouraged her to go on studying. She chose to attend a course in hairdressing, which might give her a chance to get a job outside the home.

In the end, although she qualified, she decided not to leave us. She had a baby while she was living with us, but didn't get married and her daughter Carola grew up as one of the family, eventually going to the same school as Manuela and Amanda. I never felt too guilty about having Monica's help – not only because it was completely 'normal', but because she did have enough independence to live her own life, and I think she was relatively happy with us. However, looking back, I can see that the fact that she clung to us was a symptom of a perverse system, which produced emotional as well as financial dependence.

Since opening in 1965, the Peña de los Parra in Carmen 340 had established itself not only as an original and important centre for a new sort of song movement but also as a natural meeting place for people with left-wing opinions. It gained the reputation of being full of revolutionaries – from Marxists to a new breed of left-wing

Christians. It was a place where most of the young men wore beards as a gesture of solidarity with the Cuban revolution.

Gradually walls were knocked down to enlarge the original space, and the remaining ones became covered with graffiti which, if only you could read them in the dim candlelight, were a written testimony to the breadth of support for the Peña, the political opinions of its audiences, and the great variety of its visitors – from all over Latin America, and later the world.

As right-wing repression hit other Latin American countries, it became a refuge for singers from Brazil, Uruguay and Argentina. I remember also a delegation of Vietnamese women who visited the Peña, fragile and beautiful, but each of whom had won medals fighting in the war. It became a place where craftsmen and -women could show and sell their work, a permanent exhibition of popular art.

In the restaurant at the back, the walls were hung with Violeta's tapestries and posters of song festivals in Cuba. The menu was expanded to include *anticuchos* and *mate con malicia*, home-made bread and *pebre*. I became an expert in helping in the kitchen during the hours I spent there. In those early years I often accompanied Victor, but when we arrived he would disappear out to a little shed at the back of the patio where he shut himself in to play the guitar and warm up, because he had little time to do so during the rest of the week. He was always uncommunicative before he had to sing, very concentrated, talked to nobody. Only afterwards would he relax and be sociable.

The Peña became fuller and fuller. There was usually an overflow of people waiting in the corridor for someone to come out. Such concentrated humanity meant that it was never cold in winter, although icy draughts tended to whistle through the ill-fitting doors and windows of the other rooms. People kept warm by huddling together over a *brasero* – an open dish of burning charcoal – wrapped in ponchos, toasting their feet and drinking mate.

After singing, Victor used to wait for the Peña to end, when all the artists sang and played together in an improvised grand finale. Sometimes this acquired such momentum that they would go on playing all night, long after the audience had gone home. There were compensations for the long hours and sleepless nights.

However, although it was becoming more and more of a meeting place for music, the Peña was not yet really connected with the outside world. It had no links with the labour movement or the working class as such, although the key figures there were all of working-class background and very faithful to that. It remained an experimental laboratory with a small, rather élite audience. Nevertheless, through the opportunities it provided for artists to work together and inter-change ideas, that laboratory provided the environment in which a new musical movement was growing up, firmly based on a real Latin American tradition.

Violeta had returned from Europe to find this initiative of her children already flourishing and well-established. Although she had sung with them there when she first arrived in 1965, she was already planning a project of her own which she had always cherished. At last she obtained the support of the local council of La Reina, where she lived in the outer suburbs of Santiago, to erect a circus tent which she converted into her own cultural centre, with folklore, handicrafts and popular art. The circus tent attracted a different audience from Carmen 340. It was very remote and we went there only a couple of times. Once, I remember, we found Violeta busy cooking in a primitive open-air kitchen, preparing for the evening session. The other time was at *Fiestas Patrias*, when all the folksingers instinctively gathered round Violeta. But the tent was a huge, cold place, lacking the intimacy of the Peña. Even the name and reputation of Violeta Parra was not enough to fill it.

Although in the mid-sixties she was an important figure, and her years of work as an investigator were looked upon as an example to be followed, Violeta had a strong and difficult personality. Only in 1966, shortly before her death, was the full impact of her stature and creativity felt among the younger generation of composers. I remember sitting in the Peña late one night when Angel played the newly published record of her last songs and we heard 'Gracias a la vida' for the first time. Victor for one was moved to tears. A few months later, on 5 February 1967, Violeta committed suicide alone in her circus tent. Only then did she begin to receive the general recognition she deserved.

As Victor said later, 'None of us could say, while Violeta lived, that she was an artist of the people. We even criticised her. But time and the people themselves will recognise her. She lived the best years of her life among them – the peasants, miners, fishermen, craftsmen, the indigenous people of the Andes in the north, the islanders of Chiloe

in the south. She lived with them, shared their lives, their skin, their
flesh and blood. Only in that way could Violeta have created songs
like "¿Qué dirá el Santo Padre?" or "Al centro de la injusticia" and
others which will remain in the history of our country as the birth of
a new type of song . . .'

The example of the Peña de los Parra spread like wildfire. By 1967
there were peñas all over the place. Some were regular venues, like
the established Chile Rie y Canta of René Largo Farías, others were
one-off fund-raising events for left-wing causes, but the majority
were in students' unions in the universities, one of the first and most
important being that of the State Technical University.

Victor was always being invited to them and always found it
impossible to say no. A peña actually had to coincide with his work
in the theatre for him to refuse, much to my annoyance sometimes.
At weekends it might mean visiting two or three in the same evening,
and they all went on into the small hours of the morning.

One weekend in the winter of 1966, Victor was at a peña in
Valparaiso. He had just finished singing and was on his way out,
weaving between the tables with his guitar over his head, when one
of a noisy party of young people stood up and waved to him, inviting
him to come and join their group. He recognised Eduardo Carrasco,
his brother Julio and their friend Julio Numhauser, three of the bearded
young men who frequented the Peña de los Parra, and had recently
formed their own group with the unusual name of Quilapayún. They
were being coached by Angel, and that evening were celebrating their
first success, at an amateur song festival in nearby Viña del Mar called
'Chile Multiple'.

They wanted to invite Victor to sing at the peña of the Technical
University. Victor accepted and stayed talking and joking with them
until the small hours of the morning, and eventually, amid jokes and
laughter, Eduardo asked him if he would become their artistic director.
Although he was doubtful about fitting the rehearsals into his already
overloaded timetable, Victor was interested in the proposal . . . 'It
must have been the atmosphere in the group, the frankness and spirit
of companionship that attracted him,' Eduardo commented much
later, 'because it was obvious that there was not yet much musical
achievement.'

Although none of them was a musician – Eduardo for instance was
a student of philosophy – they had decided to form a musical group

to develop the trend set in the Peña, using indigenous instruments. They wanted a stronger image than the traditional folk groups like Cuncumén, and a more authentic one than the commercial 'neo-folk' ensembles. They looked for an indigenous name with a strong masculine rhythm – the stress on the final syllable – and came up with 'Quilapayún', which in the Mapuche language means 'three beards'. Both Angel and Victor commented that it was difficult in both sound and spelling for people to remember, and there was quite a heated discussion about it. But time has proved them right.

For the next three years, until 1969, Victor worked with Quilapayún as their artistic director. They began by rehearsing in the Casa de la Cultura de Ñuñoa, late at night after Victor's classes had finished, in a cold hall which was used for our dance classes, huddled round a paraffin stove.

The first thing he had to teach them was to work seriously, because one of their main characteristics was a tendency to giggle and turn everything into a joke – so much so that he had to allow a break for fooling about in the middle of the rehearsal, so that while they were working they could really concentrate. He worked with them not just as a musician, but also as a theatre director, helping them to identify with what they were singing, to create an atmosphere, so that the essence of each song was brought out in the attitude and movement of each member of the group as well as in the music and voices. This method of working gave Quilapayún a very strong quality and stage presence which was accentuated by their virile voices and their dramatic visual presence with beards and black ponchos – an image which, as Eduardo put it, was 'masculine, but not *machista*'. With their youth and their air of determination they seemed the personification of effort in a common cause. It was something new and seemed somehow to embody the spirit of the time.

With Quilapayún, Victor tried to explore the expressive possibilities of folk music without distorting and destroying its traditional character by 'prettified' arrangements like those of the neo-folk groups such as Los Cuatro Cuartos. They aimed at the multiplication of sounds, not only in the voices, but by use of the different indigenous instruments that they were learning to play. It was a shared adventure in which he taught them to enhance rather than drown the original quality of the traditional music but at the same time to feel free to develop it.

Victor did not, of course, see his role as artistic director to mean imposing his own ideas. He taught them a great deal about folklore, but he also applied the same methods of stimulating a collective creativity that he always used in the theatre. 'That is why our work in that period was so fruitful,' Eduardo told me. 'The group acquired its own style and was guided in a very profound artistic sense. We made discoveries with Victor which were really very daring in relation to what was being done musically in that period. Victor had a very delicate sense of harmony and used chords which nobody used then, spontaneously, instinctively.'

The group still had nowhere to perform as they were almost unknown. After rehearsing all week, on Saturday nights Quila, their girlfriends, Victor and I would all set out in a caravan of ancient citronetas in search of an audience. Perhaps someone knew of a peña being held in some students' union for the evening, and off we would go. On arrival, negotiations would take place with the organisers. Usually the answer was yes, because most peñas were open-ended, so then the instruments were unloaded and the long wait began while a string of other singers and groups performed. When Quilapayún finally did sing, they usually acquired a new set of fans.

Within a year, of the original trio only Eduardo remained. But he was joined by Carlos Quezada, a designer, with a wonderful tenor voice, Patricio Castillo, younger and rather a rebel, but a superb musician, Hernán Gomez, very quiet and a specialist *charango* player, Willie Oddo, a solo singer and natural comic, and finally Rodolfo Parada. These six completed the group as it remained for many years. While the numbers multiplied, generally the three beards remained constant, although they moved from chin to chin.

It was on these rounds of the peñas that Victor first came into contact with Inti-Illimani, a group which had been formed a year later than Quilapayún in the peña of the Technical University. Their speciality was the music of the altiplano, with *quenas*, *zampoñas* and *charangos*. All five were students, studying subjects like engineering, but they also did field research in folklore and spent their holidays, when they could, in the regions where these instruments were played. Vocally they were weaker than Quilapayún, but they, perhaps more than anyone, were responsible for popularising the particular haunting sound of the quena and the brilliance of the charango, a tiny stringed instrument made from an armadillo shell.

But it was with Quilapayún that Victor was more closely associated at this time. Sometimes the whole group came to our house to celebrate an occasion like someone's birthday or a festival won. They would arrive loaded with food – meat to cook over charcoal in the garden, *chuicos* (demijohns) of wine – and with their musical instruments. Willie and Carlos were usually the cooks, specialists in marinating the meat and making the traditional salads and dressing with chopped fresh coriander and chili. Jokes, improvisation and a kind of Latin American jam session would follow, sometimes ending in a *machitún*, an invocation to the pagan gods to bring luck. There were processions round the garden, drums and pipes playing, follow-my-leader round the trees and over the fallen tree trunks and then out into the patio and the street at full blast, dogs barking, children happily dancing along with them. Needless to say, Manuela and Amanda loved them. They were a collection of mustachioed and bearded 'uncles' who were the envy of the other children of the neighbourhood.

They were all young and optimistic, sharing a spirit of rebellion against empty conventions and out-of-date formality. They loved shocking people and doing outrageous things. It was Eduardo's idea to cultivate consciously a special brand of humour as a way of creating unity in the group and while separately they might be quiet or even shy, together there was no stopping them. Sometimes this unity seemed exclusive and won them enemies, but it helped to give them their strong stage presence and magnetism.

In those days invitations to perform came in a very haphazard way, so Victor was very impressed one day by a letter, on embossed notepaper, announcing a Latin American Song Festival in the city of Victoria in the south and requesting his participation, together with Quilapayún. It was sponsored by the town council – unusual in those days – and sounded both important and interesting. After a lot of pressure from Victor, Quilapayún agreed to cancel a previous engagement in Valdivia, which left the organisers of that event tearing their hair out and swearing that the group would never again be invited to the town – and they never were. However, having made up their minds to go to Victoria, they all anxiously awaited news from the organisers.

Eventually another letter came – there were certain cash problems and would the artists please buy their own train tickets. Victor's spirits were low as he boarded the train for the long journey south with the group already regretting their decision and blaming it on him. When the train finally chugged into Victoria some fourteen hours later, all of them peered out looking for the crowds of people who should be arriving for the festival, but the wooden platform was deserted. They unloaded themselves and their instruments and were standing there, unsure of what to do next, when they saw a rather small boy approaching them.

'Victor Jara?' he said politely. 'Thank you for coming. I am a member of Form IV-B, organisers of the Latin American Song Festival. Will you please follow me?'

Their troubles were only just beginning. The festival took place in the hall of a local convent school and in charge of the sound equipment were nuns. When Quilapayún broke into Violeta's song '¿Qué dirá el Santo Padre?' ('Whatever would the Holy Father say?') the nuns were so shocked that every time the chorus with these words was repeated, they cut off the microphone and left Quilapayún mouthing the words without volume.

At the end of a long programme – there really were other guest singers and groups – they were all packed into a couple of citronetas and taken to the station. It was a cold and rainy night in mid-winter and their hosts were in a hurry to be home, driving off quickly. Once again they found themselves on the wooden platform, surrounded by their instruments, only to find that the train would be six hours late – a not uncommon occurrence. Victor was not the most popular person in Chile at that moment.

Perhaps this rather comic incident was a symptom of growing friction between Victor and Quilapayún. It certainly revealed differences of attitude. By himself, Victor would probably have had quite a good time in Victoria. He admired the enterprise of organising such an event in a small provincial town, and in fact he returned the next year to support a repeat of it.

Although the group often accompanied Victor in his songs, and they performed together in many concerts, he never wanted to become absorbed into it as a performer. But as time went on, Eduardo began to insist that Victor should give up singing as a soloist and become a member of Quilapayún. He refused to do so and found himself being criticised for being interested in individual fame. Worse, he was made fun of for his constant awareness of the fact that he had been born a peasant and brought up in an urban slum, and for his insistence on acknowledging his family background, which was the corner-stone of everything he did.

It was a situation which forced Victor to analyse his reasons for singing. He was hurt and would come home very upset from rehearsals and discussions with Quilapayún, wanting to talk things over with me. He was very self-critical, but he began to realise that there were some factors which inevitably distanced him from the group. Although he was only a few years older than most of them, his experience of life was far greater. They were all university students from comfortable homes, whose political commitment sprang from intellectual conviction but not from a first-hand experience of deprivation. He found it difficult to bridge the gap.

Victor's own particular gifts as a composer and a performer were profoundly individual, even though he put them at the service of a cause in which he believed. But he saw very clearly and taught Quilapayún to cultivate the strength of their collective image, many-sided but in unison, realising that in those days of incipient mass struggle, it could produce an impact far beyond that of any individual singer.

Meanwhile, Victor's work as a theatre director brought him other opportunities. His success with *The Knack* and *La Remolienda* led to an invitation from the British Council to spend some time seeing British theatre companies and drama schools. It was at the end of January 1968 that I left Amanda and Manuela in the care of Alfonso, Patricio and Monica and took a plane to meet Victor at Kennedy Airport where he would be waiting for me at the conclusion of a tour of the United States with ITUCH.

I can still remember my happiness as I saw him bounding down an escalator as I was on my way up. For some reason, we had almost missed one another and Victor's face exploded into his radiant white-toothed smile when he caught sight of me. He was wearing the inevitable khaki-green duffle coat, the same one that he had brought back from his first journey to Europe, and a peaked sailor's cap of the same vintage, embracing his guitar in a brand-new case.

La Remolienda had been the big success of the tour among the Spanish-speaking population of the West Coast and New York, but on the campuses of Berkeley and UCLA, Victor had had the strange and interesting experience of trying to communicate, through his music, with audiences of American hippies, into Ravi Shankar and smoking pot. He tried to tell them something about the problems of Latin America and found them to be a sympathetic audience. The Vietnam War was then at its height and most of them were protesting about the draft: they had their own fight and their own cause. Victor felt that politically they tended to be very naive, that they would never achieve a revolution, not even of 'flowers' – the drugs would take care of that, defusing what might have been a powerful movement of rebellion.

Although there was as yet no equivalent in Chile, Victor was not shocked by the bare feet, long hair and lack of cleanliness and inhibitions. He had written to me already in a letter, 'It seems to me that the hippies are a normal and justifiable reaction against this sinisterly hygienic and mechanised world . . . The American people are imprisoned in a kind of plastic cage which crushes them with its own weight.'

Our arrival in London a few days later, after visiting my old haunts of Ballets Jooss in Essen, was greeted by pouring rain, but it was an emotional experience for me because it was the first time that I had been back since 1958. It was strange to arrive in London and have no home, to be a foreign tourist, finding difficulty in thinking and speaking in English, and certainly finding that in the ten years I had been absent there had been a startling change in atmosphere. It was Victor's first visit and he was anxious to rid himself of the preconceived clichés about England and the English people which were so prevalent in Chile, and to get to know the land of the Beatles.

It was really like a honeymoon for us, one of the very few occasions when we could spend time together with no professional, political or family responsibilities. Carefree and feeling very provincial, we gaped and gawped, walking hand-in-hand around 'Swinging London'. It was shocking to be thrust into the midst of a highly-developed consumer society, on a high peak of wealth and abundance, after the poverty and isolation of Chile. We were dizzied by the barrage of commercial propaganda, colour television with live news reports from every corner of the earth (except Chile, it seemed), lavish shop-window displays, the blaring music, the flora and fauna of the Earls Court Road where we were staying, and of Carnaby Street, then at the height of its glory.

It all brought home to us very forcibly just how limited was our vision of the world in Chile, through the mediocrity of the media, where the left-wing press was too poor even to be linked to the international cable system, and in order to keep up to date with international news you had to buy the right-wing *El Mercurio* and try to discern the objective facts behind the propagandistic reporting. Here in England, the news reports were an assault on the senses and the emotions.

To this was linked our awareness of the sexual liberation which had taken place in Europe and which was so utterly lacking in Latin America. We had come from a prudish society, which not only found it necessary to censor a song like 'La beata', but in which the cult of machismo was taken for granted even by otherwise progressive people. Both Victor and I felt attuned to a real equality between the sexes. A man doesn't have to spend his time proving his masculinity in order to survive and a woman shouldn't have to frustrate all her own potential in order to serve him and be constantly available.

After a month of going to the theatre and exploring together the scenes of my childhood which Victor wanted to see, our holiday together came to an end. Victor had to sign on with the British Council and I had to return to Chile because my work was awaiting me. For some time I had been increasingly anxious to get home. Although we had received only good news about the girls, I was filled with apprehension about them and had been having nightmares in which, for some unknown reason, diabetes played a part. When I did arrive in Santiago, it was to a warm homecoming . . . the house was full of flowers, the garden and the mountains were beautiful. It was a relief to be back with my daughters and I never voluntarily left them again.

During the next three months, Victor was able to sit in on rehearsals of various productions by different companies: Worthing Repertory Company, the Richmond Theatre, the Arts Laboratory and the Royal Shakespeare Company in Stratford-upon-Avon, as well as seeing all the performances he had time for and visiting drama schools.

He suffered somewhat, as probably all Latin Americans did at that time, from being confronted by complete ignorance about his country. He told me about his arrival at Worthing Rep, very nervous about his first assignment. 'One of the actresses said to me, "Oh, how nice to meet you, you look so civilised!" It could have made me angry, but I just laughed. People think Latin America is all mystery, jungle, voodoo and cannibals. When I told them that the work of Pinter was very well-known in Chile, one of the actors asked me if it were acted in translation. "Of course," I said, "our language is Spanish." He then laughed theatrically and exclaimed, "Oh, how priceless! Pinter in Spanish!" "No more priceless than Chekhov in English," I told him.'

In his letters to me, Victor constantly expressed his preoccupation with the atmosphere he felt around him:

> . . . I sometimes think it must be more difficult to live in a country where you have the world in your hands through the media, with such 'instructive' and 'impartial' information, than to live in a country such as ours where everything is more insignificant and parochial, even though the news is manipulated by the country which dominates us. At least you don't feel so oppressed by the uselessness of your existence. Otherwise I can't explain to myself this generation of young people who seem to be trying to escape from themselves with drugs, or who commit suicide to find the only truth of being alive in death. All the time you feel that you are being pinned to the wall: with the hole in the throat of Martin Luther King, with the sight of his widow weeping beside him, with the bombing of Vietnam, the sinking of a ship with few survivors, the première of a new film by Tony Richardson, the colour of the lipstick that will be worn this week or the latest dog biscuit. You haven't time to choose or think about your choice. If you don't act immediately you will be left behind for ever. It seems that nobody dares to be themselves. They are afraid of solitude and because of that, everyone is alone in a mass of lonely people . . . Apart from being in the hands of the United States and having other defects, Chile is at least a place where bread is bread and earth is earth; a place where one can find oneself and find other people with a compass which is that of real life, natural life. Hopefully they will never 'civilise' us. I prefer it as it is – raw, open and wild.

Despite his professional interest in all he saw, Victor was impatient to be back at work in his own country where there was so much to do. He criticised himself for sitting around like a connoisseur while the whole world seemed to be on the point of exploding.

Our separation was accentuated by the fact that a long postal strike in Chile interrupted communications. It was at this moment that I discovered that Amanda was diabetic. I say 'I' discovered it, because her symptoms were classic ones and it was I who suggested to our family doctor that her blood sugar should be tested. In Chile the illness was considered very unusual in such a young child – she was only three and a half – but I found out afterwards that many children of working-class families died of malnutrition or in a coma before the illness was diagnosed or any treatment could be made available.

I could scarcely believe that my nightmares had proved prophetic. The shock was terrible. I felt, quite wrongly as it happens, that any chance of happiness had gone for Amanda and for all of us. During those first dreadful days, I carried on in a trance, learning to manage insulin injections and all the time worrying about how I was going to break the news to Victor. It certainly meant that Amanda's life and mine were going to be bound by an inescapable routine for many years to come and that from then on I had to have very strict priorities.

It cost me blood, sweat and tears to write the letter which I posted as soon as the strike was over. Meanwhile I had received letters from Victor by hand, through friends, so I knew that he was in Stratford-upon-Avon. It was there, sitting on his bed in an English 'digs' that he wrote a song which was to become one of his most famous. 'Te recuerdo, Amanda' was created, not as a direct result of hearing the news of his daughter's illness, but because he was in a state of acute sensibility about family ties, about the importance of love. That song contained a mixture of the past and the future, with that strange sense of prophecy which characterises some of Victor's songs. People ask, was it for his mother or his daughter? I think specifically for neither, though it contains both his mother's smile and the promise of his daughter's youth:

I remember you, Amanda,
when the streets were wet,
running to the factory
where Manuel worked.
With your wide smile,
the rain in your hair,
nothing else mattered,
you were going to meet him.

Five minutes only,
all of your life in five minutes.
The siren is sounding,
time to go back to work.
And as you walk
you light up everything,
those five minutes
have made you flower.

And he took to the mountains to fight.
He had never hurt a fly
and in five minutes
it was all wiped out.
The siren is sounding,
time to go back to work.
Many will not go back . . .
one of them Manuel.

Victor was lucky at that moment to be in the warm atmosphere
of the Royal Shakespeare Company where he was sitting in on
rehearsals of *Dr Faustus*. He had made many friends among the
actors, accompanying them in their daily training and also on their
visits to the local pub, the Dirty Duck. Seeing him suddenly so quiet
and preoccupied, Alan Howard asked him what the matter was. When
Victor told him about Amanda, Alan was able to reassure him about
the illness, of which he had personal experience, telling him that it
was perfectly possible to lead a normal life, even though it was still
incurable, and how hereditary factors determined its appearance in
a family.

Victor was always deeply grateful for this help and understanding
and when he wrote to me he managed a letter full of support and
encouragement, and swore that he would never separate from us
again for so long a time. 'Our home must blossom with us inside
it, both of us and our children, with all our limitations, virtues and
defects, but *together*, each one of us profoundly a part of the others,
so that our small daughters are not afraid of the future, that we have
the chance to prolong our happiness as long as we can, trying to give
the best of ourselves, but without ever separating again.'

6

SONG AS A WEAPON

By the late sixties, Victor's songs were no longer autobiographical but dealt much more with the general problems, tasks and objectives facing the peoples of Latin America – even though they were very often about individual human beings. Perhaps the most obvious example of this, and one of the first, was 'El aparecido', a song which he composed at the beginning of 1967. It appeared in March of that year on a single record, with the dedication 'To E.(Ch).G.' – a more explicit mention of Ernesto 'Che' Guevara was not possible because the record was issued by Odeon, the Chilean equivalent of EMI.

After Fidel Castro's speech announcing the departure of Che Guevara from Cuba, there was continuous speculation about where he had gone, and everyone was asking in what part of Latin America was he fighting for the liberation of oppressed people. He seemed to be everywhere and nowhere, like some revolutionary will-o'-the-wisp, an almost mythical figure already, evading the remorseless and powerful enemies who were hunting him down . . . This was what Victor tried to convey in this song with its urgent *galope* rhythm, the idea of pursued and hunters, 'the eagle with the golden claws', the enemies who have put a price on his head and will eventually kill him. Only a few months later came the news of Che's death in Bolivia.

While the guerrilla movements in so many Latin American countries were certainly an inspiration to many people, Victor among them, such means of struggle had not been adopted by the traditional left in Chile, the Communist and Socialist Parties. These had decades of experience of mass struggle through the largest and most united labour movement in Latin America, and they saw no reason abruptly to change their methods now.

Because the working class in Chile was so well organised and both students and peasants were now joining in the struggle, it still seemed possible that revolutionary change could be brought about by the force of numbers within the framework of a parliamentary democracy. There was intense discussion and disagreement about *vias* – roads to socialism – even between the Communist and Socialist Parties, a debate which had been stimulated by the Tricontinental Congress in Cuba attended by Salvador Allende, when he was president of Chile's Senate.

Victor was criticised by the Communist Party for having dedicated a song to Che Guevara at that moment, even though the song itself was not so much a call to arms as an expression of admiration for Che's heroism and a denunciation of the methods and motives of the USA in protecting its interests in Latin America. Although Victor was essentially a man of peace, a non-violent person, he had a passionate awareness of the real violence of deprivation. I know that he didn't rule out the possibility that one day it might be necessary to resort to arms in order to put an end to that violence.

In another song of the same period, which Victor didn't sing himself, but arranged for Quilapayún, a different aspect of this problem is reflected. 'El soldado' ('The soldier') touches a vital theme which, although it was talked about, was never taken into account as it should have been. The song seems strangely prophetic:

Soldier, don't shoot me,
don't shoot me, soldier!
Who pinned those medals on your chest?
How many lives did they cost?
I know that your hand is trembling,
don't kill me,
I am your brother.

Since the beginning of the Cold War, the Pentagon had forged closer and closer links with the armed forces of Latin America. Their guiding doctrine had been changed from one of national defence to the idea of national security, with the enemy defined as the insurgent, the supposed internal agent of international communism.

The arms supplied by the United States tended more and more to be anti-insurgent weapons, small arms, riot gear, armoured cars. Chile's special police squad trained to suppress demonstrations, the Grupo Movil, owed their methods and their equipment to the USA, just as the arms used to kill Chilean miners and their wives at El Salvador in 1965 had been 'Aid from the USA'.

Camps were opened in Panama and other parts of Latin America where officers and NCOs from the continent's armies and police forces were indoctrinated in the concept of the 'internal enemy', and taught to fight against their own people, against internal rebellion, revolution or dissent. This was very different from the simple patriotic doctrine which Victor had assimilated when he did his military service. He had found nothing especially offensive about the idea of defending the frontiers of his own country. But this was different and much more sinister.

There had already been military intervention in Guatemala, at the Bay of Pigs and in Brazil. The US Marines had actually invaded the Dominican Republic in 1965 and US special forces like the Black Berets and the Green Berets were used widely as military advisers and interrogators. Even so, the illusion persisted that the Armed Forces of Chile were apolitical and would protect the constitution and the elected government of the country.

The political parties analysed the class structure of the Armed Forces, noting that the officers were all of upper- and middle-class background, while the lower ranks – the majority – were drawn from workers and peasants. But there was a grave miscalculation of the power of psychological indoctrination and the effectiveness of military discipline.

Victor's first song with a choral character, also composed for Quilapayún, showed his awareness of the need to prepare with urgency. In 'Somos pájaros libres' ('We are free birds') he urges, 'Brothers, it is already too late, let us fly to the mountain peaks!' For Victor too it was as though time had begun to accelerate.

Meanwhile the most visible facet of US policy to combat revolution in Chile during the sixties was an intensification of the cultural invasion. The mass media were filled with propaganda for the 'American Way of Life', newspaper stands were plastered with cheap American comics; the radios swamped with American pop music; television with American soap operas; the cinemas with Hollywood B movies . . . and because of the importance of radio in their lives, the poorest and most deprived people were perhaps most vulnerable to this propaganda.

One of Victor's songs, written in 1969, personifies this problem. '¿Quién mató a Carmencita?' ('Who killed Carmencita?') was based on the true story of a young girl who committed suicide under the influence of drugs. She lived in the same sordid district where Victor had grown up.

> With her best dress carefully ironed, she walked along
> trembling with anxiety, tears streaming down her cheeks.
> In the distance, barking dogs and motor horns,
> the park was dark, the city slept.
> Hardly fifteen and her life burnt out,
> home stifled her and school was boring,
> only queuing outside the radio stations
> did she come alive,
> her eyes dazzled by the idols of the moment.
> The cold-blooded dealers in dreams,
> grown fat at the expense of youth,
> had distorted her ambitions and riddled her with lies,
> canned happiness, love and fantasy.
>
> She fled,
> Carmencita died,
> on her temples a bleeding rose,
> she went to meet her last illusion.
>
> She didn't realise that her mind was being poisoned
> by false dreams that didn't belong to her,
> that world of marihuana and private swimming pools,
> 'Fly to happiness with Braniff International!'.
> Her world a sordid workers' district,
> dreary streets full of shouting and quarrelling,
> home cramped and crowded, working in the kitchen.
> While she was dying, others made their fortunes.
> The newspapers declared 'Causes unknown'.

The term 'protest song' was very much in fashion at the time. But although Victor was often called a protest singer, the song movement in Chile owed little to the commercialised version exported by the United States music industry. Of course, singers and songwriters like Pete Seeger, Malvina Reynolds and others who had stood up against the war in Vietnam were very much admired, but the Chilean song movement *per se* had its roots deep in its own cultural tradition and dealt with its own problems. It was at about this time that Victor commented:

> The cultural invasion is like a leafy tree which prevents us from see-ing our own sun, sky and stars. Therefore in order to be able to see the sky above our heads, our task is to cut this tree off at the roots. US imperialism understands very well the magic of communication through music and persists in filling our young people with all sorts of commercial tripe. With professional expertise they have taken certain measures: first, the commercialisation of so-called 'protest music'; second, the creation of 'idols' of protest music who obey the same rules and suffer from the same constraints as the other idols of the consumer music industry – they last a little while and then disappear. Meanwhile they are useful in neutralising the innate spirit of rebellion of young people. The term 'protest song' is no longer valid because it is ambiguous and has been misused. I prefer the term 'revolutionary song'.

A revolution was what the political climate of Chile seemed to be demanding. Discontent with the government of Frei was growing rapidly. Among the progressive sectors of the Christian Democrat Party there were increasing signs of dissatisfaction with the policies of their leaders.

One outward sign of this discontent was the demand for university reform which began in 1967 in the most reactionary and élite of all the 'seats of learning' – the Catholic University of Santiago. Although it started as nothing more than an expression of the students' desire to have a greater say within an authoritarian system, it quickly became politicised. It was a crucial time in the universities. The strong youth movements of the late sixties were also present in Chile and if the revolution in hair styles, fashion and sexual behaviour came rather late, the influence of the real revolution in Cuba was much stronger and more direct.

By the beginning of the university year in March 1968, the reform movement had spread to the University of Chile. The Faculty of Music and Scenic Arts, our Faculty, was one of the many university buildings to be occupied by students and teachers demanding change. By May, telegrams of solidarity were being exchanged with the students in Paris and other universities around the world, but what was happening in Chile was different, I think, from the situation in other countries. While in France, for example, the French Communist Party and the trade union movement remained outside the students' uprising, in Chile the leaders of the reform in both the University of Chile and in the State Technical University were communists, both in the student movement and among the academics.

They were urging that the universities be opened up to the children of workers and peasants, but although not everyone agreed with this, and there were many shades of opinion about how profound the reforms should be, in general the movement was one of consensus of all but the most reactionary forces in the country. Most people were agreed that there was a need for more democratic structures and that the universities should maintain a critical attitude towards society, rather than being the servants of the *status quo*.

Although the Chilean universities had great prestige in Latin America, they were not fulfilling the needs of the country. Increasingly, study and research programmes had become dependent on foreign subsidies and were designed to suit the interests of the multi-nationals and the US government. It was very clear that this had to be changed and that the problems and needs of Chile should be given priority.

It was a time of great turbulence and excitement into which Victor was immediately plunged on his return from England. It touched him and all the members of Quilapayún and Inti-Illimani very closely because they were all involved in the universities, either as students, or in Victor's case as a teacher in the Theatre School and a director of ITUCH. All of them took an active part in the assemblies, planning sessions and street demonstrations and by singing in the peñas which sprouted like mushrooms in all the students' unions and faculties. As artists they were identified with the reform movement.

Their songs were sung in street demos in which they themselves took part, being rushed by the riot police and attacked with water-cannon and tear-gas. Out of these experiences came a song which

Victor composed and sang together with Quilapayún – 'Movil Oil Special' – the title being a play on the name of the riot squad and that of a certain multi-national company very present in Chile. It became one of the songs of the reform and was later recorded with background noises of a student demonstration and the crump of exploding tear-gas grenades. The song movement had begun to emerge from the intimate atmosphere of the peñas, bound up with a mass movement which seemed to swell up and sweep them along with it. Victor could really feel that his songs were playing a part in daily struggle.

By October, the battle had been won in the University of Chile and elections were announced to choose the new authorities. The Faculty, which had been occupied all the winter by the students and teachers, returned to work with radical changes. Just one small symptom of the changing times was the fact that in December of that year a recital of Victor with Quilapayún was included in the official season of Chilean music, under the auspices of the University's Instituto de Extensión Musical.

The song movement had found mass audiences among the students. Now an even more important step in its development was about to take place, product of the particular social and cultural climate existing at the time in Chile, and even more of the fact that the labour movement had always maintained a tradition of fostering cultural activities. In the early years of the century, the movement's founding father, Luis Emilio Recabarren, helped in the formation of workers' theatre groups and encouraged poetry and song at political meetings – especially important at a time when many working people were still illiterate. Since then the tradition remained – political and trade-union meetings and rallies almost always included some form of artistic expression.

The upsurge in the struggle for social change which occurred in the late sixties, and the new links which were being forged between the students and the trade-union movement after the university reform, made it possible for Victor, Quilapayún and the others involved in the song movement to reach audiences of workers and peasants. Bypassing the hostile media, they could reach the people with whom they really wished to communicate.

By 1969, Victor was constantly fulfilling invitations from trade union organisations. The occasions varied. It might be a celebration, an anniversary, to support a strike, or simply because they liked the music. For example, the workers of a large cement factory, El Melón, were accustomed to invite singers who were in the 'Top Ten' to their annual party. That year, rather daringly, the organisers invited Victor and he took Quilapayún along with him. Their tremendous success took everyone by surprise because, even then, people still doubted whether this sort of music, non-commercial, Chilean-sounding and without electric guitars, could really be popular.

It was one of a succession of concerts throughout the country. They sang in big cities and remote country places, from the oil-fields in Tierra del Fuego to the mines of the northern desert. Emerging from the peñas, this new kind of music was part of a social and political movement which took it to its heart. It had found a function as a weapon in a revolutionary struggle. As Victor said, 'An artist must be an authentic creator and therefore in very essence a revolutionary . . . a man as dangerous as a guerrilla because of his great power of communication.'

On Sunday, 9 March 1969, at 7.00 a.m., by order of the Minister of the Interior, Edmundo Pérez Zúcovic, two hundred and fifty armed police, under the command of the acting governor of the province of Llanquihue, Jorge Pérez, attacked a group of ninety-one peasant families who had occupied a patch of wasteland, Pampa Irigoin, about two miles from the centre of the city of Puerto Montt.

As they approached the settlement, the police tripped over the primitive alarm system installed by the peasant squatters. The rattling of the tins tied to the barbed wire fencing woke the sleeping families. Shouting to each other, dragging children still half asleep out of their improvised shelters, the women hurriedly gathered up their babies. The peasants ran hither and thither, trying to find a way out of the police cordon. Some grabbed their working tools with the idea of resisting – spades, picks, whatever they could lay their hands on; others tried to reach the neighbouring settlement, Manuel Rodriguez, where they hoped to find shelter. But the police had already surrounded Pampa Irigoin. They began to lob tear-gas grenades and then opened up with machine guns. Many men and women fell to the ground wounded as the police set fire to the primitive huts which had been their homes. Seven peasants were killed and a baby of nine months died suffocated by tear-gas. Sixty were injured, mostly in the chest and stomach, because the police were shooting indiscriminately against unarmed people, and they were shooting to kill.

The peasants, all of them homeless, most without work, had occupied the land which belonged to the Irigoin family five days previously. The autumn rains of the south had already begun to turn it into a sea of mud; the improvised huts hardly provided shelter from the rain, but they were the only homes the people had. They were tired of waiting for the right to live better than animals. They hoped that by occupying the land their plight would at last be noticed by the authorities. But the answer of Pérez Zúcovic had been to order the police to 'do their duty' to evict the peasants from the wasteland, and to use firearms if necessary.

Pérez Zúcovic was a wealthy businessman on the right wing of the Christian Democrat Party. He was responsible for the Grupo Movil and all the other repressive machinery of the police which had been used on countless occasions against demonstrators, striking workers and their families and students. Even before the massacre of Puerto Montt he was one of the most generally unpopular political figures of the day.

In Santiago, as Victor read the news, he became enraged and hurt as though it had been his own family which had been attacked and ravaged by the police. Immediately, he took his guitar and began to compose a song of accusation against Pérez Zúcovic, seeing in him a symbol of the distorted values of the society we were living in.

The general outrage caused by the massacre of Puerto Montt inflamed an already tense political situation in the country and in the following days there were violent clashes between student demonstrators and the police in Santiago, very much centred round our Faculty building and that of Political and Economic Sciences nearby. A great protest demonstration was called by the Student Federation and the trade unions for Thursday, 13 March in Avenida Bulnes, a wide avenue leading directly south from the Moneda Palace.

Speakers and artists were on the platform to express their condemnation of the horrible crime and their sympathy with the widows and mothers of the victims, who had travelled to Santiago from the south after the mass funeral of their relatives. A gigantic crowd of people, perhaps a hundred thousand, packed many blocks of the wide road.

It was there that Victor sang his song 'Preguntas por Puerto Montt' ('Questions about Puerto Montt') for the first time in public. I was standing at the back of the stage when he sang. I could see him, legs tensed apart, singing as though his life depended on it, to a sea of faces disappearing into the distance in the growing dusk, a sea which responded, on the last notes, with a roar of pent-up feeling.

In the weeks that followed, wherever he went, Victor was asked to sing this song. It began to take on a political life of its own, and before long Victor was to have his first intimation of the personal consequences. One evening I was waiting for him outside the Faculty building in the centre of the city, sitting in the citroneta with the engine running. I saw him coming through the glass doors of the main entrance, rather noticeable with his halo of curly black hair and not very conventional way of dressing. Out of the corner of my eye, I also saw a group of young men emerging from the headquarters of the National Party opposite and realised that they were pointing at Victor. One in particular was very tall, wearing a camel-hair coat, wide-shouldered and belted. All of them had sleek hair and suits – the uniform of the momios. Suddenly they crossed the road and surrounded Victor. I saw their raised fists and shouted at him from the car. He pushed them away and managed to get into it, while I drove off. It was just a passing incident but it was the first of many. They had threatened that they would 'get him' if he persisted in singing subversive songs.

A couple of months later Victor was invited to give a recital at St George's College, one of the best known and most expensive secondary schools for boys in the barrio alto. It was to be part of a week of debate and cultural activity whose main theme was to be a questioning of the traditional values inherent in the Chilean educational system. Victor's first instinct was to refuse because, as he himself admitted, he was prejudiced against such an audience, but he realised that it was a challenge that ought not to be ignored.

He suggested that he should give a joint recital with a poet, a friend of his called Jaime Gomez, allowing time for a frank and open discussion with the students. Victor and Jaime arrived at the school at around two o'clock in the afternoon of 8 July to find that the recital had been transferred to the larger assembly hall of a neighbouring girls' school. About eight hundred students had already assembled when they arrived and Victor felt that there was a rather strange atmosphere. Groups of students outside the building observed their entry in silence and he felt that they seemed hostile. After all, he had already had some experience of that.

He told himself not to be paranoid and suggested to the organisers that Jaime and himself should install themselves in the body of the hall rather than isolate themselves up on the stage, in order to create a more direct sense of communication. However, they were strongly advised against this, and perhaps luckily, deferring to them, Jaime and Victor went up on stage to begin. Songs and poems alternated. They began gently and the applause at the end of each number was normal. Victor had not prepared a specific programme. On these occasions he preferred rather to rely on the feel of the audience to suggest his next song to him. He wanted to get to know them and to judge their reactions to a song like 'El arado', which spoke of the very topical problems of the peasants, or 'Te recuerdo Amanda', a love song with a sub-text. He was genuinely interested in their opinions and had no wish simply to hear polite applause nor to provoke a violent reaction.

He felt the atmosphere becoming tenser and more polarised between one section of the audience and another. The students were beginning to show their real feelings, some applauding loudly, others hissing and shouting, until a fist fight broke out in the gallery. There was a great deal of confusion upstairs and Victor stopped and asked for quiet, to be allowed to finish the recital, suggesting that afterwards there might be a discussion. Insults were shouted at him from the gallery.

'El aparecido' was sung against the noise of growing conflict and he again pleaded for reason rather than violence, being answered with shouts of 'communist', 'subversive' and strings of obscenities. Then he became really furious and went straight into the song which expressed his feelings most strongly at that time, 'Preguntas por Puerto Montt'. As he sang, a large stone, flung from the gallery with great force, hit him on the chest and bounced off his guitar. Then a shower of stones rained on to the stage, one grazing Jaime's head. Victor stood up as a group of students began running down the aisle with the obvious intention of storming the stage. Other students and teachers rushed to form a protective wall around the performers and to try to stop the others from climbing on to the stage. Victor and Jaime were hustled out of a back door by the organisers who were very apologetic about what had happened but wanted to get them away as soon as possible.

Aggressive groups of students had already gathered outside, so Victor's citroneta was brought to him and as he and Jaime drove off, a large car came skidding out of a side road and crashed into the mudguard, leaving a large dent and a rattling noise as a souvenir of that afternoon. Only after he came off stage did Victor learn that the younger son of Pérez Zúcovic was a student at the school and had been the focus of a counter-demonstration organised by ultra-right elements there.

There was a sensation in the press which lasted for days and had long-term repercussions. The Parents Association of St George's reacted with declarations which made front-page headlines in *El Mercurio*, protesting about 'incidents provoked by Marxist infiltration' at the school. Victor was derided as a 'so-called artist' and they complained that their sons were being brainwashed with Marxist philosophy, demanding the sacking of the sociology teacher who had been responsible for the week of activities. The principal of the school, however, put up a spirited defence of the school's educational policy and informed parents that if they did not like it they were at liberty to take their sons away.

It made Victor realise very clearly just what he must expect if he continued to express in his songs what he felt had to be said. But there is no doubt that his commitment and his resolve were strengthened rather than weakened by it. He took a step forwards rather than backwards in the face of violence, taking the risk with his eyes open.

In mid-1969 the whole world was in a state of expectation because a man was about to step on the moon. But in Chile the country was bursting with social and political conflict. The papers were full of reports of acts of violence, especially those attributed to the left-wing MIR, who were following the example of the Tupamaros in Uruguay. There was rather less mention of the armed and organised aggression of the large landowners who were still determined to prevent the implementation of the very modest land-reform programme initiated by the Frei government. Groups of them were setting up road blocks on the longitudinal highway, terrorising and occasionally shooting peasants – acts for which they were never brought to justice. There were rumours, well-founded ones, that they had castrated an official of the Ministry of Agriculture, and later they murdered another, Hernán Mery. Among the ring-leaders of this activity was the pituco I had met soon after my arrival in Chile, who had pursued me over the fields in his dressing-gown to apologise for his outburst against communists.

But these violent extremes seemed almost irrelevant when set beside the massive upsurge of social unrest which was taking place. A new and powerful factor within this ferment was the growing awareness and involvement of the younger generation. Students, not just at university level, but in secondary schools as well, plunged into political activity, and all the political parties of both left and right had strong and growing youth sections. Perhaps as a result of this and of the growing importance of the song movement, in 1968 the Young Communists had taken the daring step of setting up an alternative record company – La Discoteca del Cantar Popular, or DICAP as it was usually called. Although nothing like it had been attempted before in Chile, it was a logical development of the priority the communists had always given to cultural activity. It had begun as a tentative experiment with the release of *Por Vietnam*, an album of international political songs, sung by Quilapayún, which had not the slightest chance of being released by a commercial company.

Victor's *Pongo en tus Manos Abiertas* ('Into your open hands'), released in June 1969, was the second album on the new label. 'Preguntas por Puerto Montt', 'Te recuerdo Amanda' and 'Movil Oil Special' would never have passed the political censorship barrier. The song which gave the album its title was dedicated to the founder of the Chilean labour movement, Luis Emilio Recabarren, and it included, too, Daniel Viglietti's song for Camilo Torres, the revolutionary priest, killed while taking part in the guerrilla war in Colombia.

The success of these first two albums was to be followed by a flood of others which would convert DICAP within the next five years into a flourishing enterprise which gave a solid base to the song movement and created new channels for reaching mass audiences.

At the time of the release of *Pongo en tus Manos Abiertas* and soon after his visit to St George's College, Victor was preparing to take part in a festival which was to prove of historic importance in the development of the song movement. It was the initiative of Ricardo García, a disc-jockey who had always shown an interest in folk music and had the vision to perceive that a strange phenomenon was occurring in the field of popular music, as though the mass media, for all its manipulative powers, were somehow out of touch with public taste.

The First Festival of New Chilean Song, as it was called, was sponsored by the newly established Vice-Rectoria de Comunicaciones of the Catholic University. It was conceived as an investigation into the current situation of Chilean popular music, with round-table discussions between composers, record producers and representatives of the mass media. It was also to include a competition between twelve invited composers who would submit songs to be judged by a distinguished jury.

That the festival had no left-wing bias was evident from the fact that the guests of honour were to be Los Huasos Quincheros, one of the most 'traditional' groups, now celebrating thirty-two years of their existence, and from the decision to exclude Quilapayún because their repertoire was 'too political'.

Although the festival was organised as a conventional competition, the rivalry which developed was not between the individual composers taking part, but rather between two different and opposing concepts of what constituted Chilean song: the new music, with songs that were critical and committed to revolutionary change, or the 'apolitical' songs which gave the impression that nothing needed changing. It was the first musical confrontation.

Considering the non-political character of the festival and the kind of media coverage expected, Victor might have chosen to enter a safe song. But that wasn't in his character. He plunged straight into the challenge of the event by composing a song which *El Mercurio* later called 'explosive'. 'La plegaria a un labrador' was a call to the peasants, to those who tilled the soil with their hands and produced the fruits of the earth, to join with their brothers to fight for a just society. Its form, reminiscent of the Lord's Prayer, was a reflection of Victor's newly reawakened interest in the Bible for its poetry and humanist values, at a time when a deep understanding was growing between progressive Catholics and Marxists in Latin America.

Stand up,
look at the mountains,
source of the wind, the sun, the water
– you who change the course of rivers,
who, with the seed, sow the flight of your soul,

stand up,
look at your hands,
give your hand to your brother so you can grow.
We'll go together, united by blood,
today is the day we can make the future.

Deliver us from the master who keeps us in misery,
thy kingdom of justice and equality come.
Blow, like the wind blows the wild flower of the mountain pass,
clean the barrel of my gun like fire.
Thy will be done at last on earth
give us your strength and courage to struggle.

Stand up,
look at your hands,
take your brother's hand so you can grow.
We'll go together, united by blood,
Now and in the hour of our death.   AMEN.

In spite of their being officially excluded from the competition, Victor invited Quilapayún along as his accompanying group, convinced that 'La plegaria' would benefit from a larger-scale presentation. He worked especially closely with Patricio Castillo, the youngest member of the group, on the development of the music and this was the beginning of a fruitful collaboration which was to last even after Patricio left Quilapayún and indeed to the end of Victor's life.

Early on the evening of the festival, the members of Quilapayún began to assemble at our house for a last rehearsal. Such was the excitement that at the end of the run-through Carlitos suddenly burst into an improvisation on the drums, wailing out a kind of invocation to the gods. All of them joined in with whatever percussion instrument they had to hand, until a kind of voodoo ceremony was under way and they were dancing and singing in unified ecstasy.

That night was the first of many times that Victor sang in the Estadio Chile, that large dilapidated building in the heart of the district where he grew up, near the Central Station. The auditorium was a basket-ball court with the stage jutting out at one end. It had a regular working-class audience and for the festival local people mixed with workers, students, middle-class intellectuals, office workers – almost a complete cross-section of the population.

The moment came when I had to leave Victor, who was nervous and withdrawn as always before a performance, and dive under the rope separating the stage from the public. The jury were already installed in the front row, rustling papers and looking important. Fernando Castillo Velasco, the Rector of the Catholic University, spoke a few words, explaining that it was in the spirit of the reform movement that they gave their sponsorship to this festival of popular music. Then Ricardo García took over and the festival was under way.

It is difficult to remember the emotions of that evening without mixing them up with subsequent events, but there is no doubt that the principal feeling was one of celebration, of working people and students, en masse, having a rare chance to show their recognition and affection for their own artists – those who were expressing what they wanted to hear.

Isabel singing Violeta, Angel, Rolando Alarcón, Patricio Manns, Richard Rojas, Victor, Inti-Illimani, Quilapayún, one by one received ovations which seemed to lift the roof, but it wasn't a personal triumph for the artists themselves, and I'm sure that none of them interpreted it in that way. Rather it was a victory for a very profound social movement, with its own cultural expression which at that moment was gaining recognition, recognising itself, reaffirming its own identity.

In the end the jury couldn't come to a unanimous decision but decided to divide the prize between 'La plegaria' and a lively song dedicated to a heroine of the fight for independence from the Spanish, 'La Chilenera' by Richard Rojas, with the rhythm of a *sirilla* to which the audience could stamp its feet.

As I queued up, among the crush of people pushing to hug and congratulate Richard and Victor, I did feel that something important had happened. Our lives had reached a turning point and, although we loved each other as much as ever, we were irrevocably a part of a process bigger than ourselves, of a great multitude working in a common cause. The inspiration of 'La plegaria a un labrador' belonged to that time of optimism and commitment.

The year following the first Festival of New Chilean Song was a crucial one in our lives, just as it was a crucial year for Chile. The

massive popular success of the song movement had at last forced
the media to take notice. Victor found himself thrust into promi-
nence as a composer. He was interviewed extensively by the press,
his songs began to be played on the radio and for the first time
he was offered television programmes. It was a break-through for
the whole song movement, and enormously widened the scope of
Victor's work.

But there were less pleasant consequences too. Victor began to be
a target for the more sensational right-wing press, who wasted no
opportunity to attack and ridicule him. And political reactions began
to have a direct effect upon his work. At the Casa de la Cultura
de Ñuñoa, the Academy of Folklore was now functioning perfectly.
Victor and Maruja Espinoza had three groups of students studying and
investigating; the performing group had won popularity and prestige in
numerous recitals all over the neighbourhood and beyond; new soloists
and even composers were emerging. But there was a new mayoress in
Ñuñoa, Balbina Vera, for whom Victor's presence was like a red rag
to a bull. She had decided that the Casa de la Cultura was a hotbed of
reds and political agitators and was determined to put a stop to it. That
the majority of the students and teachers had left-wing views was, of
course, true, but that they spent their study time in political meetings
was not, as even the most conservative students testified. However,
Balbina Vera had decided, at whatever cost, to get rid of the author
of 'Preguntas por Puerto Montt' and 'La plegaria a un labrador', and
she demanded Victor's resignation.

The staff responded unanimously that if Victor resigned, they would
all resign too and she would be left without teachers. Her reaction
was simply to close the Casa de la Cultura, declaring it to be 'under
reorganisation', thus ending the most fruitful and lively period of
its history.

Despite the growing importance of music in his life, Victor throughout this period had continued his work as a theatre director, both
with ITUCH in the university, and with a number of independent
companies. When he returned from England he plunged into the
direction of *Entertaining Mr Sloane* by Joe Orton with the Compañía
de los Cuatro, which was a great success. At the moment of his dismissal
from the Casa de la Cultura he was immersed in a production which
was to be his last with the Theatre Institute. I had often observed
rehearsals of Victor's plays, but on this occasion I had the chance

to work alongside him, both as choreographer and in preparing the actors for the special physical demands of the play.

Vietrock was the product of a workshop for dramatists in the Open Theatre in New York, the final version of a collective creation about the war in Vietnam, written and published by Megan Terry. The war was almost at its height, and after the terrible bombing attacks on the cities of the north and the use of napalm against the civilian population, the news, photographs and film coming out of Vietnam were horrendous. Victor was very glad to have the chance of directing a play which provided limitless possibilities for expressing the depth of his feelings on the subject.

As a play, *Vietrock* was essentially the result of collective improvisation with no logical structure. Instead it gave the spectator a global vision of the birth, life, passions and death of the protagonists in the war.

Although I was billed as choreographer, Victor needed very little help in that sense – he had an extraordinary sense of movement, of space and rhythm – but my chief and indispensable function was to prepare the actors before rehearsal. This involved more than merely getting them physically into training. They had to be brought into a state of kinetic sensibility in which they were capable of doing much more than they thought they could – a state of relaxation and surrender to the physical demands of their imaginations, getting rid of their normal inhibitions. They had to be ready to throw themselves about, to explode into the air, wriggle on their tummies, run, roll, jump, collectively convert themselves into helicopters, flowers and explosions. For obvious reasons Victor had chosen a cast of predominantly young actors, but even the more mature members of the cast threw themselves with great enthusiasm into a production that made demands on them of a kind they had never before experienced.

We steeped ourselves in documentary material – not too easy to obtain in Chile – not only about the war, but also concerning the reactions and attitudes to it in the United States. It was impossible not to become identified with the Vietnamese people who were fighting for their own liberation against a powerful aggressor. Victor wrote:

. . . *Vietrock* cannot be reproduced 'as seen in the USA'. Here no copies are possible. The author doesn't go further than a rather primitive pacifism from a North American point of view; she doesn't perceive the imperialism of her country with the same eyes as we Chileans and Latin Americans see it. The play has a very free outline, and the position that we have taken in relation to it is one of judgment, of criticism and condemnation of imperialism. We are not North Americans and there is no reason why we should share the distorted vision of the author. There seem to be apparently progressive North Americans who cannot free themselves from their twisted – and fundamentally imperialist – vision of the Third World. But the value of the play is that it is a portrait of the war in which thousands and thousands of Vietnamese are being killed day by day in the defence of their country against the invaders from the Pentagon. And it is much more than that, it is also the drama of a large part of the American people, of mothers, of soldiers who are sent to fight a war which has nothing to do with them.

I had always admired Victor as a director – quite objectively, I think. Now I had the opportunity to watch him at work throughout the long rehearsal sessions. I saw his capacity for drawing people out, quietly guiding, quietly but strongly motivating, rarely dictating, never losing his temper. If there were conflicts with the actors, he was always very controlled in dealing with them, never letting his own pride or irritation intrude. Sometimes I would accuse him of being 'a Buddha', because the more disturbed or furious he was about some problem, the quieter and calmer he would get. The actors worked with him eagerly and with a sense of dedication to a common task.

Vietrock was very much a product of the university reform which had also affected the Theatre Institute. After 1968, Victor himself had been elected to the new governing council and he participated energetically in the discussions about reorganisation, proposing radical changes in the method of work and programming. After his visit to England he felt that it would be more logical to function as a repertory theatre with mobile productions. He was enthusiastic about the possibilities for change and for reaching wider audiences, but at the same time impatient with the slow pace, the conservative attitude of many of his colleagues and the endless meetings and theoretical discussion that the reform generated.

He began to feel that time was running out and that he personally could be of more use to the cause – which he held to be more important than his own career – if he could have more freedom to get out of Santiago, to travel and move around the country with his guitar – impossible if he was responsible for a large production in the Antonio Varas Theatre. He wanted to explore to the full the possibilities of communication through popular song and music and the potential for harnessing that work to the fight for revolutionary change.

Neither of us thought of it as an irrevocable decision. Victor was still full of ideas about what he wanted to achieve in the theatre. But at that particular moment it was more relevant to work with music and song. The same considerations led him at the same time to leave the Peña. He found it restricting to be tied to Santiago every weekend, and singing there was rather like preaching to the converted.

Just as Victor was deciding to leave the University of Chile, I was being tempted to return to it. The reform had brought very radical changes to the new Dance Department, which included both the school and the ballet company, and Patricio had been elected its new director. A delegation of students came to see me to persuade me to return to the Dance School, even if it were only on a part-time basis. With the new direction and the flexibility that the reform had introduced, I felt that it would be easier to work within the university than before, and I accepted.

Shortly afterwards, the grant we had been receiving from the Municipality of Las Condes for our Taller de Danza – choreographic workshop – was abruptly cut off. No reasons were given, but I suspect that some of our work may have had too left-wing a flavour for the taste of some of the councillors. However, there was a spirit in the group which made it impossible just to give up and abandon everything we had created together, so we were glad to accept when the new Dance Department at the University offered us a place to rehearse and the loan of tape recorders and other essential facilities.

We decided unanimously to change the name of the group to Ballet Popular, in order to reflect the role we wished to play, taking dance out of the conventional theatres and into the community. So far our activities had been confined to the barrio alto of the capital, but our aim was to extend the enjoyment of watching dance to the widest possible public, as a prelude to their active participation in the actual experience of dancing. This, we hoped, would become possible if Chile had a popular government.

Perhaps the only negative factor in all this was that my friend Alfonso did not accompany us in this development of our work. He had always been more interested in working with small children and therefore had not been so directly involved with the workshop itself, but even so, it was symptomatic of the way in which the political situation had begun to separate even the closest of friends. It seemed that one had to take sides.

The campaign for the September 1970 presidential elections in Chile began to gather momentum more than twelve months beforehand. By then both the right-wing National Party and the Christian Democrats had named their candidates, Jorge Alessandri and Radomiro Tomic respectively. But the new alliance of Marxists, Christians, social democrats and progressive independents called Popular Unity took longer to make its choice.

Popular Unity did, however, reach agreement on a basic programme of forty measures designed to transform the economy and put an end to the more glaring injustices in society. The nationalisation of Chile's natural resources, notably the American-owned copper mines, together with state ownership of the banks and the most important monopoly industries, were to be combined with such essential measures as a free half-litre of milk every day for each child — which by itself would almost guarantee that no more Chilean children would grow up mentally deficient through malnutrition — free medical care, education and adequate housing. Chile was to have an independent foreign policy and to renew diplomatic relations with Cuba.

This programme represented a real challenge to the power and influence of the United States. It placed the interests of the majority of the Chilean people before those of the multinationals and the oligarchy — a socialist and, in the best sense of the word, a patriotic programme.

While discussions about the leadership were still continuing, in October 1969 we were surprised by an attempted military coup. I say surprised because never, during all the years that I had lived in Chile, had anything similar happened. I knew that Chile's history had seen military take-overs, like that of General Ibañez in the 1930s, but since then respect for the constitution had been considered a fundamental part of military tradition, and something that distinguished Chile from many other states in Latin America. However, the attempt was a serious one, mounted by an ultra-right faction within the army led by General Viaux.

Within twenty-four hours the trade-union movement had called a general strike. The Central Unica de Trabajadores, CUT, Chile's TUC, which until that moment had been engaged in a permanent struggle against the repressive and devastating economic policies of President Eduardo Frei, now called out its entire membership to protect the constitutional government. The country came to a complete standstill and the coup was averted, more than anything by the strength of numbers and political awareness of the Chilean working people.

In mid-January 1970 the forces of Popular Unity reached agreement and Dr Salvador Allende of the Socialist Party was declared the presidential candidate of the coalition. On a warm summer evening, a gigantic multitude gathered in Avenida Bulnes to mark the nomination and to launch Allende's election campaign.

As usual, in addition to speeches from the leaders of all the Popular Unity parties, an integral part of the event was a cultural programme with performances from many of the well-known artists and groups that supported the campaign. Victor, of course, was there, but for us dancers it was especially symbolic, because it was the first performance of Ballet Popular under its new name. We felt that it was a good beginning. Just eight months were left to convince and mobilise the people of Chile in the face of the barrage of right-wing propaganda. The other candidates had a start of many months.

That summer, in February 1970, on the eve of a period of intense activity for both of us, we took what was to be our last family holiday together. Contulmo, Lake Lanalhue, the Pensión Jost on the shores of the lake, remain intensely in my memory, perhaps because of that and because we were very happy there: happy as a family, happy as lovers, happy because we had come for the second time to this incredibly beautiful and unspoilt region of Chile where we were lucky enough to find friends like Angelita Huenumán.

We re-discovered the plants that grow along the lakeshore, the quietness of the water, the wide sky, the walks over the hills, the majesty of the virgin forest of Nahuelbuta with its trees a thousand years old rising up into a dim cathedral of vegetation above our heads . . . it was a moment of pause before we plunged into the maelstrom.

I can't say that we were a completely carefree family. We were full of anxieties, including financial ones. Victor had internal conflicts about his relative responsibilities for his family and to the cause he believed it necessary to fight for . . . sometimes it seemed difficult to reconcile the two, although we both knew that they could only be one and the same . . . and anyway I was also there to make my share of the responsibility. Amanda, 5 years old now, was still a rather sad-looking little girl, but gradually her illness was coming under better control and she herself was more used to her regime. Manuela, already 9, was doing well at school, but tended to be shy and unsure of herself, rather deprived of attention, I am afraid, because Amanda's blood sugar got so much – we always seemed to be concentrating on it.

Victor would have loved to spend more time with us, to have had more chance to talk to Manuela, to play with Amanda and take a more active part in their development, but we all considered that this inhuman pressure of activity separating him from us was a temporary situation, that it wouldn't always be like this. Since his return from England, Victor had suffered from an inner anxiety about leaving us, and had periodic nightmares which grew worse and more frequent as time passed, when he would wake up in a cold sweat or cry out as though he were in agony.

By mid-February we were back in the baking heat of Santiago ready for the fray. It is not easy to convey what a presidential election meant in Chile. I had already experienced two, but this one outstripped them all in intensity, length and degree of polarisation. It penetrated every corner of the country, every aspect of life, every place of work and study, every neighbourhood, every home. Families could be broken up, people lost their jobs, found new ones, quarrelled with their friends, found whole new circles of them, were obliged to make up their minds on a series of vital issues, and in general were subjected to a continuous bombardment of dramatically opposing points of view.

The character of Popular Unity, with its broad base in the working class, the peasants and a majority of the young people in the country, and its lack of economic power, made its election campaign essentially dependent on mass mobilisation. Thousands of local campaign committees were set up – the CUPs or Comités de la Unidad Popular – which were responsible for the tremendous variety of grass-roots activity carried out all over the country during the long months of the election campaign and after.

Every neighbourhood, office, factory, university, school had its own CUP. Sometimes more than one. In La Faena, for example, a very poor shanty-town on the outskirts of Santiago, there were thirty-eight – so many supporters of Popular Unity that almost every block had its own committee. In our neighbourhood there was only one, and semi-secret at that.

Most trades and professions also had their own CUP. Painters, folklorists, dancers, perhaps for the first time were working together in a co-ordinated fashion. About this work Victor said in an interview:

> The most important thing was our desire to work together, to unite our efforts to win a popular government. This common aim led to artists of different fields getting to know one another. Artists are used to working alone, their worries are individual, at most discussed with others in the studio. But now as never before, artists of the same political persuasion have got together, and this personal contact, to know ourselves to be friends in a common fight, has been felt by abstract painters, modern dancers, investigators of pure folklore, just as much as by those who sing revolutionary songs. We have felt that, as human beings, we could work hard together for something that before was just a thought, an idea, a dream, but which now has been converted into a reality, a strong force in action.

Meanwhile, out of the need to counterbalance the influence of the media, heavily weighted, of course, against Popular Unity, a new form of popular art was being born. It began simply enough as the rough scrawling of slogans and symbols on empty walls. In the urgency of the election campaign speed was of the first importance, because anyone painting graffiti for Popular Unity was liable to be attacked by right-wing gangs or arrested by the police. Wall-painting teams or *brigadas* sprang up all over the country, the first and most famous of them being the Brigadas Ramona Parra or 'BRP' as they signed their paintings, set up by the Young Communists. Soon all the Popular Unity parties had their own brigades.

Groups of young people would go out at night, in paint-stained boiler suits and protective helmets, sometimes on foot, but mostly in

Joan in a break during the rehearsals of *Surazo*, 1961

Violeta Parra

Dancing a *sajuriana* with Silvia Urbina on the 1961 tour

Attending celebrations of Shakespeare's birthday, Stratford-upon-Avon, 1968

Victor singing in the May Day demonstration, 1967 (photo by Patricio Guzman)

ccompanied by Eduardo Carrasco playing the *bombo*, 1967 (photo by Patricio Guzman)

Singing 'La plegaria a un labrador' with Quilapayún in the First Festival of New Chilean Song, July 1969.

On holiday in Lanalhue 1969

President Salvador Allende with his friend Pablo Neruda

Las Noticias de ULTIMA HORA, jueves 27 de agosto de 1970

Victor singing in the 1970 presidential election campaign

In one of the many poblaciones around Santiago, Victor remembers his own childhood

Winter rain and cold make life harder in the shanty-towns (photo by Andres Boerr)

Travelling around in a *micro* with Inti-Illimani and other artists during the parliamentary election campaign in March 1973

On one of the stops, Inti-Illimani performs to the crowd of workers in the street

In Peru, above the ruins of Macchu Picchu. One of the last photos of Victor, taken by
Mariano Sanchez Macedo, July 1973

an old lorry or with some form of transport which would ensure a rapid getaway. They became adept at jumping off and clinging on again in an emergency. While one person, the *loro*, kept watch, a leader, best at drawing, would trace out the design of the slogan on a chosen wall, and each member of the team would have a particular area to paint.

Several walls could be painted in one night, but they had to be continually renewed because they would be erased or painted over by rivals. A real battle went on to gain control of the best and most prominent sites and it was good to see some of the mansions of the barrio alto suffering from nocturnal visits which left them proclaiming Allende on their garden walls.

In the end it was Popular Unity, with its massive human resources, which won the battle of the walls of Santiago and the other cities of Chile, and which could afford to elaborate, to paint images as well as slogans, to fill in the thick-drawn lines with patches of bright colour, and to create a whole new visual expression of the aims and wishes of the people. It was a new art-form based on writing, on the shorthand of essential symbols, with boldness and economy of line and colour, born out of the need to cover large areas of wall rapidly.

The members of Ballet Popular, too, put themselves at the service of the election campaign, which involved giving hundreds of performances all over Santiago and the surrounding countryside. At first we didn't know how to break the barrier of unreality and idealisation which tended to separate dancers from the public and made it difficult for people to feel that they also could participate. It was a period when trends in modern dance were towards more abstraction, more movement for movement's sake, so that we would perhaps have been considered very old-fashioned in our attempts to make reality and everyday life the sources of the dances we created. But we were sure that it was right in the context in which we were working. And our audiences proved the point.

We discovered by trial and error how to give performances under all sorts of conditions and circumstances, sacrificing some of our professional standards perhaps, but learning so much in the process that it was well worth while. Dancing on dusty ground in the open spaces of a shanty-town, on the scorched earth of a football field in summer with dogs and children joining in, in the cramped space of a wooden hut which was the local mothers' centre, or in a church, on wobbly, improvised platforms – the worst – or on the vast open stage at a political demonstration with a public of something like half a million people, our choreographies had to be elastic – stretchable or shrinkable.

Temperatures varied from freezing cold to unbearably hot. Costumes had to be as much like everyday clothes as possible, as well as hardy and durable. We had to be ready to dance in shoes or with bare feet, according to the floor surface. We had unfortunate experiences at first when the audience had such attacks of giggles at the sight of girls or men in tights that they couldn't pay attention to the dance. After that we kept to trousers and track suits.

For music, we knew that if we used songs and instrumental pieces by Victor and other composers of the new Chilean song movement, half our troubles were over. We immediately had the sympathy of the public and it was a way of integrating our work with theirs. A choreography of mine which became almost the signature of Ballet Popular during the election campaign, and which we called *Venceremos*, was based on an instrumental piece of Victor's. In it, in order not to look like midgets from very far away in the great demonstrations, the human figure was magnified by the use of bright colours and long banners which we converted into bonfires, collective washing and other symbols. It was danced with great vitality and optimism and was full of collective feeling. Through it a number of well-known dancers were able to express their support for Popular Unity in a simple and effective way. The audiences seemed to love it.

The best experiences were when we could hear the comments, exchange opinions with the audience, and try to respond to questions about dance that came from young people who were seeing it for the first time. I used to watch the faces of the public during the performance to see their reactions to each moment . . . the tired, haggard faces of women, so many of them toothless and old before their time, lighting up with the music and movement; the children, ragged and under-nourished, clapping and jumping about with joy, even hard-boiled adolescents clustering round after the performance to ask how they could learn to dance.

We began to realise how urgent it was to initiate cultural activities in the poblaciones – a need on a par with that for better food and housing and access to medical care. We promised that we would try to come back, that we would send them teachers, knowing that if Popular Unity won the election there would be more facilities for doing so. But after our first visit we often heard again from the people of the población, and sometimes it was to tell us that without waiting for help they had formed a group and made a choreography . . . could we come and give them an opinion about it?

Just occasionally Victor came with us and shared the performance, singing and talking between one dance and the next. He had such a wonderful way of talking to people, of getting them to respond, to tell their own problems or just to exchange jokes. He always seemed to know how to get over what he wanted to say in very simple terms, but directly and strongly, and to relate it to his songs. He used to sit down on a corner of the stage, if there was one, talking to the children who always crowded into the first row, almost on top of the performers. Victor would get them clapping and singing in no time, and sometimes we would manage to get them dancing too.

In those intimate performances we also managed to reduce our focus to the real people sitting in front of us. It would have been easy to get depressed about what we were doing in the sense that we might feel that it was useless or irrelevant to the priorities of their lives and needs, but their reaction was so warm and enthusiastic that we realised that there was something we could give them, even if at that moment it was only an expression of solidarity. Our best way of fighting was to do everything in our power to ensure the victory of a president who would make the neglected and under-privileged people the protagonists of history.

The violence that dogged those months came from the right rather than the left. Popular Unity seemed to take pride in peaceful demonstrations, disciplined, spirited, but peaceful. Even the MIR had quietened down and were considering rather half-heartedly giving their support to Salvador Allende.

The fascists maintained paramilitary groups in both the cities and the rural areas, smuggling arms over the mountains from Argentina. But the Frei government vacillated in bringing the influential landowners to justice. There were mass demonstrations against the continuing violence, and in one of these Miguel-Angel Aguilera was killed. Miguel-Angel was only eighteen. He belonged to the Brigada Ramona Parra and had come to the demonstration in response to a call from his trade union. He was standing peacefully on the corner of Plaza Tropezón with his work-mates when he was shot by a plain-clothes policeman who had mingled with the crowd.

This crime inflamed an already red-hot political atmosphere. The funeral was a massive march of hundreds of thousands, filling the wide avenue leading to the cemetery, filled with rage and a sense of resolution which had been increased rather than diminished by this needless death. It was for Miguel-Angel Aguilera that Victor wrote his song 'El alma llena de banderas' ('Our hearts are full of banners'), which exactly captures that spirit and expresses the sense of an epic struggle in which even death had to be faced.

This song was Victor's contribution to the Second Festival of New Chilean Song, which took place in August 1970, shortly before the election. The tone of the festival was different from the first one. There was none of the relative political tolerance of the previous year. Any performer known to support a candidate other than Allende was whistled off the stage.

By now there was no doubt that the 'sound' of Popular Unity was that of the indigenous instruments that Inti-Illimani and Quilapayún had done so much to popularise. But it was also necessary to have a marching song for the campaign, and so 'Venceremos' was born. Sergio Ortega was asked to write the music and in this first, campaigning version, the words were Victor's.

It was all done in a tremendous hurry. I was present at the recording of it, late one night in a basement studio. Musicians from various groups took part, and accompanied Victor by singing the choruses. DICAP had the job of producing the record and distributing it at lightning speed so that the song could be used in the marches of Popular Unity. By the time of the election, huge crowds were capable of singing at least the choruses. Later the words were re-written and the song became the 'hymn' of Popular Unity.

If one has never experienced them, I think it must be difficult to imagine what it was like to be a part of those mass demonstrations which completely took over the centre of Santiago when they occurred. They played such an important part in the political process, perhaps too big a one. Everyone became obsessed with numbers. People were continually being counted, in workplaces, neighbourhoods, universities, and at meetings large and small. It was a tremendous boost for our morale to see that the supporters of Popular Unity were capable of creating far larger crowds than the ruling Christian Democrat Party. The right wing, en masse, never showed itself on the streets. Their power lay in other fields, which

I think we naively failed to calculate. If they did come out, it was in small groups to commit or provoke violence.

But more important than the mere counting of heads was our experience of seeing and touching each other, of sensing the physical presence of so many people whom we knew to be compañeros. We were able to shout together, and if we marched down the Alameda or the elegant Avenida Providencia, there was the satisfaction of showing the momios just how many we were. It was all very exciting and also very primitive, and at each call to demonstrate, even though it was after a hard day's work, there we all were, honour-bound to be present, to swell the numbers.

7

THE DOORS OPEN

4 September 1970

Election day at long last ... The campaign has been over for
twenty-four hours and an unnatural quiet reigns, like a lull in the
storm. With the memory of the last gigantic demonstration of Popular
Unity fresh in my mind it is impossible not to feel optimistic. It was the
biggest, most festive, most combative ever, stretching for the length
of the Alameda, from Plaza Italia, past the Santa Lucía Hill, on down
towards the Central Station. Some day there were as many as 800,000
people there, and I can believe it. It was incredible to hear all those
people singing 'Venceremos'.

People are going early to vote – our neighbours went out long
since. Most of them vote in Las Condes, but Victor has to go to
the First District in the centre of town, because he is registered in
his place of work. Monica has gone too, and I am alone here with
the children, Manuela, Amanda and Monica's daughter Carola. I am
the only one who has no vote – as a resident foreigner I can take part
in local but not in national elections. I tell myself that if Allende is
elected, it will be worth going through all the bureaucracy involved
in taking out Chilean nationality.

Everything is quiet, even though it is such a crucial day. But
election days in Chile usually are – after all the demonstrations,
violence, disorder of the campaigns, the actual voting takes place in
a calm and orderly fashion ... Everything depends on what happens
today. If Alessandri wins it will be the end of all our hopes. If Tomic

wins, nothing will change. It's hard to believe that after so many attempts, Allende could really be elected President. If he is, the people of Chile will have their own government, and the workers, the underprivileged, the rotos will come to power . . .

Must get lunch for the children. There are sure to be long queues at the polling stations. It will be ages before Victor gets back.

I couldn't bear to have to listen to the triumphant hooting of our neighbours' cars tonight. It is horrible when the right wins an election. They take to the streets in their limousines and race around with horns blaring, shouting insults at anyone who doesn't support them. There has been a very hostile atmosphere in the neighbourhood lately. Manuela has noticed it even among the children – she is very sensitive to it. There are other Popular Unity supporters among the neighbours, but they keep quiet and try not to be noticed. No chance of that for us. Not many people round here dare to put a poster for Allende in their window, although there are plenty for Alessandri and Tomic. Actually our nice family doctor is a Tomic supporter, I notice. But he isn't hostile towards us. On the contrary, he is very friendly and often goes to the Peña.

But there is the hum of the citroneta . . . Victor has come home. It seems strange that he has nothing to do but come home and wait. Amazing that we can all have tea together.

It is agonising to listen to the radio. A spokesman from the Ministry of the Interior is reading out the first results. I'm nervous and can't sit still and listen to them, but Victor is installed in an armchair by the log fire in the living room with the radio next to him. He has a pencil and paper and tries to note them down as they come in. They are very partial at first . . . No computers here . . . They begin by giving the counts from individual voting tables which are segregated by sex so that it is easy to see the different voting patterns for men and women. Even now the women tend to be more conservative . . . The women's tables they are announcing seem to give a majority to Tomic, but these results are from Santiago . . . Maybe it will be different later, when the votes from the north start coming in.

It's already dark. Victor has forgotten to put the light on – he hasn't even noticed he's sitting in the dark. He seems to have given up the idea of writing everything down. I sit on the floor beside him and put my head on his knees. He strokes my hair gently and says, 'Mamita, what on earth shall we do if Alessandri

wins?' . . . Then, after a pause, 'And what on earth will they do if
Allende wins?'

That horrible official voice drones on, giving the returns, now from
all over the country. It's impossible to tell who is going to win. It is
obviously a close race, and maybe the government is controlling the
order in which it announces the results. Still, Allende seems to be
doing very well. Every victory for Alessandri makes us shudder, but
perhaps we are keeping level. So far it seems fairly evenly matched,
and the results from the north are still not complete. They *must* be
mostly for Allende.

The phone rings. It is a friend of Victor's to tell him that Allende
has practically won. It doesn't seem to tally with what we are hearing
on the radio. We look at each other and I squeal with excitement
and start jumping about. We hadn't dared hope until now. Monica
is back. She shares our excitement. One good sign: there is no sound
of celebration in our neighbourhood.

We change stations on the radio to see if any of the commentaries
support the idea of a definite victory for Allende. The Ministry official
certainly hasn't made any such announcement . . . The children are
in bed now. We can't bear the suspense any longer and decide to
go out. Victor's friend says that there is a gathering of Popular Unity
supporters outside the FECH, the old Students' Federation building
in the Alameda, a decaying dump soon to be demolished, opposite
Santa Lucía Hill. Monica will stay at home.

We come out into the night to find the other houses all in darkness.
Our canasta-playing neighbours seem to have gone to bed. The noise
of the citroneta starting up seems very loud and noticeable. We are
the only people about. It gives me the creeps – usually on election
night people are running in and out of each other's houses. Victor
backs out of our car port, making the usual loop to get out of the
courtyard, avoiding the tree which I often manage to bump into,
and off we go. An Alsatian barks and Don Juan, standing sentinel on
the corner, raises his hand as we go out. He is a stout and enigmatic
ex-policeman who acts as night-watchman for our group of houses.
We are not sure whether he is a friend or not, but he certainly knows
everything that goes on in all the houses.

There is no one on the street. Down Avenida Colón, the mansions
are in darkness with the shutters closed. Even the floodlights in the
large gardens have been turned off, although it is not very late. In the

Alameda there is little traffic, but, yes, outside the FECH building a large crowd is gathered. We park the citroneta behind the building and I follow Victor as he pushes his way through the crowd. People recognise him, slap him on the back as we pass, and joke about the possible result. Nobody seems to know for certain what is happening, but there is an air of subdued celebration.

The people guarding the door open it for Victor and we are suddenly inside the building. A gloomy, ill-lit staircase, and adjoining rooms full of untidy filing cabinets and shabby furniture. It seems that all the well-known faces of Popular Unity are here – leaders of the parties, senators, deputies, artists – chatting quietly in groups, sitting on the staircase, awaiting confirmation of the rumoured victory . . . I see the Communist leaders, Lucho Corvalán, Volodia Teitelboim, and then I realise that Salvador Allende himself is there.

I think about how many times, over how many years, they have awaited election results, over how many years they have campaigned and hoped for a popular victory. Many are working-class, elderly, with a life of struggle behind them. Some are young . . . Outside now you can hear the noise of the growing crowd, shouting slogans.

At five minutes past twelve the message arrives: Salvador Allende has won the presidential election, and the *Jefe de Plaza* – that is, the Army Chief in charge of election arrangements in the capital – has given permission for Popular Unity to hold a public meeting. The people are already here. The celebrations are under way. The Alameda is packed again. People are climbing lampposts, trees, parapets, and flooding up the hill opposite, hoping to get a glimpse of Allende when he speaks.

Inside, all is joy, embraces, tears. I find myself swept off my feet. Everyone is hugging and embracing one another. People push to get near Allende to congratulate him. Then it is my turn. I give him what I feel to be an uninhibited bear-hug, but he says to me, 'Hug me tighter, compañera! This is no time to be shy!'

A few minutes later, Allende steps out on to the tiny balcony of the FECH building to speak as the President-Elect of Chile. It is a small, insecure-looking balcony – there is barely room for him to stand . . . Someone has managed to rig up a microphone, not a very good one . . . The crowd roars and chants 'Allende! Aye-N-day! Aye-N-day!' People are dancing in the street, holding hands, making chains, circles, lighting bonfires . . . the broad streets of the city centre are suddenly full of horses and carts which have come in from the surrounding shanty-towns loaded with people to celebrate together.

Victor and I can't bear to be inside the building any longer, and rush out into the street to be among the crowd. Spontaneous processions begin with improvised torches . . . we find ourselves marching down the Alameda towards the Moneda, the Presidential Palace. Suddenly from the opposite direction a contingent of soldiers appears in armoured cars. It seems like an omen, a menace, but they pass by with nothing more than a gesture from some of the troops looking down on us from the trucks.

Among the crowd we see many young Christian Democrats with their banners. They have come to offer their congratulations and support to Popular Unity . . . We are not drunk, but there is a feeling of unreality, it is like a dream. When have we ever seen the people of the shanty-towns, with ragged, barefoot children, celebrating like this in the centre of the city? . . . Occasionally we meet someone we know – more embraces . . . This is going on all night . . . But we must go home. Perhaps Monica will be waiting up to hear the news.

As we drive home once more, east of the Plaza Italia, up towards the mountains, everything is silent. We have left the festive atmosphere behind us and here we are alone. I wonder what is going on behind the closed shutters of the mansions. As we drive into our deserted street, I wonder with what faces our neighbours will greet us in the morning . . . or perhaps they will not greet us at all. Tomorrow we shall see.

We are happy, but apprehensive, too. Will the fascists and the CIA really let Allende take power? After all the violence of the past few months we know that it is not going to be easy . . . Those troops on the streets, were they friends or enemies? We snuggle down to sleep with a feeling that the world is turning upside down.

The morning after the election our happiness was already tempered by the knowledge that right-wing forces in Chile would stop at nothing to prevent Allende taking power. Fiestas Patrias that September seemed different. Most of the ordinary people taking their traditional family picnic to the Parque Cousiño and dancing the cueca in the fondas, seemed to feel that it was a special celebration, that they were cele-brating Chile's Second Independence – this time not from the Spanish empire, but from the multi-nationals and the oligarchy.

The Armed Forces were cheered with special fervour as they marched in the traditional parade on the 19th. Marching behind the taller and slimmer professional officers, the short, stocky conscripts seemed to be compañeros, young men from peasant and working-class families who must surely be supporters of Popular Unity.

The Commander-in-Chief, General René Schneider, made a speech in which he declared his support for the democratic process and defined the role of the Armed Forces as that of upholding the constitution. The Schneider Doctrine, as it came to be called, was the main stumbling block for those anxious to provoke a military coup – a very real threat in the two-month period between the election and the day when Allende would formally take over as President from Eduardo Frei.

The final count had given 36.3 per cent to Allende, 34.9 per cent to Alessandri, and 27.4 per cent to Tomic. Under the Chilean constitution, if, as so often, the winner were short of an absolute majority of the votes, Congress must confirm the result and could in theory choose to name the runner-up as President. Now began a series of manoeuvres to persuade Congress, where the Christian Democrats held the balance, to break with tradition and proclaim Jorge Alessandri, not Salvador Allende, President.

The first stage was the economic pressure – the self-produced panic on the stock exchange, the massive withdrawal of funds from banks and building societies, the closure of private industries while their owners 'fled' to Miami or Ecuador, speculation on the black market in goods and dollars, and hoarding of food and other necessities to create artificial shortages. On the few walls that they had managed to paint during the election campaign, the right had promised 'Allende = Chaos'. Now they were determined to make their prophecy come true.

Many of the larger mansions in the barrio alto were put up for sale and the contents sold off while their owners complained about the cruelty of fate. Small groups of very well-dressed women in heavy mourning demonstrated in the centre of the city, waving black handkerchiefs and crying, 'Save us from communism!' It was impossible to feel sorry for them. No one was harming them or forcing them to leave the country. Toilet paper disappeared from the shops overnight. This was Jorge Alessandri's contribution to the situation – as owner of the Papelera de Puente Alto he had a monopoly of paper production in the country. The threat of socialism meant that we had to make do with old newspaper.

But these actions were only the tip of the iceberg. Underneath, more complex plots were being hatched. Alessandri was courting the Christian Democrats, promising that if they voted for him in Congress, he would immediately resign the presidency, leaving the way open for another election. This time Frei would be eligible to stand again, and if he, rather than Tomic, received his Party's nomination, he could count on the votes of a united opposition to defeat Allende. The idea must have appealed to the right wing of the Christian Democrat Party, and not least to Frei himself.

The weeks between the election and the vote in Congress were so fraught with political tension that it was difficult to concentrate on work in the university. The forces of Popular Unity and the trade-union movement had to be constantly on the alert to prevent moves to overthrow the constitution. There were many calls to assemble for meetings and demonstrations to show that the people would not allow themselves to be cheated of an election victory won in a fair and democratic contest. Classes were often interrupted while teachers, students and auxiliary workers marched to the Plaza de la Constitución to gather with other trade unionists from all over Santiago. The election had to be defended by constant mobilisation. Chile's oligarchy respected democracy only so long as they were the winners.

Santiago was full of foreign journalists. For the first time we felt that the eyes of the world were on Chile – perhaps now at least people in Europe would discover where it was on the map. Allende's victory was already having repercussions in the rest of Latin America, and the possibility of achieving socialism and independence by peaceful means had given new hope to mass movements everywhere.

In the midst of all this excitement, Victor had to go abroad. He left the country with reluctance, because he didn't want to be away while so much was happening. He had been invited to an International Arts Festival in Berlin, more in his capacity as theatre director than singer. There he would have the chance to see the Berliner Ensemble, and he had invitations also to sing in Czechoslovakia, Colombia, Venezuela and Peru. As he kissed me good-bye at the airport, he regretted missing Amanda's sixth birthday, but swore to be back for 24 October, when Congress should confirm Allende President.

Victor's heart and thoughts were so much in Chile during this journey that perhaps he didn't take as much advantage as on other occasions of what he saw and experienced. He was very surprised and moved when, sitting alone in his hotel room in East Berlin, he heard his own song, 'Preguntas por Puerto Montt', being sung in Spanish by a duo of German singers.

Meanwhile at home the drama continued. CIA agents were said to be pouring into the country. A plot to assassinate Allende was uncovered and the police seemed strangely slow to act against right-wing terrorists. Within the Christian Democrat Party the left wing won the day and it was announced that their casting vote in Congress would be in favour of Allende.

But on the morning of 22 October, only two days before the crucial vote, General René Schneider was the victim of an attempted kidnapping in which he was critically wounded. His car was hemmed in by three others as he travelled from his home in Calle Martin de Zamora towards the centre of Santiago. When he drew his revolver to defend himself, he was shot. It appeared that his would-be kidnappers, a group of right-wing terrorists related to the same fascist network as General Viaux, either panicked or exceeded their orders. Certainly General Schneider had been an obstacle in the way of those plotting a military coup. But this attack had the opposite effect to that intended.

Victor, still in Peru, heard the news in a typically distorted version which suggested that the left was responsible and that this was the inevitable result of Allende's being elected. Cutting short his programme, he took the first available flight home and arrived on the morning of 24 October, just in time to hear the news that Congress had indeed confirmed Salvador Allende as President of Chile.

General Schneider, however, lay fighting for his life in a Santiago hospital, and such was the state of consternation and concern that there was no celebration of the vote. A national vigil accompanied the Commander-in-Chief until his death on 26 October. He was given the funeral of a popular hero, but seeing Alessandri and Frei marching behind the coffin among the chief mourners, together with Allende, one wondered what their true feelings were, and whether they too had been involved in the kidnapping plot. General Carlos Prats, who was now appointed Commander-in-Chief, declared his allegiance to the Schneider Doctrine and his loyalty to the democratically elected President.

The vote in Congress had been overshadowed by this tragedy,

but on 3 November, the day that Allende formally took office and moved into the Moneda Palace, Santiago was the scene of the most incredible cultural festival which had ever taken place in Chile. On twelve open-air stages set up at different points in the city centre, in an atmosphere of festivity, non-stop performances were mounted by all the main cultural groups and individual artists. This time it was not just the politically committed who took part, but institutions like the Symphony Orchestra, the Philharmonic Orchestra, the National Ballet, the company of the Theatre Institute, and poets, choirs, comics, operetta, clowns, pop singers, folk groups, and, of course, the artists of the New Chilean Song Movement.

It was a wonderful occasion, with festive crowds filling the entire centre of the city. The streets were closed to traffic while masses of children and people of all ages strolled and looked and listened in the late spring air. Everywhere there was music, with the smell of empanadas, roasting peanuts and smoke from the barbecues, while thunderous applause echoed from one stage to another.

For the first time, Ballet Popular performed in the same pro-gramme as the National Ballet, on the largest stage in the Plaza de la Constitución, where Victor also was singing. Many of our ballet colleagues who had not voted for Popular Unity, and had never performed at a demonstration, became infected by the feeling of joyful, popular celebration, and even the most reactionary of them had not the heart to complain of such an appreciative audience. I remember that when Victor came out on stage, dedicating his songs to 'our Compañero Presidente', Allende suddenly appeared on the first-floor balcony of the Moneda Palace, on the opposite side of the square, and waved a salute at him across the multitude of people. It was a celebration like no other for a new sort of president. The people felt that they had entered the Moneda Palace with him.

From this moment on, our lives were to be coloured by the political context, completely bound up with day-to-day events. When things were going well for the Popular Unity government we were happy, when they were going badly we were personally affected – so great was the political feeling and the sense of being part of an important struggle.

Much of the work that both Victor and I had been doing in our different spheres, against the odds, unsupported, almost subversively,

suddenly became official policy. It was as though a door against which
you had been battering suddenly burst open and you found yourself
on the other side, staggering, but free. It was wonderful, but it took
a bit of getting used to.

At first there was a momentary pause in Victor's song-making.
After protesting and denouncing for so long, to have a real cause
for celebration and so many constructive tasks to perform was in
some ways disconcerting. He couldn't go straight on like a machine,
churning out positive pamphlet songs. He had to take time to get used
to the new conditions, absorb the new atmosphere. But as he started
to get into gear and to become immersed in the new situation, songs
began pouring out.

He called his next album, published in April 1971 with DICAP,
El Derecho de Vivir en Paz ('The right to live in peace') a title which
emphasised his feelings about the situation we were living in, although
the actual song from which it came was dedicated to Ho Chi Minh and
the people of Vietnam and had been written while he was producing
Vietrock.

Many people took part in the production of the album: Angel
Parra, Inti-Illimani, Patricio Castillo, as well as Celso Garrido Lecca,
a distinguished composer who was teaching in the Faculty, and even
a pop group called Los Blops, who accompanied Victor in two of
the songs with electric guitars and a synthesiser as an experiment in
'invading the cultural invasion'. It was a time when everyone was
happy to work together, in a spirit which was neither commercial nor
competitive, encouraging and criticising one another without worries
about relative status or importance.

Meanwhile, thousands of students were going out into the country
in their summer vacation to help with the harvest or to take part in the
campaign to eliminate adult illiteracy, while Ballet Popular and many
other artists were travelling in a 'cultural train' along the longitudinal
railway and its branches, stopping at small villages and large towns
with theatre, dance, exhibitions, concerts and workshops.

We had working-class Cabinet Ministers; we had celebrated the
dissolution of the Grupo Movil – their water-cannons had been taken
into the poblaciones to supplement water supplies; the distribution
of free milk to all growing children had begun, putting an end, we
hoped, to malnutrition. Many children and even adults were having
a holiday and seeing the sea for the first time in their lives because

the government was setting up primitive but adequate holiday camps
for workers on some of the beautiful beaches up and down the long
coast of Chile. We felt optimistic and confident that anything could
be achieved. The opposition seemed to be in retreat.

I remember a phrase from that time which seemed to express the
feeling of it. Someone said in a speech at a mass meeting – I think it
was Luis Corvalán, leader of the Chilean Communist Party – 'The
house is yours . . .' – meaning that it was time, at last, for the great
mass of working people to take possession of, be responsible for and
enjoy their own country. Victor, listening, made an elaborate doodle
around that phrase which he noted down because he liked it.

Something else from that time that expressed all our feelings: a
cartoon with one roto saying to another, 'Even the smog seems
beautiful now.' And another with a couple of pitucos exchanging
notes: 'So they're not going to shoot us?' 'No, worse than that,
they're going to make us work!'

These are not so much symptoms of a 'communist repression', nor
of an overbearing sectarianism, but rather of the fact that the people
who had been underdogs for so long and erred, if anything, on the
side of excessive humility, needed to be convinced of their right to
take a lead, a right which they had won in democratic elections.

One of Victor's new songs, 'Abre tu ventana' ('Open your window'), addressed to a woman of the shanty-towns, contained this
idea:

> Open your window, let the sun
> bring light into every corner of your house.
> Look outside – our lives weren't made
> to be steeped in shadow and sadness.
> Maria, look,
> it's not enough to be born, grow up and fall in love
> to find real happiness . . .
> The hardest part is over
> now your eyes are full of light, your hands of honey . . .

Other songs, too, were filled with a spirit of happiness and optimism
which seemed to exude from him. It wasn't because it was the 'party
line' or anything like that. It was what he and so many others really
felt. Victor wrote, 'I should like to be ten people, in order to do ten

times as much of all there is to do. We have this wonderful chance of creating a socialist society by peaceful means and we mustn't squander it . . . The world is watching us to see if it is possible.'

'BRP', a song with music by Celso and words by Victor, was written in tribute to the painting brigades which had come into being during the election campaign. These had developed from painting simple political slogans into creating elaborate and beautiful murals. Sometimes they were helped by famous painters, like Roberto Matta. Local people took part both in discussions about the content and in the actual painting. All over Chile, in poblaciones, along the embankment of the Mapocho River, by factory gates and in provincial cities, dull walls were blossoming with brightly coloured symbols relating to everyday working life and the programme of the Popular Unity government: ears of wheat, copper bars, mothers with babies, miners in their helmets, hands clasped in friendship and peace, doves, stars, guitars. The same basic technique was used and developed, with thick black lines tracing out the forms, filled in with simple bright colours – a technique which became almost a recipe for a visual image, because it allowed for communal painting.

I found it impossible not to take pity on some of my dance students as they hung exhausted on the barre in the morning with little energy or concentration after a long session of wall painting. César, in particular, was the leader of a brigade and one of the pioneers of design in this particular form of street art. He explained to me that the dimensions of the walls made the act of painting rather like dance, because the whole body had to be used to wield the brush. With a dozen or so people working together in a group effort, co-ordinated in unison and counter-point, painting a mural became very like a choreography.

'Ni chicha ni limona' ('Neither one thing nor the other') was a very topical song which became so popular that it reached the Chilean equivalent of the Top Ten. It made fun of people who were sitting on the fence, afraid to commit themselves to Popular Unity, even in order to oppose right-wing terrorism and sedition. It was directed more than anything at the Christian Democrats who were being forced, against their will, to confront that crucial decision. (The issue was a very sensitive one: Popular Unity was in a minority in both the Senate and the House of Deputies, and the Christian Democrats held the balance of power; parliamentary elections did not coincide with presidential ones, and the next chance to alter the balance of power in the legislature would not be until March 1973.) Victor's exuberant voice invaded the air-waves just at this moment, with his catchy refrain accusing people of being 'wishy-washy' and inviting them to join him 'where the potatoes are burning' – the Chilean equivalent of 'where it's all happening'. People loved the song and joined in singing the chorus. We always wondered whether it really did persuade anyone to vote differently. In any case, at the municipal elections in April, there was a marked leftward swing throughout the country, and Popular Unity emerged with an absolute majority.

During the summer, Victor and I had made a combined effort to translate Malvina Reynolds' 'Little Boxes' – a song which had attracted him since he heard it sung by Pete Seeger. Victor made a Chilean adaptation ('Las casitas del barrio alto') in which this rather gentle satire on life in the rows of villas overlooking San Francisco was applied much more caustically to the barrio alto of Santiago. He added one extra verse which shocked people out of their laughter, referring to right-wing gangsters in Austin Minis who made a sport of murdering generals. It made a sinister contrast with the bright little polka tune. Later Malvina was to refer with approval to the 'political elevation' of her song. Victor was baiting the right wing, using humour as a weapon.

Victor was always concerned with the visual appearance of his albums. The sleeve had to reflect what he wanted to convey with the songs. Sometimes he specifically commissioned photographers to produce pictures which would do this. He chose a photo of the work-torn hands of a peasant for *Pongo en tus Manos Abiertas*; for *Canto Libre* he insisted on the outer cover being a close-up of a decayed, padlocked door, and when the sleeve was opened, a flying dove seemed to soar out of it.

Now, for *El Derecho de Vivir en Paz*, he wanted a sensation of wide-open space and bright colours. He found an ink drawing of a galloping, playful horse to give a sense of joy and freedom. The album was launched in great style, thanks to the enormous popularity of the New Chilean Song Movement and the consequent expansion of DICAP and its power of organisation and publicity. It was odd to find oneself confronted with posters of Victor in the street announcing a recital. A theatre director is a much more anonymous person.

At about this time Victor was asked to compose and record new signature music to be used as linkage between programmes on the National Television Channel. It was to replace the insipid airport type of music that had been in use since the channel opened. From 1971 until 10 September 1973, the instrumental music familiar to every Channel 7 viewer was Victor's, although probably few people realised it. There were also tunes to accompany a series of cartoons based on a popular doggy character called Tevito, who forecast the weather and made announcements. Victor had great fun with this, making short variations on the same theme, using different instruments, sounds and rhythms to give each one its specific character.

In all these recordings and in his instrumental pieces, Victor worked with many different musicians, but above all with Inti-Illimani and with Patricio Castillo who had now left Quilapayún. The first music that Victor composed for Channel 7 was later published on a single record with the name 'Charagua' and became the first music using indigenous instruments to reach the Top Ten. It became so well-known and popular that when Inti-Illimani performed it in one of their recitals in a remote place in the northern desert, the audience thought that they were cheating, that they were playing the record over the loudspeakers. The people couldn't believe that a group important enough to be in the charts would actually come and play to them.

Victor's relationship with Inti was informal, but close and very friendly. He greatly admired their musical talent and their work in investigating the indigenous music of the altiplano, and he also valued them as friends. It was impossible not to like them. They were all students of the Technical University and in their early twenties, except for the youngest, 'Loro' Salinas, who was still in his teens. Later he became the musical director of the group and meanwhile was making his first experiments in original composition.

Victor too had become linked to the Technical University through its rapidly expanding Department of Arts and Communications. Since his resignation from the post of theatre director in the University of Chile, our income had been somewhat haphazard, but he wanted to avoid becoming financially dependent on his music. The Technical University offered the ideal solution: together with other artists and groups such as Isabel Parra, Quilapayún, Inti-Illimani and Cuncumén, Victor was to receive a modest monthly salary, in return for which he committed himself to contribute to the massive cultural extension

programme of the university, with its branches and colleges throughout the country and its radio network.

Unlike the other Chilean universities, the UTE – the State Technical University – had a certain tradition of contact with the working-
class and trade-union movement. Since the reforms of the late
1960s it had made great strides in making its courses accessible to
the sons and daughters of peasant and working-class families. It had
begun to decentralise, opening branches all over the country. The
university itself was leading a campaign to end adult illiteracy, with
brigades of students acting as instructors. And in co-operation with
the trade-union movement it was responding to specific local needs
– courses in tractor driving and maintenance, technical courses in
agriculture and forestry, first aid for attendants in rural health clinics,
while in the cultural field it was providing instructors in folklore,
theatre and many other activities. The enlightened support that it gave
to Chilean artists through the Department of Communications helped
them to rationalise their work and enabled them to support the many
spontaneous initiatives of working people all over the country.

Between the Technical University and DICAP, Victor now had a
solid base from which to develop and expand his work for the next
three years. What before had been the result of individual effort,
improvisation, chance and sheer will-power, now came to be based
on much more solid structures and organisations.

Amid all the bustle of the local election campaign and the rehearsals
and recordings of *El Derecho de Vivir en Paz*, I remember one of
the largest parties we ever held at home. It was to celebrate the
completion of a workshop studio which we had built in the garden,
because there were never enough places to rehearse. Although it was
made of whitewashed brick, rather than adobe, it looked something
like the house of Victor's childhood in Lonquen, with the traditional
curly clay tiles which we had rescued from some old houses being
demolished nearby. From now on it was to be a place of constant
activity in both dance and music.

All the young men of Inti-Illimani came to the party, with their
girl friends; the whole of Ballet Popular, just back from their long
tour of the south by train; Marta and Angel and others from the Peña;
Patricio and students from the dance and theatre schools – plenty of
people to play the guitar and sing . . . and there was dancing too.
We grilled meat over a charcoal fire in the garden, ate corn on the

cob and melons, drank wine . . . It was a brilliant starry night such as you can only get in Chile. There was the anticipation of so much wonderful work to be done, such unlimited possibilities . . . We had plenty to celebrate.

Meanwhile, my own relationship with the University of Chile had come full circle. After resigning from the ballet in 1964, from the Dance School in 1966 and then spending three years working in Ñuñoa and Las Condes with no connection at all with the Faculty, I had returned to it in 1969, after the great changes brought about by the reform movement.

I was free to do so because Amanda had just entered the kindergarten of Liceo Experimental Manuel de Salas, where she would be at the same school as Manuela for most of the day. Even at 5 years old she was a sensible little girl and had got relatively used to her injections and her diet. Manuela was a skinny 9-year-old with perhaps too much sense of responsibility for Amanda, but a large circle of friends of her own . . . and Monica was coping with the housekeeping.

We were lucky to have been able to get the girls into one of the nicest schools in Santiago. It was, as its name suggests, an experimental school, belonging to the University of Chile and closely associated with the Pedagógico – the Teacher Training Institute. Its teaching methods were more modern than those of most state schools and its atmosphere was less snobbish and pituco than that of the private schools created by the foreign colonies. At any rate, any snobbery attached to Manuel de Salas was of an intellectual kind, because it was difficult to get into, but it had the great advantage that it was free. The majority of the parents were professional people, artists and intellectuals, and inclined to be progressive.

Back at the Faculty, I found myself facing enthusiastic students and a lot of responsibility in leading an experimental project to train dance teachers who would work in the community, teaching children and amateurs. It was a project which had an important place in the new programme of the Dance Department, with the full support of the Faculty, and was part of the new cultural agreements between the University of Chile and the trade union federation, the CUT.

Working people were no longer content with merely watching dance or theatre, but felt that they had a right to take part, to experience it, to make their own plays and choreographies. We were not yet ready to respond to the enormous demand for teachers of amateur groups, but my work was geared to that aim, through a special course for mature students with previous dance experience.

The Dance School was a different place now. In general, there were more young adult students, even young men, very often inspired by having seen Ballet Popular and realising that dancers were human beings capable of relating to society. The little girls, being trained as ballerinas, were still there – indeed now they had a teacher from the Bolshoi – but more priority was given to widening the whole social base of dance in the country. The first step was to train good amateur teachers, and the second to open 'satellite' dance schools in working-class areas for children and young people who might later be interested in dance as a career.

I found that the concepts I had learned in my own dance training with Sigurd Leeder were the best guide to developing a system of amateur community dance specifically adapted to the people involved and the environment in which we were working. It was important to give physical training as well as the experience of dancing, and very often we found ourselves faced with the visible effects of malnutrition. We realised that it was necessary to co-ordinate our work with the new 'polyclinics' which were being set up in many of the poblaciones. Conditions were often far from ideal or even possible in normal terms. Concrete floors, cold and draughty rooms, rickety boards, not enough space or too much . . . We had to be prepared for anything, just as in the performances of Ballet Popular.

The Dance School was now my main priority, although I continued to work with Ballet Popular occasionally. The latter still had an important role to play because it continued to be more mobile than the larger National Ballet and could perform in smaller places. Gradually, however, its work was becoming fused into the official programme of the Dance Department, as the whole focus of dance was directed towards more mass participation, both within our Faculty and in the dance school of the Ministry of Education which had been established in 1969.

A programme called 'Art for Everyone' brought regular performances of ballet, orchestral music, folklore, theatre, poetry and mime to the outlying working-class districts of Santiago in a circus tent or on a large, mobile, open-air stage. Some people criticised this policy as being paternalistic, with artists, instruments, equipment, descending upon a población like some *deus ex machina* and then suddenly disappearing after a few days, leaving only a fleeting experience behind. Perhaps it was, but at least it was a start, and it was accompanied by longer-term programmes, like the one in which I was engaged, which hopefully would introduce real participation.

The National Ballet also began to give massive numbers of performances and lecture demonstrations to audiences of school-children and students, reaching out to much wider audiences. For the first time, it travelled to the far south, to Coyaique, Punta Arenas and Aysen, where no ballet company had ever been before.

The atmosphere in the Faculty had changed too. The rather rigid, authoritarian structures had disappeared and been replaced by a democratic organisation in which there was more participation. There was a sense of comradeship which linked the solo dancers of the Ballet with the boy who worked the lift and the woman whose job it was to clean the floor; it linked students and teachers beyond the timetable of their classes and a new spirit of interchange and comprehension seemed to spring up. Under the Popular Unity government, the spirit of the reform movement was enhanced by a new concept of society and the role of the university within it. The Faculty was a highly politicised community in which everyone had a part to play.

This new spirit was put to the test during the first winter. One evening in June, the coldest month of the year, black clouds gathered over the cordillera and during the night a violent storm developed, with a howling gale and torrential rain. Lying in our warm bed, listening to the rattling of the wooden shutters in the high wind, we knew that in the poblaciones makeshift roofs were being lifted from improvised shelters, that whole families must be exposed to the wind and the rain, losing their few possessions. If the river Mapocho flooded, they were in danger of being swept away by the flood. Every winter the same thing happened – babies might die of cold or pneumonia, but the same conditions continued to exist and, apart from a dose of charity, a distribution of jumble and old blankets, no drastic measures were taken to help the victims and to prevent it ever happening again.

Now, however, under a popular government, the response *had* to be different. And it was. Governmental organisations, trade unions and even the universities were mobilised to bring immediate help to the victims of the storm which had affected a wide area and left many poor areas devastated. Rescue work was co-ordinated so that each Faculty was responsible for a different area. The students of the Technical University had many skills which were invaluable, in directing the construction of emergency housing, water supplies, drainage and so on, but even musicians and dancers could offer unskilled labour and muscle.

As always happened, when the clouds cleared the day after the storm, revealing the cordillera covered in glittering snow, a penetrating cold descended on Santiago. All the Faculty vehicles were mobilised to take supplies of paraffin and food, as well as rescue teams, into the población of Renca, but it was found that only jeeps would be of any use. Low-lying land and unmade roads had produced thigh-deep mud. It was impossible even to walk. The high winds had left many families homeless and they were trying to shelter in the only larger and more solid building in the community, which was a church. Babies and small children, poorly clothed and bare-foot, were in immediate danger of serious illness.

A more drastic solution was called for and it was decided to evacuate the children to the Faculty building and to use the large ballet studios as dormitories. This enterprise, which sounds logical if you consider that children's health and even lives were in danger, was nevertheless unheard-of and completely revolutionary.

It was organised and animated by a wonderful woman who was an example to us all. Quena was perhaps a prototype of that very small but significant number of people from aristocratic families who were committed to revolutionary changes in Chile. She was a handsome woman, usually dishevelled, whose language tended to be filthy and who slopped around in a parka and old trousers. In her youth she had spent some time as a land girl working on a farm in the Cotswolds and had ventured round the world relying on her own efforts to earn a living, renouncing her family background. Now she worked in the Dance Department as an administrator and in this emergency she became the life and soul of the rescue operation.

She rallied all of us, even the most reluctant and lazy, to do something useful. The secluded realm of the ballet was invaded by ragged, howling children who had never before seen an ordinary bathroom or toilet. Many were suffering from dysentery. They were undernourished, dirty and scared at being separated from their families, although their spirits soon revived after hot food.

It was the first time that the real tragedy of poverty had touched our comfortable, privileged world, and I am sure that for many of the dancers it was an important experience. Even though we might have been politically and socially aware before this, and had often made the usual collections of old clothes and blankets 'for the poor', it was not the same as actually caring for these young creatures, seeing them eat so ravenously, and after having the matted strands of their hair washed and combed for lice, emerge as beautiful children.

One of the babies brought to the Faculty became the subject of a song by Victor. Luchín was seriously ill with pleurisy and needed constant nursing, day and night. Quena had found him on one of her many journeys to the población, a dirty little bundle of rags on the muddy floor of a shack where he lived with his numerous family. A horse, the family's only precious possession and source of their precarious livelihood, shared the room. Luchín was almost a year old, but tiny for his age. He needed a long convalescence before he could be reunited with his family, so Victor and I took him home and cared for him for some weeks, until later, with the consent of his parents, Quena adopted him permanently.

Fragile as a kite over the roofs of Barrancas,
little Luchín was playing,
his hands blue with cold,
with his rag ball,
the cat and the dog . . .
and the horse looked on.

His eyes brimming pools of green,
his brief life spent crawling,
little bare bottom in the mud.

The horse was another toy for him
in that tiny space,
and it seemed that the horse enjoyed his job,
with the rag ball,
the cat and the dog,
and Luchín wet through.

If there are children like Luchín,
who eat earth and worms,
let's open wide their cages,
so that they can fly away like birds,
with the rag ball,
the cat and the dog,
and with the horse, too.

('Luchín')

But the rescue operation didn't stop with the evacuation of the children. As soon as the weather made it possible, voluntary work parties were organised, and with the government providing the materials, students, teachers and performers worked together with the people of the población to improve the roads and to erect emergency wooden houses – palaces in comparison with those that had existed before, because they had real floors.

These were only emergency measures – later the población would have to be entirely rebuilt – but they were carried out with great energy and a sense of comradeship rather than charity, while the local organisations, including those of the women of the población, gained strength as they tried to solve their problems together, with all the support that the government could give them in health care, housing, transport and education.

These events coincided with a very festive atmosphere in the country as a whole – 11 July 1971 was called the 'Day of National Dignity', to celebrate the nationalisation of Chile's copper mines. It was the day when the people of Chile took over from the multi-nationals natural resources which brought in almost three-quarters of the country's entire export earnings. It was a red-letter day which was like a second Fiestas Patrias. The measure was such a popular one that even the right-wing National Party didn't dare to vote against it in Congress, and it was passed unanimously.

It was a good time. Political divisions were forgotten as people were swept away by enthusiasm. Cuecas and other songs were composed in honour of the occasion. Allende went to the mining town of Rancagua, headquarters of the Braden Copper Company, and was cheered by a gigantic, festive demonstration – although, as so often happens in Chile, a serious earthquake, centred on Valparaiso, marred the celebrations.

The new, more flexible conditions in the Faculty had made it possible to undertake a wonderful dance project in which Victor also was involved. It made him, with his inevitable green duffle coat and peaked fisherman's cap, a familar figure in the Dance Department. The idea was not a new one. It was in the early sixties that Patricio first approached Victor about composing the musical themes for a ballet based on the universal legend, which is also present in Chilean folk mythology, of the young peasant who has to complete seven trials to rescue the heroine – maiden, princess or whatever – who is kept a prisoner by a horrible monster – in this case down a well.

In *Los Siete Estados* or 'The Seven Stages', Patricio had used this idea as a symbol of the liberation struggle of the people of Chile, with seven stages or scenes in its development – down the mines, in the cities, on the land, in the desert, and so on. At first, Patricio had suggested that Victor be entirely responsible for the music because he wanted it to have an absolutely authentic folk character, but Victor had refused, knowing his own limitations. However, he composed many of the themes and songs and these were now being worked on by Celso Garrido Lecca who was developing them, in close consultation with Victor, into the complex musical structure that the ballet demanded.

Victor had been swept more and more, almost without willing it, into the field of composition. He had begun to regret his musical illiteracy, but on the other hand he felt that it was not possible to begin again at the beginning, that if he began to study in a conventional way, he might lose his instinct and be unable to compose at all. Certainly he thought he would lose his folk authenticity. He was very happy therefore to have the chance of working with Celso from whom he could learn so much in a very direct and practical way. He was as enthusiastic as a child at seeing all the possibilities that could develop and transform his simple themes through electronic treatment.

Los Siete Estados was a major, full-length work and demanded the participation of many people: Victor, both as composer and performer on stage; Inti-Illimani, who contributed to the musical arrangements and were also to take part on stage; Celso, as the main composer of the music; members of the Symphony Orchestra, and of course, the whole National Ballet. Directing all this was Patricio who was the author and choreographer of the whole project.

I often went upstairs to watch rehearsals. From what I saw of the choreography and heard of the music as it was completed, I felt that it was going to be something of a masterpiece, the best Patricio had ever produced, and the music quite a new synthesis. The première was to be in October 1973.

Everything I write about the years of Popular Unity is subjective, almost passionately biased, unrecognisable for people who had a different viewpoint. I don't apologise for it. It is Victor's truth and my truth. And truth is something that has to be fought for, as we painfully learned during those years.

The enormous economic power of the opposition gave them the upper hand in the mass media, whatever small gains were made by Popular Unity – such as the opening of a radio station belonging to the CUT, or a new director for the National Television Channel. This last was important because most of the resident producers had been installed there by the Christian Democrats when the channel opened in 1969. Even the modest invasion of the mass media by the New Chilean Song Movement, as a result of its sheer popularity, was important, but over-all, the balance was heavily weighted in favour of the opposition, who used their power without scruple.

Through the decades of right-wing government, the left had acted as constant agitators against the establishment, encouraging strikes and demonstrations, usually peaceful ones, putting forward a radical point of view, and using, I suppose, their propaganda machine to the full extent of its chronically small resources. But that had been like using pea-shooters in comparison with the Big Berthas that the opposition now brought to bear – with the aid of generous subsidies from abroad.

El Mercurio, for example, received hundreds of thousands of dollars from the CIA to maintain its propaganda campaign against Allende's government. It was incredible and infuriating to witness, not only how facts could be distorted to influence public opinion, but how events could actually be precipitated by lies and false rumours. It was very easy, for example, to produce scarcities. I remember one occasion when a newspaper – La Tribuna, I think it was – carried a front-page story about an imminent and permanent shortage of toothpaste. The shops were full of toothpaste at the time, but of course people, especially the better-off, rushed out to buy mammoth quantities of it, and inevitably it disappeared from the open market.

The same sort of thing happened with cigarettes, detergents, Nescafé. It was made easier by the fact that most people had more money to spend. Hoarding, speculation, a black market, were fomented by such means, creating artificial scarcities which were then converted into real ones.

There was no proper libel law in Chile, no real protection against calumny. Gross lies about people could be invented with impunity. Any public figure of the left was open to such attacks, and Victor was no exception. Since the time of the incidents in St George's College, some of the right-wing newspapers had been publishing snide little comments about Victor, using adjectives to suggest that he was a homosexual, an accusation which in a thoroughly *machista* society was understood by everyone as the worst possible insult. Although it couldn't affect us very deeply it was unpleasant, especially as it was generally accompanied by a spate of obscene and menacing telephone calls. I always tried to persuade him to take it as a compliment. It showed that he was hitting them where it hurt.

One morning, as we were having breakfast, a friend who lived nearby came to see us with the news that Victor was in the headlines. The front page of *La Tribuna* – seditious gutter-press to us, voice of the National Party to others – bore a banner headline with the story that Victor had been caught at an all-night homosexual party with little boys, 'dancing a perverted cueca'. He was supposed to have been arrested and taken to the police station. The story didn't end there. It was taken up gleefully by *La Prensa*, the Christian Democrat paper and by UPI which sent out an international cable in which the original story was embroidered with the announcement that Victor had been expelled from the Communist Party. This must have been the revenge of the right wing for songs like 'Las casitas del barrio alto' and 'Ni chicha ni limona'.

It would have been funny if we hadn't known that however false a calumny, something of it always sticks. At the time it was maddening, because there was no redress. Victor could only counteract it by going on the offensive and making a public declaration, writing some verses in the style of the folk poets. His reply was published in the left-wing papers, but of course ignored by those who had originally invented the story. He received many letters of support from individuals, organisations and institutions, including the Communist Party and the Theatre Institute of the University of Chile. The whole incident

highlighted how much the reactionary forces in Chile hated Victor
and to what absurd lengths they would go to try to discredit him.
Victor's declaration was as follows:

> In choosing to be a member, as I am and shall continue to be, of the
> Communist Party of Chile, the principal enemy of the reactionary
> forces of the country, and hated by them, I am prepared to suffer
> persecution and personal attacks far worse than the unwarranted
> insults which the voices of the reactionary conspiracy, *La Tribuna*
> and *La Prensa*, have directed at me.
>
> I understand the desperation that must exist among those whom
> these newspapers represent, because of the political isolation in
> which they find themselves and the envy they must feel for the
> monolithic character of my Party. In order to attack it, they resort
> to trying to discredit the reputation of one of its popular singers.
> If they give me so much importance, I suppose it must be because
> the songs aimed at those who murder generals and those who are
> sitting on the fence during this vital period of our country's history
> have had more impact than I had modestly expected.
>
> You know very well that the growing isolation in which you
> find yourselves is due to your constant betrayal of the Chilean
> people. In any case, your attacks on my person, which are also an
> attack on the Communist Party and on Popular Unity, stimulate
> me to continue to compose such songs.

In the verses which followed, Victor referred to a 'one-handed'
Christian Democrat Party and a 'tottering' National Party, trying to
pull each other up by their chins, while sinking slowly in the mire. This
was a graphic, if perhaps vulgar, way of expressing it. The Christian
Democrat Party had lost its left wing, which had peeled off to form
the Christian Left Party, affiliated to Popular Unity, in impatience
and disgust at the leadership's policy of conspiracy with the National
Party and even with the fascists. The National Party itself had lost its
electoral support and in defeat was resorting to any means to retain a
hold on power.

We were on the eve of an offensive of street violence and terrorism,
accompanied by an orchestrated campaign to produce chaos and an
atmosphere of hatred, in which the right-wing media played a vital
part. All those who supported the government were concerned and

frustrated at the lengths to which the opposition was allowed to go in publishing false information, inciting violence and civil disobedience, presenting a distorted version of the situation and the intentions of the government. Freedom of the press is an important principle, but as Allende put it, this was 'not liberty but licence'. Even so, he was reluctant to curb freedom of expression and only on one or two occasions was any action taken against the media – such as the closure for a day or two of a radio station which had called for civil war, and was inciting the Armed Forces to mutiny.

Yet although during Allende's government almost too much freedom of expression existed, and certainly far more than had ever existed before, this did not stop the right wing from mounting an international campaign to propagate the idea that they were being repressed, that freedom of the press was in danger in Chile. On his journeys abroad, Victor had seen for himself the distorted image that was being projected of events in Chile via the international cable system.

In response to this situation, the artists of the New Chilean Song Movement were now called upon to play an international role, both in Latin America and in Europe, as representatives of Allende's Chile, as 'cultural ambassadors' of their country, helping to counteract the propaganda campaign against Popular Unity. Quilapayún and Isabel Parra had made an extensive tour of Europe in this capacity at the time when Allende took over as President; Inti-Illimani had given performances in Ecuador where they were needed to counteract the influence and disinformation of the momios 'fleeing' from Chile, many of whom had settled there.

In November 1971 Victor set out on a long concert tour of Latin America, not to promote himself as a singer, but to represent his country. He sang, and in introducing his songs, talked about Chile, in all sorts of places: in large concert halls, on radio and television, in trade-union meetings and at universities, travelling all over the continent from Mexico to Buenos Aires.

For him, typically, perhaps the most moving experience of the whole tour, as he described to me at length in his letters, was in Costa Rica, when he was taken in a tiny plane from San José down to the coastal jungle, to give a concert to the workers on the banana plantations of the United Fruit Company. On an open-air stage within sight of the management buildings – for Victor one of the symbols of US exploitation – he sang to a mass of black workers, who received his songs with such enthusiasm that the concert ended in an ecstasy of mutual solidarity, with many of the workers climbing on to the stage to sing with him and then carrying him off shoulder high, among cheering crowds shouting 'Viva Chile!' and 'Viva la Unidad Popular!'.

In Venezuela, considered a democratic country, Victor was shocked at the presence of soldiers armed with machine guns at his recital in the University of Caracas. In Chile at that time, and indeed ever since their foundation, the autonomy of the universities was considered fundamental, and there was a public outcry whenever the police attempted to go into university precincts. Here too, in spite of the military presence, the recital ended in a demonstration of solidarity with Chile, the audience on their feet singing the national anthem of Venezuela. It was an indication of what Popular Unity meant to the young people of Latin America and, as the tour continued, it was the same in every country – huge audiences, demonstrations of support and a spirit of fighting optimism.

Victor came home just before Christmas, completely exhausted, but very happy. He felt enriched and strengthened by all his experiences and all the friends he had made. It had been both a political and an artistic success, and he had opened doors for other Chilean singers and groups to make the same journey through Latin America. The New Chilean Song Movement was spreading over the whole continent, linking up with and influencing similar movements in every country.

8

'WHERE THE POTATOES
ARE BURNING'

While Victor was out of the country, Fidel Castro came to Chile for a month-long visit, the first that he had been able to make to another Latin American country since the Cuban revolution. He was given a tremendous reception. Festive crowds lined the whole route from the airport to the city centre. Everyone wanted to meet him and many had the chance to. He travelled to almost every corner of the country, usually accompanied by Salvador Allende, talking to workers and peasants, students and shanty-town dwellers in what was more like a series of mass political discussion workshops than the formal rallies of a state visit. Some were very impromptu, whenever Fidel chose to make an unscheduled halt in some remote hamlet, or to join in a game of basketball.

The opposition were furious and determined to mount a counter-offensive, something they now felt strong enough to do, having recovered from the demoralisation they had been feeling since the elections. They chose the same tactics that had been used with such success in Brazil in 1964, in preparing the overthrow of President Goulart – the mobilisation of middle- and upper-class women in protest marches against the government.

The first one took place while Fidel was still in the country, and, as in Brazil, became known as the Saucepan March. To symbolise the hunger that a socialist government had supposedly brought them, the women all carried empty saucepans which they beat like drums with wooden spoons. The march was well prepared. The idle,

canasta-playing, cocktail-circuit ladies of the barrio alto had at last
found something to do. In our neighbourhood, the activity was
noticeable. Women had become political agitators, running from
house to house, gathering on street corners. They organised a series
of chain telephone calls urging the neighbours to join in. Through
the grape-vine of the maids and the children, we knew that servants
were being offered a free evening and money to go out for a meal
and to the cinema if they took part with their employers. Rumour
had it that brand-new little saucepans were being acquired especially
for the occasion.

For Popular Unity rallies, the crowds would gather on foot, in buses,
or even in horse-drawn carts. But on the day of the Saucepan March,
the approaches to the city centre from the barrio alto were jammed
with shiny cars. These well-dressed, well-fed women, whose freezers
were probably full of hoarded food, some of whom were perhaps
handling a saucepan for the first time in their lives, were egged on
by a real fear of losing their privileged life of comfort, but the sight
of them was sickening, insulting even, to those women who had seen
their children grow up stunted through malnutrition and who knew
what hunger really was.

Around the fringe of the march, allegedly to protect the women,
filed the paramilitary brigades of Patria y Libertad ('Fatherland and
Freedom'), Chile's main fascist organisation. Armed with sticks, stones
and catapults, they set about creating a riot in the city centre, aiming
to provoke police action 'against defenceless women'. The right-wing
press had a field day.

The battle to win the support of women was to be a constant theme
in the months to come. There was scarcely any specifically feminist
activity in Chile, in spite of the work of early women pioneers who
had broken the male monopoly of the professions. Women seemed
to play an active part in politics as members of their class rather
than their sex, although they tended to specialise in the problems
and fields traditionally regarded as women's concerns. The women's
vote had always been more conservative than the men's (and as it
was counted separately, was immediately identifiable). The opposition
now counted on being able to win the hearts of Chilean women. Yet
the reverse occurred. Allende's share of the women's vote actually
increased between 1970 and 1973.

It was not really surprising, as the majority of women were better off under Allende than they had ever been. In spite of difficulties caused by hoarding, a lucrative black market and, later, by difficulties in distribution caused by those who owned and controlled the transport system, there was a notable improvement in the standard of living of the poorest. The beggars who had haunted Santiago ever since I could remember – mothers with babies in their arms, knocking on the door to ask for a crust of bread, the children who sang on the buses or who slept under the bridges – all but disappeared, because men's wages were worth more and they could actually support their families.

Unemployment was drastically reduced and women were encouraged to go out to work, to find jobs in factories. In the nationalised industries, much effort went into providing crèches and canteens serving hot food. There was even an experimental scheme in which women workers could collect a hot meal from the canteen to take home for the family's evening meal. To become a domestic servant was no longer virtually the only opening for a woman with a baby who needed work. Indeed, maids were becoming increasingly difficult to find, at least in Santiago, and they were forming their own union in order to fight for better wages and conditions.

The textile industries, which traditionally had a large percentage of women workers, were among the first to be nationalised, so some of the first worker-directors were women. Victor was invited to the celebrations on the occasion of the nationalisation of Chile's largest textile factory, when the personal flag of the multi-millionaire Yarur family was taken down. Of course such a celebration had to be accompanied by folk-song.

Until then, before being taken on the payroll, workers had to swear absolute loyalty to the Yarurs, with their hands placed on a human skull kept especially for the purpose. Now, the factory was managed by the people who worked in it and owned by the whole country, with a Chilean flag flying over the roof. Naturally, Victor made a song for the occasion and sang it there – it was called 'How times are changing'. He discussed with the women workers how they felt. They told him how different it was, taking a pride in working harder and increasing production as their contribution to the revolution, as a patriotic duty, instead of feeling that they were being exploited for profit by private owners.

I saw these changing attitudes in women whom I had known for years. For example, Rosita, a woman who came to do washing in our neighbourhood, had to travel for miles across Santiago, taking at least two different buses, loaded down with a huge bundle of washing, usually a baby as well, and with a small child tagging along. Her older children, meanwhile, ran wild at home in the distant población of San Miguel. Her husband was usually out of work and drank a lot. A typical story. Like Victor's mother, she was the mainstay of the family and would work incredible hours in order to keep them from starvation. I visited her home several times – typical visits of a middle-class patrona – taking her old mattresses or a paraffin stove we no longer used. It was one of the poorest poblaciones, with improvised wooden huts set very close together, unmade roads, one tap for every ten houses. Rosita had no ambition in her life, none for her children – she was almost resigned to them growing up to be thieves and pickpockets. There was nothing else. Her own life was one long round of drudgery to scrape a bare minimum of existence. Like so many Chilean working-class women, she had lost all her teeth at an early age and looked much older than her forty-or-so years.

We lost sight of her for a time, but in 1972 I met her again. She was living in the same district, but with such a difference. No miracle had happened to her physical surroundings, except that the house looked cleaner and in much better repair, and proper drains and water were being laid. It was Rosita herself who was transformed. She was working in the local organisations, active and busy, feeling that she was contributing to her community and to her family. When she called me 'Compañera Juanita' instead of 'Señora', not only was this a great compliment to me personally, but it epitomised her changed attitude to life and to society. It was a sign of a new-found confidence in herself. She was anxious to organise a performance of Ballet Popular in her neighbourhood and to follow it up with dance classes for young people in the local community centre – this, instead of shirts and sheets, was the subject of our conversation, and it was my responsibility to follow up her suggestion.

In Popular Unity circles, there was certainly awareness of the need to integrate women more into the community, into the workforce, into politics. We had women Cabinet Ministers – it was an especially fine moment when Mireya Baltra was appointed Minister of Employment, for example – women senators, women deputies. But this, in itself, wasn't new. There had long been a place for a few women near the top in Chile, especially for those who could pay other women to do the inevitable 'women's tasks'.

But even with a socialist government, ingrained attitudes persisted. A woman activist presiding over a meeting would have to rush off to cook her husband's supper. He would expect it to be waiting for him when he got home and with her in attendance, even though he was a socialist and theoretically believed in women's rights. A government campaign to convince people to eat more fish, which was plentiful and cheap, instead of meat which was scarce, was spearheaded by photos of working women, enthusiastically frying fish in the streets. The image presented was that of faithful women, alongside their men, carrying out the tasks for which they were prepared, to work for the revolution.

We had no objection at the time. Rather, women were glad to feel that they could make a useful contribution, and indeed, women's organisations were already beginning to play a vital role in helping to fight the black market and in setting up alternative distribution systems. We were compañeras, and had our place in the struggle alongside the men . . . Our enemies were the same.

Victor's and my bio-rhythms, or at least our daily timetables, were chronically staggered. I'm one of those dreadful people who wake up before seven in the morning, bright and active, ready for anything. It comes, I suppose, from years of having to inject some life into inert students at early-morning classes before beginning my own day's work as a dancer. Victor, on the other hand, although capable of getting up very early, even after going to bed at three o'clock in the morning, was never totally conscious until almost lunchtime. Our quarrels almost always took place in the morning and conversations would go something like this:

ME   (*Having already been up about two hours and taken Manuela to school . . . Quite tactfully.*) Papi, I've got to go out in about ten minutes. (*Not strictly true. Knowing what was going to happen, I always lied here.*) Are you coming with me? (*Taking a bus to the centre meant waiting at least half an hour and perhaps hanging on suicidally to the outside all the way.*)

VICTOR   (*Having just wandered vaguely downstairs, is eating his breakfast*

– *always a cup of tea and a boiled egg – and grumpily reading the*
newspaper.) Uurgh!

ME   (*After eight minutes with no sign of movement. Slightly louder and*
more emphatic.) VICTOR, I have to go out NOW, or I shall be late
for my class!

VICTOR   (*Seemingly becoming conscious of what I am saying.*) Aaaaaahhh
. . . Wait for me, Mamita . . . I'm just coming.

ME   All right, but HURRY. I'm going to start the car. (*Always a lengthy*
procedure.)

(*Victor's back, clad in his green towelling dressing-gown, disappears upstairs*
. . . I hear him going into the bathroom . . . noises off . . . splashing . . .
singing . . .)

ME   (*Ten minutes later, infuriated, revving the engine, shouting up at the*
bathroom window.) VICTOR, I AM GOING NOW, THIS MINUTE.
YOU KNOW I CAN'T BE LATE FOR MY CLASS. FOR GOD'S SAKE,
HURRY UP!

Up to this point the situation was completely predictable. The ending
varied according to Victor's mood . . . and to whether or not I was
really as late as I said I was.

Sometimes Victor would stump out within a bearable interval, cross
and silent, take the driver's seat and vent his rage on the car, as he
drove into town, with me in the passenger seat heartily regretting
having shouted at him. He'd drop me off at the Faculty, without
saying a word, and drive off to his various engagements. Sometimes
there was just a roar of rage from the bathroom, telling me to bloody
well go without him. Sometimes, more rarely, because I really wanted
him to come with me, I would be as good as my word and drive off
leaving him behind, knowing that he was going to be late for whatever
appointment or rehearsal he had. One of the few times that I did this
I actually crashed the car into the tree in the middle of the courtyard;
on another occasion, I almost took the carport with me, so I must
have been really angry.

But whatever happened in the morning, by midday Victor would
either appear at the Dance School – sometimes I found him waiting
for me, grinning, as I came out of my class – or ring up to ask how
I was. Our quarrels never lasted and were usually about completely
stupid things.

Unfortunately, at the other end of the day, I was as incapable as Victor was at breakfast-time. He could be full of life, singing and conversing at two o'clock in the morning, while I would be in a coma, my conscious efforts limited to stopping myself falling asleep.

Even so, if I were at home in bed, I lay awake until I heard the hum of the car drawing up outside the house and the wonderful sound of Victor's key in the lock. I would listen to him going into the kitchen to see if there was anything to eat, sticking his head in the refrigerator, and then his steps on the stairs. He would come in quietly, thinking I might be asleep, but if I stirred, he would begin to tell me about the performance or the meeting, all the latest news and gossip. Only when I felt the warmth of his body as he lay down beside me and embraced me could I relax, knowing that he was safe and sound.

Apart from a nagging, constant anxiety about Victor's safety, I had every reason to be happy. We had maintained our loving relationship and now it was enriched by a sense of each of us having our own place in a common cause. We were compañeros as well as man and wife.

I participated in his work, always emotionally, sometimes more directly, or as a critical audience. I had helped him through bad times, he had always given me loving support when I needed it. He always respected my work timetable and never expected me to wait on him, although he was always so enthusiastic when I did cook him a meal or had time to accompany him on some of his working expeditions that I suspect he would really have liked me to be a more conventional wife.

The worst thing about those years was that there never seemed to be any time to talk. Victor was always rushing from one engagement to another, and if I wanted to talk to him, I usually had to queue up, as it were, behind ten other people who were waiting to ask him to do something. Naturally it caused friction in our relationship, although when we were able to have a quiet time together, everything got sorted out. I did not resent Victor's activities, but I did wish he didn't have so many. I always looked forward to some imaginary time when we should have just a little more leisure.

Home was a busy place now. It was usually full of people of assorted ages. Chilean children seemed to live out of doors or in each other's houses, but always in fairly large groups which would descend on one house or another like a swarm of bees, groups which transcended the political rivalry or even hatred of their parents. Manuela and Amanda each had her own group of friends.

Then, since we had the workshop in the garden, it was continually being used for music rehearsals and dance workshops. Cups of tea and coffee sustained people or after a work session everyone would eat *onces* (literally translated 'elevenses'), that peculiarly Chilean custom of eating in the afternoon but which bore no resemblance to 'afternoon tea'. Large cups of hot milk coloured by a strong infusion of stewed tea, rolls, toasted if they were more than a couple of hours old, with butter, cheese, mashed avocado pear or a thick sweet 'cheese' made from quinces.

If Victor had been to the market recently, there might be *arrollado* – spicy slices of pork with chili and lots of garlic. It was Victor's main contribution to the housekeeping to get up very early once a week, usually on Saturdays, to go to the Vega or vegetable market. He really enjoyed it and felt completely at home there. The atmosphere was just the same as when he was a little boy helping his mother in her restaurant in the Western Market. He was a regular and got to know the stall-holders. He would come home laden with his favourite food . . . *porotos granados* – fresh haricot beans to be cooked in the Chilean way, with corn, pumpkin and a touch of fresh basil; goat's cheese; enormous tomatoes for tomato and onion salad; *corvina*, a fish something like a large halibut, native to the Pacific, delicious and one of the few things I knew how to cook well; then, in season, all the wonderful fruits that are cheap in Chile: melons, grapes, all sorts of peaches and nectarines, cherries the size of pigeon's eggs, apricots, custard apples . . .

Victor loved food, although he often went all day without it, with no time to eat; he loved dancing, always kept himself in training as much as possible, went to classes when he could, used to make us laugh with his funny improvisations; he loved giving presents and always came home from a tour with his suitcase full of things that he had found in markets on his travels – handicrafts, ponchos, pottery. I still have an embroidered dress he brought me from Mexico, a beautiful poncho from Peru, delicate needlework from Paraguay. He loved swimming, being on holiday, eating seafood on the beach, exploring, hosing down the whole family with cold water on a hot summer's day in the garden, going to the fondas on 18 September to dance the cueca, being with his friends at home, making a log fire and roasting chestnuts . . . all the things that most people like doing. He was no workaholic, even though he worked inhumanly hard. His enthusiasm was contagious, just as his laugh and his smile were.

Manuela's relationship with Victor had always been good, but it improved even more as she grew older. He was a friend as well as a father. He sometimes used to go into her room when she was doing her homework or listening to music, to sit on the bed and gossip with her. He asked her advice about whether he should accept an invitation to go and sing at her school. Perhaps they would talk about the latest hits on the radio – Victor was a Beatles fan – or discuss her school work, her laziness or otherwise and the reasons for it. His occasional appearances at Manuel de Salas when he went to fetch her caused a minor sensation, because only Manuela's closest friends knew that Victor was her second father.

Of the experiences that we shared as a family during the years of Popular Unity, one of the most important was a visit to Cuba early in 1972. Victor had been invited to give recitals all over the country and I to teach in the modern dance school. With characteristic Cuban generosity, the invitation included the whole family.

Cuba had become much more accessible with the opening up of diplomatic relations, but it was still not possible to fly there direct, and a change of planes in Mexico City involved being taken one by one into a rather sinister passageway in the airport to have our photos taken, before being allowed to board the Cuban plane. I can only suppose it was the long arm of the CIA at work.

It was my first visit to the island, and Victor had not been back since he went there with *Parecido a la Felicidad* just after the revolution. Now he had an intense programme of recitals, both in Havana and in the interior of the island, where he met singers of the Nueva Trova, the post-revolutionary musical movement, working with the peasants and volunteer student groups in the Sierra Maestra.

Meanwhile I stayed in Havana with the girls and gave classes to the modern dance company and school. Set in a park full of tropical plants and trees, it seemed a paradise compared with our cramped quarters in the centre of Santiago, especially as the students had residential hostels and were selected from all over the country on the basis of talent alone. Once admitted, they had no financial worries to interfere with their studies.

We met Haydée Santa María, who had been among the small group of revolutionaries accompanying Fidel in the assault on the Moncada Barracks in 1953. Now, as Director of the Casa de las Americas, she invited Victor to give a recital there. She loved his songs and his singing, and I can understand why, because hers was the phrase 'Some musicians only love their music, but others love the people . . .'

We had a wonderful time in Cuba. Thirteen years after the overthrow of Batista it seemed to be a society with opportunities for everyone. Impressive were the number of new schools and crèches where babies could be left in the care of experts while their mothers went out to work; the amount of new housing where the economical system of building with prefabricated blocks was used, with open-sided galleries full of tropical plants, producing light and attractive buildings. Impressive, too, was the attitude of ballet dancers, teachers, actors, everyone we met, who did their stint helping with the vital sugar harvest every year and also undertook military service, always on guard against a repeat of the Bay of Pigs invasion.

However, with so much happening, out thoughts were never far from Chile. Victor was impatient to be home. I confess as we took the plane back to Santiago to a feeling between impatience to be back 'where the potatoes are burning' and a sense of great trepidation.

Although we had been away only a few weeks, things were happening so fast in Chile that we already felt a change in the political climate. The opposition was really getting itself together. We heard how they had taken advantage of the session of the UNCTAD in Santiago and the presence of many foreign journalists to organise a big protest march – a development of the Saucepan March of a few months previously – with the slogan 'Junten rabia, ciudadanos!' or 'Get angry, citizens!'. It had been answered by another of Popular Unity, three times as large, and the biggest ever until that time.

But the bad news, especially for us, was the result of the recent elections in the University of Chile for the new Rector and other authorities, which had resulted in a swing to the right, not just against Popular Unity, but against the reform itself. The new Rector was the Christian Democrat Edgardo Boeninger.

The University of Chile was of such importance as a national institution that this election was of great political significance. The contest was not so much between individual candidates as between different political forces, and the media coverage, with television debates and interviews, was intense, equal to that for a parliamentary election. Luckily our Faculty had shown itself to be on the side of reform and of Popular Unity, but the general result was a set-back for the government.

Many people were blaming this, I don't know how justly, on the divisive action of the ultra-left groups during the election. Although numerically small, they were very active among the students and in the campaign had attacked both Popular Unity and the right-wing candidates with the same enthusiasm.

On the other hand, during the winter of that year, other important elections showed overwhelming victories for Popular Unity – for instance in the trade-union federation, the CUT, in the Technical University and in a by-election for the Senate in the northern province of Coquimbo where Amanda Altamirano, a Communist, was returned with an absolute majority.

But the attacks from both right and left were beginning to affect the relationships between the political parties which made up Popular Unity and this was the most disturbing new factor. In May 1972, soon after our return, Victor found himself involved in a situation which had developed in the university city of Concepción, where the MIR had been founded and where it continued to have its greatest strength.

Declaring the programme of Popular Unity to be completely out of date, the MIR had succeeded in persuading local branches of some of the Popular Unity parties, especially the socialists and MAPU, to defy the national policy of their own parties and of the government. They were calling for the creation of 'people's assemblies' to replace the constitutional structures of government and had declared Concepción to be *Territorio libre de America* – a liberated zone. They wanted to prohibit a demonstration called in the city by the Christian Democrats, which would undoubtedly provide an opportunity for Patria y Libertad to provoke disorders and chaos. Their threat was to combat violence with violence.

It was a complex and difficult situation and in the midst of it Victor was called upon to give a recital in the University of Concepción, the centre of the rebellion against the government. Under the circumstances, such a recital had also to be a political statement, and in the course of it Victor called for unity to support the government, thus bringing down on his head the anger of the ultra-left.

However much he might have sympathised with the impatience of the students with the fascist violence which appeared on the streets during opposition demonstrations, Victor was clear – and said so – that the confrontation which Patria y Libertad was so obviously seeking should be avoided. Violent suppression of the right of the 'democratic' opposition to express itself was not the means of winning over the majority of the people to support revolutionary change and indeed the opposition were doing their best to represent themselves as the victims of 'Marxist repression'. Above all, any divisive movement within Popular Unity itself would be fatal.

The first such divisive episode had occurred almost twelve months previously, in June 1971, while conversations were proceeding between Popular Unity and the leadership of the Christian Democrat Party to reach some sort of truce. A new left-wing splinter group calling itself the Vanguardia Organizada del Pueblo or VOP chose that moment to assassinate Edmundo Pérez Zúcovic, the Minister of the Interior in Frei's government. Their action put an end to the talks and placed an insurmountable barrier between Popular Unity and the Christian Democrats. No wonder people thought that the VOP must have been set up by the CIA.

It had been a horrible moment when we heard the news on the radio. Victor came home pale and upset. In spite of the murder of General Schneider, political assassination was still at that time alien to Chile. We were naturally appalled by this act and Victor was especially concerned because some people tried to put the blame on him because of his song 'Preguntas por Puerto Montt'.

After the trouble in Concepción came another incident involving the MIR. A police search for wanted criminals in the shanty-town of Lo Hermida was met by organised armed resistance from the inhabitants led by the MIR, and when Allende went in person to talk with them they physically barred his way. (After 1973 one of the leaders in this incident, 'Comandante Raul', emerged in rather different colours as one of the principal torturers for the DINA, the secret police of the military junta.)

It was a bad moment. Just as the opposition stepped up its campaign and conspiracy against the government, the forces of Popular Unity were full of internal differences and conflicts. The tensions between the political groups could be strongly felt even in our Faculty. The bitter atmosphere seeped even into classes and rehearsals as the months passed, to say nothing of the frequent assemblies which were called in answer to some political crisis and all too often turned into three-way battles between Popular Unity and the ultra-right and ultra-left-wing minorities.

It seemed that only in the frequent and massive marches to keep the fascists off the streets of Santiago was sectarianism put aside and a spirit of unity fostered. Marching together with an almost physical contact; in the excitement of being part of an active mass of people, differences could be forgotten for the moment. It was now, just as the spirit of unity was endangered, that the slogan 'El pueblo unido jamás será vencido' ('The people united will never be defeated') began to be heard. It was later incorporated into a most effective song by Sergio Ortega and sung by Quilapayún, but it was first heard in 1972 on the streets of Santiago as a cry of warning as well as of determination.

August and September saw a further increase in street violence by right-wing gangs. In the massive and orderly march of Popular Unity, celebrating the second anniversary of Allende's election, for the first time we marched through the heart of the barrio alto, down Avenida Providencia, past the tall blocks of elegant apartments, with some of the inhabitants shouting insults and threats from the balconies and the crowd below responding with roars of defiance and rude jokes.

Only a few days before, the same avenue had been filled with smoke and tear-gas, while groups of fascists from Patria y Libertad overturned trolley buses, set fire to them and made barricades out of burning tyres. Providencia was their own district and the leaders of Patria y Libertad often congregated in the Restaurant Munich in the very heart of it.

In the Faculty, too, we were in the midst of street disturbances caused by the opposition, and sometimes by the ultra-left. From the upper windows of the building we could look down and see the paramilitary brigades of the National Party lining up and drilling in the street below with complete impunity and on one occasion, a Senator from the same party waving a gun as he egged on demonstrators outside the law courts.

A constant cause of conflict was the proposed educational reform, the project for an Escuela Nacional Unificada or ENU, in itself scarcely more radical than comprehensive schools in Britain, but particularly controversial because it threatened the autonomy of the large number of schools run by the Catholic Church. Gangs of secondary school students, mostly from the private schools of the barrio alto, seemed almost daily to overrun the centre of Santiago, causing disturbances and carrying on a running battle with the police. Some of them were barely 12 or 13 years old. Luckily in Manuel de Salas classes continued normally and only a few students stayed away. Even in Manuela's age group it became a patriotic duty to study harder than usual and never miss a day's school.

The nationalisation of the copper mines in July 1971 had been perhaps the most important and certainly the most massively popular measure the Popular Unity government ever undertook. A civil service commission was set up to assess the compensation due to Anaconda, Cerro and Kennecott, the three US companies that had owned the mines. This ruled that from the final amount of compensation should be deducted the excessive profits which the companies had made during the preceding years.

Popular and just though this decision was, it set alarm bells ringing in corporation headquarters in New York and other financial capitals. If Chile could assert its sovereignty and fight back against the robbery of its natural resources, how many other developing countries might not follow the example? Now the corporations began in earnest to plan revenge and gave backing to the destabilisation plan already launched by the CIA and ITT.

In October 1972, the Kennecott Copper Company instigated an international embargo on Chilean copper, and Chilean ships were 'arrested' in European ports, unable to proceed or unload. At home, the powerful lorry-owners' organisation came out on strike, supposedly against the threat of nationalisation and the scarcity of spare parts and tyres, but in reality in a co-ordinated effort to bring the country to a halt and overthrow Allende's government.

Because of Chile's strange geography, the interruption of traffic along the one longitudinal highway could quickly cause havoc. The strike was a highly organised operation. Fleets of lorries were taken off the road and collected in camps at strategic points. It was frightening to see hundreds of large lorries lined up, usually on slightly higher ground, guarded by groups of armed men.

It was impossible for the police to disperse or requisition them without a confrontation and, of course, the lorry-owners had the co-operation of the landowners. Not only were the vehicles out of action, but from the camps the highway could be controlled. Armed bands set up road blocks, attacked any lorry that might still be on the road and scattered *miguelitos*, deadly little devices made of bent nails which could rip a tyre to shreds.

With the large fleets of petrol-tankers out of circulation, petrol immediately became like liquid gold and in order to buy a few litres, it was necessary to wait for hours, pushing the car in the queue in order not to waste a drop. Paraffin, which was vital for both heating and cooking in the poblaciones, disappeared; essential goods like flour for bread, milk for children, rice, potatoes, sugar, to say nothing of things like meat and eggs, became almost unobtainable; the owners of the largest dairy ordered thousands of litres of milk to be poured down the drain in order to add to the crisis.

There was an immediate and massive response to the emergency. A considerable number of lorry-owners, usually those possessing only one or two vehicles, did not want to join the political strike. These formed their own independent organisation, MOPARE, to try to resolve some of the problems. It was very moving to see these old and much-used lorries − they reminded me of Pedro Morgado's − rattling along in convoys, their drivers knowing that they risked being attacked by gangs from the lorry camps, despite the occasional police escort. Tyres were slashed, windscreens shattered and many drivers injured.

Workers, students, teachers, artists and many professional people joined in the voluntary effort to counteract the effects of the strike. The students of the Technical University, all over the country, made a greater contribution than anyone in distributing food and paraffin to the poblaciones, but the members of our Faculty were also mobilised.

Our job was to load and unload trains at the goods depot of the Central Station. I remember Victor working with Quena in the organisation of the different teams of people, answering the most urgent needs . . . such-and-such a población completely without paraffin, a vehicle urgently needed . . . four hundred sacks of flour to be unloaded at the goods depot . . . milk to be transported to another población . . . and so on.

Victor didn't just spend his time sitting by the telephone or singing while other people worked. I have a vision of him standing on a heap of flour sacks, sweating as he heaved them up one after the other as a long line of people − mostly dancers and actors − brought them from the train. Stacking them in an orderly fashion was heavy work, but

Victor looked happy and cracked jokes with the people around him, who were infected by his good humour. Because of my back trouble, I could carry and stack only the much lighter boxes of spaghetti – even so it was exhausting. But we all felt that we were doing something useful and morale was high because we knew that all over the country hundreds of thousands of people were doing the same.

Inevitably, however, the strike began to have dire effects on the economy. The spring sowing was delayed because the seeds couldn't be transported to the right areas on time, output was lost because of the lack of raw materials in the factories. To make matters worse, other sectors of the middle classes joined the strike . . . the shop-owners, bus-owners, the Medical Association and other professional groups. But the volunteers worked harder, workers tried to break production records, doctors who supported Popular Unity formed their own 'patriotic front' and worked double shifts to replace their striking colleagues, shops tried to stay open in spite of being liable to have their windows smashed.

There were many ugly incidents. I remember the rather unusual case of the Coppelia, an elegant ice cream parlour in Providencia, whose clientele, because of its situation, tended to consist of teenagers from the barrio alto, and whose ice cream was both delicious and expensive. The owner, a Swiss Jew, was a progressive man. At the time of the strike the business was being run as a workers' co-operative and of course it stayed open. During one of the rampages of fascist gangs through the district, it was violently attacked, its plate-glass windows and machinery smashed, and the workers inside injured. Violently anti-Semitic insults were shouted by the mob and published in the right-wing press.

Public transport continued to function, although with difficulty because of the scarcity of petrol and the fact that vehicles were likely to be attacked and overturned. The majority of buses were privately owned and these joined the strike, making it very difficult to get to work. People walked enormous distances or crowded into the backs of old lorries. If one was lucky enough to have a little petrol for the car, it was impossible to travel without giving lifts to people attempting to get to work. I never felt nervous about this because the fact that they were trying to do so meant that they were compañeros. The car became a kind of collective taxi for the duration of the strike.

The Juntas de Abastecimiento y Precios, or JAPs as they were popularly called, were community organisations licensed by the government to control the black market, hoarding and speculation. In some poblaciones JAPs had been functioning successfully for months, but in our neighbourhood only the strike forced women to take the idea seriously. The majority of our neighbours not only could afford to pay black market prices, but consciously boycotted any initiative of the government. As women who supported Popular Unity, we used to meet in each other's houses, almost in secret, to discuss problems and appoint the people who would be responsible for co-ordinating supplies from a central distribution point.

The idea was to get retailers in the district to work with us, to receive and sell the food in the normal way, but under our supervision and at official prices (often one-third or less of the black market rate). One of the main problems was that none of the shops wanted to co-operate with us, either because they were anti-Popular Unity or because they were afraid of reprisals from right-wing gangs. Butchers who would work with us were almost impossible to find − most of them had a flourishing black market trade going under the counter, and had no wish to have snoopers from the JAP around.

Only Alberto, a young red-headed grocer of Yugoslav origin, was ready to work with us and it was from his tiny shop that we sold the fortnightly supply of groceries and frozen chicken. It was a kind of rationing because the amount we received was in relation to the number of families registered with the JAP.

We organised the rotas of duty in the shop, unpacking and serving, checking to see that each household was served only once. We were only a small group of women in a predominantly hostile neighbourhood, but it felt good to be doing something and to be in contact with one another. By working in the JAP or even registering with it − although anyone could do so − people were exposed as supporters of Popular Unity and therefore put on the black list of the Junta de Vecinos, the local neighbourhood organisation set up by the Christian Democrats and completely controlled by them. As time went by they seemed to work more and more closely with the local gangs of Patria y Libertad, of which there were plenty.

It was during the October strike that the beatings of the railings began − a variation on the Saucepan Marches. In the evening, just as it was getting dark, the noise would begin − 'Bang, bang, bang!' − a loud clanging which started in one place and then spread from block to block, echoing round and round, until the whole district was full of it, like sinister, metallic tom-toms.

Some days were very bad; everything seemed to be coming to a halt – the shops shut, no transport, queues everywhere for basic necessities, riots and violence in the streets – but the massive voluntary effort continued and eventually, in spite of all the dollars pouring into the country to finance the strike, it came to an end quite ignominiously. The Commander-in-Chief of the Armed Forces, General Carlos Prats, joined the Cabinet as Minister of the Interior, a guarantee of order and peace until the next parliamentary elections, due in March 1973. In spite of the disaster for the economy, the Popular Unity government and the mass of the people had gained a moral victory.

9

'THE BEST SCHOOL FOR SONG IS LIFE ITSELF'

In spite of the October strike and all that it signified, life and, above all, work, continued as usual. In the midst of it all, the students from my teachers' course were now doing their teaching practice in the poblaciones. We had already opened one satellite school in Quinta Normal, the working-class district behind the Technical University, and were about to open another in La Granja to the south of Santiago. About a hundred children from the neighbourhood were enrolled and classes were in full swing. It was my job to go and supervise and give advice, but the student teachers managed very well by themselves.

Loading and unloading trains and working in the JAP did not mean that we could suspend our study programmes and all the positive things there were to do, and in the same way, musicians went on making music and composing songs, songs which were useful in animating all the voluntary effort people were putting in together.

The song movement was flourishing. Quilapayún were masters of the funny, topical song. They made fun of the saucepan ladies, urged people to eat more fish, ridiculed right-wing politicians with devastating effect, and threw these songs off in their spare time, as it were. Their Chilean version of the light-hearted Cuban song 'La batea' was sung in the great demonstrations by masses of people, hands held, swaying to the rhythm like an excited football crowd. As a musical group, together with Inti-Illimani, they were the most popular in Chile. Unless they were away on some international tour, they sang at almost every important political demonstration, helping to create a festive atmosphere. If Inti-Illimani represented the musical 'sound' of Popular Unity, Quilapayún represented its macho fighting spirit as well as providing some much-needed humour.

There was quite a lot of controversy about the pamphlet or 'throwaway' songs on very topical themes. Many people, including Victor, tried them with varying success. Some were funny, some were explanatory and therefore, perhaps, useful, some were satirical, but many were just plain boring and musically unoriginal. Unfortunately, anyone can write mediocre songs and it was easy for the opposition to begin to manufacture them, tit for tat, whereas they could never match the depth, poetry and musical beauty of the best of the song movement.

People sometimes talk about the New Chilean Song Movement as though it was a homogeneous cultural phenomenon which functioned on the basis of preconceived ideas directed towards definite goals. As far as I could see, it wasn't like that at all. There were as many different points of view as there were people taking part in it. It was essentially a movement of discovery and exploration. There were discussions, often heated ones, rivalries, polemic, even quarrels. Only one thing united everyone, and that was a desire to be part of a revolutionary process and with their work help to develop a new culture which would truly reflect and play a part in it.

There were different priorities. In spite of their gift for popular, topical songs, Quilapayún often stated quite categorically that the most important aspect of the song movement was the integration into it of the academic composers like Luis Advis and Sergio Ortega, with both of whom they had worked as a group.

La Cantata Santa María de Iquique, by Luis Advis, had had its first performance in the Second Festival of New Chilean Song in August 1970. Performed by Quilapayún, together with classical musicians and an actor as narrator, it told the story of the massacre of 3,000 nitrate miners with their wives and families during a strike in Iquique in 1907. It was Luis Advis's first venture into the use of indigenous instruments, which he combined with elements of folk music in order to tell the story of anonymous working people who are so often forgotten by the official history books.

The elaborate cantata form produced a certain amount of discussion – was it really 'popular' music? – but the co-operation between academic and folk musicians could only be positive, and *La Cantata*

Santa María de Iquique obviously touched a chord with mass audiences. More so, perhaps, than more elaborate works like *La Fragua* by Sergio Ortega, which was really only suitable for performance in concert halls.

Inti's priorities were slightly different, I think. They too worked with Advis and other composers on several important projects like *Canto al Programa*, a long work based on the forty measures of the Popular Unity programme, and a homage to Violeta Parra which used her *Las Decimas* poems as its text. And they were co-operating enthusiastically with Victor and Celso on *Los Siete Estados*. But they always emphasised a musical development very closely linked to Latin American folk roots, whose riches they continued to investigate.

Victor himself was constantly on the alert against what he felt to be paternalistic attitudes, against the danger of imposing preconceived moulds from above. He believed that a true popular culture took time to mature, you couldn't go out and invent it. He thought that an artist should be less concerned with producing *the* transcendental work, than with being a kind of craftsman whose work would be as useful as a nail in making a house or a drop of oil to make a machine run smoothly. His priority was giving the people the means to express themselves and then listening to them with respect.

As he said in 1971, 'In every place where we perform we should organise, and if possible leave functioning, a creative workshop. *We should ascend to the people*, not feel that we are lowering ourselves to them. Our job is to give them what belongs to them – their cultural roots – and the means of satisfying the hunger for cultural expression that we saw during the election campaign.'

On one point everyone agreed, and that was the necessity of responding to the tremendous demand for technical help from all the new musical groups which were appearing all the time, and to contribute in a wider sense to the process of mass participation in cultural activity.

Different groups found different ways of carrying out this function. The Peña de Los Parra, for instance, as its fame grew as a symbol of 'the New Chile', became at weekends a tourist attraction. But during the week, Isabel and Angel converted Carmen 340 into a popular cultural centre where local people from the surrounding working-class district came for classes and were encouraged to compose songs and poems, do handicrafts and so on, as well as to hold meetings and discussions. It had grown roots in the local community.

The young men of Inti-Illimani did not see themselves as teachers, although they took part in the musical workshops of the Technical University, but they were always ready to help other groups and especially, as musicians, to put themselves at the service of composers who wanted to work and experiment with them. In this way, they co-operated constantly with Victor, individually or as a group.

Quilapayún chose yet another way. They decided, quite literally, to multiply themselves, creating as many groups as possible with the same characteristics, the same image, even much of the same repertoire, as the original. Each member of the original Quila was in charge of the formation of a new group so that they could multiply themselves by six. We had Quila I, Quila II, Quila III . . . and so on, with variations because there was one female group (Quilas with long black skirts instead of ponchos) and a 'Lolopayún', a group of teenagers. I must confess that to Victor and me and perhaps to others too, it seemed a very strange idea, akin to cloning. Needless to say, Quila defended themselves strongly against this criticism. They felt that it was a way of not confining Quilapayún to six particular individuals, but of giving more people a chance to be part of a group which was very popular and had a very well-defined image. It was a novel idea, and one which tended to make them ubiquitous, which was infuriating for their enemies.

Although I always mention the same names because they were Victor's closest associates and also, perhaps, the most visible heads of the song movement, there were now hundreds of other groups all over the country. They had sprung up in universities, in factories, in schools, in community centres. Victor was constantly being invited to act as judge in workers' song festivals where new composers presented their work. It was an incredible upsurge of creative activity in people who had never before been encouraged to express themselves and in an age when radio and television tended to turn people into passive listeners. The song movement was now much more than a group of well-known artists. It seemed that a whole people had learned to sing.

Victor himself worked with many different groups and individual musicians. I was especially pleased when, during 1972, he spent four months working with six girls who wanted to form their own song group. It was certainly time that women were represented more equally. We had important women soloists like Isabel Parra, Marta Contreras, Charo Cofré, but apart from the feminine version of Quilapayún which I believe started at about the same time, there was no collective presence of women. The fact that it was now felt necessary was a sure sign that women's self-awareness and independence had progressed, although I think mixed groups would have been even better. Women were still treated as a sect apart.

Four of the girls were music students from the Faculty. One, Teresa Carvajal, had a most beautiful contralto voice and was training to become an opera singer, but she was ready to put that aside to become part of Cantamaranto. Victor helped them to organise themselves and in the arrangements of their first songs and also asked them, together with Huamari, another new group, to help him in the recording of his next album, *La Población*. Isabel Parra also took part in this collective project by singing the first song of the nine which make up the whole work, 'Lo único que tengo' ('My hands are all I have').

This album was a new departure for Victor, a result of his spirit of constant exploration and his desire to be a sounding-board for the most anonymous and deprived sectors of the population. He had always made individual songs which were portraits of people within their environments, like 'Angelita Huenumán' or 'El lazo' – the old man who plaited whips in Lonquen. Now, in the winter of 1972, he began a more ambitious project, working in accordance with his belief that 'the best school for song is life itself'.

The idea came about almost by chance, when a friend who lived in a shanty-town said to him, 'Compañero, if you're looking for something to sing about, why don't you make an album about the history of our shanty-town?' Victor immediately seized upon the idea, knowing that behind each one of the shanty-town communities lay a story of collective struggle which few people knew about. With tape recorder and guitar, Victor spent weeks working in Herminda de la Victoria, where his friend lived, and in other poblaciones including Los Nogales, where of course he had many contacts. He interviewed men and women who had taken part in the original settlement and had lived through all the drama of planning and then executing the operation to seize the land.

In Herminda de la Victoria, Compañera Ana told him how before they had been living on the banks of the Mapocho river, on land which inevitably flooded each spring as the rivers swelled with the melting snow from the Andes. Made desperate by the conditions under which they were living, one day they decided to take drastic measures. Men and women working together, they loaded up their few possessions on handcarts or in bundles over their shoulders, babies and small children wrapped in blankets against the cold, and in the night spread out, as planned, along a ditch, ready to run at a given signal to install themselves in certain fixed positions which had all been given numbers so that no one should get lost. Once they were squatting with their possessions and their families, they thought it would be difficult to turn them off.

The women told Victor about their emotions at that moment as they hid in the dark and cold along the ditch, how they dreamed about having a permanent home, a real place to live with their families. Then came the signal. Men, women and children began to run, but someone had given them away to the police. Shots rang out, but nothing stopped them; they flung themselves on the ground on which they wanted to build their homes, heaps of belongings, saucepans, bedclothes around them. Somebody asked, 'How is the baby? Herminda is very quiet.' 'Oh, she's sleeping,' her mother replied. But she wasn't sleeping. A stray bullet had killed her. Compañera Ana's eyes filled with tears as she remembered that moment. The settlement had been named Herminda de la Victoria in memory of the baby who never had a chance to grow up there.

Drinking cups of tea or fizzy drinks, with a radio at full blast in the background, Victor heard the story of how the población had been built up, little by little, the struggle to get drinking-water supplies, electricity. He heard how one of the first leaky shacks to go up had been that of a group of prostitutes. He went to talk to them, to find out what they felt about their life . . . the lively song which resulted, 'La carpa de las coligüillas', was like a conversation between them and the people of the población. Another character who appears in the album is *el maestro chasquilla*, the typical Chilean jack-of-all-trades, the man who without education or proper training learns to be a plumber, a carpenter, to build a house, to keep the factories running. 'El hombre es un creador' ('Man is a creator'), with its perky tune played on paper and comb, seems to give the essence of that ability to survive against the odds, much more powerful because, as the song concludes, 'Now we are so many'.

Victor felt that by using some of the techniques of the theatre, he could develop a theme more profoundly than through one simple song. On the sound-track of the album, he included some of the recordings he made in the poblaciones, with the voices of the women telling their own story, a child reciting a rhyme, even a cock crowing and the dogs barking. He asked his old friend the playright Alejandro Sieveking to help him with the structure of the album and with the text of some of the songs. It seemed that the two threads of Victor's work were coming together and complementing each other. He saw great possibilities for further development of this method and although he was never satisfied with what he had done, he was keen to try again.

Almost immediately after *La Población* was published, and it must have been because they felt that what he had done was valid, he was approached by a delegation from the largest peasant organisation in the country, Confederación Ranquil. They told Victor that he was the artist that they felt could most closely represent them, because of his own peasant background; that he was the person they would like to entrust with the task of writing and composing a work about their history, about how their organisation had survived a terrible massacre, and had grown, little by little, into the massive confederation which was fighting for the interests of the peasants throughout Chile and helping to implement the land reform.

In November 1972, soon after the end of the lorry-owners' strike, Victor travelled south at the invitation of the peasants, making an expedition far up into the cordillera on horseback, the only possible form of transport, to reach the remote village where some of the survivors of the massacre still lived. In the tiny local school of Chilpaco he was received as guest of honour and treated to a performance which the children had prepared. He learned how some of them still had to walk miles to school every day, barefoot winter and summer; he conversed with the people who remembered the uprising against the cruelty and exploitation of the landowners; one of the old men still had the minutes book of their organisation in which was recorded an actual speech that their leader, Juan Leiva Tapia, made on the founding of the very first peasant union in Chile in 1928: 'Let us go forward, Mapuches of Lonquimay, a new sun will light up this valley of snow and forest; let us put aside the quarrels and disagreements which the landowners foment among us and give life to our union, our organisation which will fight for and defend the rights which until now have been denied us.'

Only six years after the founding of their union, the peasants began an uprising which was brutally suppressed by the police. Victor was taken to the place where the river Ranquil converges with the great Bio-Bio, a rocky gorge which the peasants had named 'the slaughter house' because it was there that, one by one, their leaders had been shot, their bodies falling straight into the icy water below; he heard about the mother who would not give up her baby and fell dead into the whirlpool with him in her arms.

The region was full of the myths and legends of the Mapuche Indians who were its principal inhabitants; the rocks, the trees, the waters of the torrential rivers, new-born in melting snow from the high peaks of the mountains, were all instilled with magical, religious significance. All this, with elements of Mapuche rhythms and instruments, Victor wanted to capture with a poetic text. In his head, he began to have a clear idea of what he wanted to do and I felt that it would have been something both profound and original — a work that would have brought out the character of the protagonists, the drama of the struggle, the remote and overpowering landscape in which it took place and the cultural inheritance of those forgotten and persecuted people. It was one of many projects which could not be realised. He was working on it in September 1973.

While he was there in Ranquil and Lonquimay, Victor discovered that the family of landowners who had been responsible for the massacre were still flourishing, in possession of their lands and exploiting the peasants as before. The agrarian reform had so far not touched them. Their territory extended to the frontier with Argentina, they had their own airstrip and were known to be smuggling arms and organising paramilitary groups. Victor spoke to many of the peasants and convinced them that it was necessary to send a delegation to the CORA, the government land-reform agency in Santiago, to ask for the expropriation of the land. He also reported the situation when he returned to the capital, and was present at the hearing when the decision to expropriate was taken. The peasants invited Victor to the local celebration, but unfortunately he could not go. To this day they remember him as an artist who was also a man of action, a revolutionary not only in words but in deeds.

*   *   *

The fortieth and last measure of the Popular Unity programme concerned culture. Among other things, it proposed the establishment of
a National Institute of Culture whose function would be to stimulate,
co-ordinate, guide and support the popular movement. This was never
carried out, although many people, Victor included, were impatient
for its implementation. As he travelled round the country, seeing all the
work that was going on in an improvised, spontaneous way, without
technical help, subsidies or planning, he saw the need for a more active
and coherent cultural policy.

This did not imply imposing norms and models from above, but
helping in practical ways so that new values, new attitudes could
emerge – not only relating to art, but also to work, to production,
to new forms of solidarity and co-operation. This was the sort of spirit
that had invaded our Faculty at the time of the storm, or that inspired
the workers at Textil Progreso after the earthquake in Valparaiso in
1971. On this occasion the textile workers had decided to donate a
day's wages to the victims in a población that had been destroyed
and then went themselves en masse to the spot to help erect the
new units, thus creating a real contact which lasted long afterwards
and culminated in a Christmas party six months later.

Indeed, although there was much impatience for even more
achievement, a great deal had already been done. The nationalisation
of one of the largest publishing houses was an example. During the
three years of the Popular government, Quimantú, as it was renamed,
published dozens of paperback editions of world literature at prices that
everyone could afford, and distributed them to the newspaper kiosks
where they competed with the US comic strips. Editions were sold
out almost immediately and you could see ordinary working people
on the buses reading Jack London, D. H. Lawrence, Thomas Mann,
Dostoevsky, Mark Twain; young Chilean poets and novelists were
given their first chance of being published; new magazines and other
publications appeared, like the popular history series *Nosotros Los
Chilenos*, which gave a vision of Chile and her people far different
from the traditional identikit picture of the roto chileno, telling
in words and pictures the story of the poblaciones, the mines, the
fishermen, of working-class struggle and repression, of the earthquakes
and natural disasters, and even of the growth of the New Chilean Song
Movement.

Victor felt that much could be done to bring together the threads of popular culture and to stimulate it even more by a type of mass theatre in which he had already been involved on three occasions. There was a certain tradition in Chile for holding pageants and spectacles in the National Stadium. The annual football match between the University of Chile and the Catholic University, *el Clásico*, was an important sporting event, but it was also combined with grandiose spectacles presented by each club at half time, which came to be quite as popular and competitive as the match itself.

The events which Victor directed were of a different nature, but owed something to this tradition. They all took place in 1972 – the first two were celebrations of the Chilean Communist Party and its youth movement, the *Jota*, the third a homage to Pablo Neruda on his return to Chile after receiving the Nobel Prize for Literature. All of them had one common factor – that the protagonists were ordinary working people who had come from all over the country to participate.

With Patricio, who was also involved as choreographer, Victor conceived and worked on a plan in which the great variety of activities in the diverse and contrasting regions of Chile could be brought together in a series of encounters of this type, to take place not only in Santiago but in all the provinces. Encounters where local folk groups, amateur theatre groups, dance groups, muralists, poets and so on could not only show their work to each other, but actually co-operate on a common project. For such an idea to be put into practice, a national organisation was necessary.

Victor was so keen on this idea that he talked of giving up his work as a singer in order to explore all the possibilities and techniques of this sort of mass theatrical event. Perhaps he envisaged the peasants of Ranquil enacting their own story, using theatre, song and music, integrating elements of Mapuche culture. He certainly felt that a whole new field of popular expression was opening up, a product of the times in which we were living.

I remember impressive scenes from the great events in the Stadium. One told the story of the massacre of Santa Maria de Iquique. The nitrate miners themselves had come from the north to take part. They became so possessed with their roles that, as gunfire rang out, they fell to the ground to a man and did not get up again, while those who were supposed to help drag the bodies away also 'died' and extras had to run on to the pitch to carry them off.

There were scenes from the time of President Gonzalez Videla, when the Communist Party was illegal and persecuted: a clandestine printing press; a football match that was really a branch meeting being played in a población, ready to break up at any moment if the police arrived; the Brigadas Ramona Parra racing round the stadium, clinging to an old lorry like acrobats, jumping off to paint lightning murals; an explosion down a coal mine, the women waiting for the dead to be brought to the surface, the miner's small son putting on his father's helmet to take his place down the mine.

Gigantic puppets, used in street theatre, were useful to make grotesque figures of the 'enemy' – members of the oligarchy, right-wing politicians, ITT and other multi-nationals. In the tribute to Neruda, people came rushing in from all sides of the stadium to form a dense block spelling out his name; masses of people swept away the black spider of Patria y Libertad – the symbol of fascism in Chile – while tens of thousands cheered.

There can be few Nobel Prize awards that have ever been celebrated in urban slums and shanty-towns. But it was so in Chile when Pablo Neruda was declared laureate for Literature, although the poet himself was abroad at the time, carrying out his duties as ambassador in Paris. He was already a sick man, suffering from cancer as we later discovered, and he returned home for the last time at the end of November 1972, to be given, on 5 December, a tumultuous welcome by the people of Chile in the National Stadium.

This mass cultural spectacle, based on the story of his life and poetry, was, I think, unique and couldn't have happened anywhere but in Chile and at that particular historic moment. For this event, working people came in delegations representing every imaginable skill and trade from every province in the country: there were nitrate workers from the desert of Tarapaca, copper miners from Antofagasta, *pirquineros* or quarrymen from Coquimbo, merchant seamen from Valparaiso, railway workers from Aconcagua, building workers from Santiago, wine-makers from Curico, textile workers from Concepción, fishermen from the island of Chiloe, dairymen from Osorno, sheep farmers from Aysen and oil workers from Magallanes in the extreme south.

The delegations began to assemble in Santiago a week before the event and were received in the Municipal Theatre, red plush and all, with a gala performance of ballet and music, and were then given their instructions for the week of rehearsals by Victor and Patricio. Most of them had distinguished themselves in their work in one way or another, perhaps by years of service or by surpassing production targets or maybe by being inventive in solving problems of spare parts in the face of the international boycott, or perhaps some had been chosen by the prevalent, although irritating, system of *cuoteo*, so many for the Socialist Party, so many for the Communists, so many Radicals and so on. At any rate these men – for they were mostly men – were highly motivated at having been chosen by their local trade union to take part in this national tribute to Pablo Neruda.

It was a massive spectacle without being gymnastic or regimented. There was no time to produce military precision with so many people, but it flowed from one scene to another in a way that seemed spontaneous and organic. Many professional performers took part but often only as guides to help during the rehearsals. Most important were the mass of working people themselves among whom the story of Neruda's life and poetry unfolded. As Neruda himself said, 'There are many poets who have received honours like national prizes or even the Nobel Prize, but perhaps none have received this supreme honour, this crown of work which these representatives of a whole country, a whole people, signify.'

One strange element was that being an official event, sponsored by the government itself, it was expected that the whole nation be represented and that included, of course, the Armed Forces. For the most part their participation was separate from the main pageant – the brass band of the Air Force, police dogs doing their show, came before it – but in one scene, which represented a famous poem of Neruda about Manuel Rodriguez, hero of the War of Independence against the Spanish empire, a group of cavalry officers took part, galloping round the stadium.

They came to rehearsals in their uniforms and stationed themselves just above the tribune from which Victor and Patricio were directing. At one point both glanced behind them at the officers, and the cold hatred and contempt that they surprised in their stare produced a sensation of forboding like an icy shower amid the warmth and enthusiasm of the rest of the rehearsal.

Apart from Neruda himself, whose speech warned of the danger of civil war that he saw hanging over us, the main speaker in the Stadium was General Prats, now both Minister of the Interior and

Vice-President, standing in for Allende, who was at that moment in New York to address the United Nations General Assembly.

That day in the Stadium, General Prats was cheered and applauded with respect and affection, but he surprised most people by giving not so much the speech of a military man as that of a scholar who had studied and admired the work of Neruda. His presence in the Cabinet as a government minister gave us a great sense of security.

10

WITHOUT KNOWING THE END

There was a momentary respite at the end of the year. The presence of representatives of the Armed Forces in the Cabinet had brought about an uneasy truce. Although we didn't know it, it was our last Christmas together and in spite of everything it was a festive occasion. For Victor to be relaxed and at home, even if it were only for a couple of days, was already something to celebrate, and apart from that there was really a lot to be happy about. Tremendous progress had been made in the last two years. Although there were so many difficulties and scarcities affecting everyone, the majority of people were better off than they had ever been. No one would go hungry that year, nor would any child be without toys at Christmas. We had our place in a great struggle which seemed to be winning through against enormous odds and powerful enemies.

Meanwhile, there was a chance to enjoy being a family for a moment and we made the most of it. Christmas meant eating out in the garden, late at night on the 24th, under a brilliant starry sky, with the smell of charcoal smoke in the air. It meant a lighted Christmas tree, a pine that we had planted several years previously which Victor decorated with the help of all of us. A warm, windless night, with the shouts of excited children in the background, a table out on the grass under the mimosa tree.

Quena was there, with Luchin asleep already, and Patricio, now a close friend of us all. Manuela was 12 years old and her first boy friend had come to dinner. Victor was quite disconcerted at how quickly time passes and small children develop. We ate a duck which

Monica's family had sent from the country and which for the last few days had been rooting up the grass in the garden. Everything was normal and homely, even though the conversation could never stray far from the political situation and the vital need to win the forthcoming elections.

When the visitors had gone and the children were in bed, there was a quiet moment when Victor and I sat outside under the night sky waiting for everyone to be asleep before playing Father Christmas. It was getting cold, and I remember Victor saying, 'This coming year is a crucial one, Mamita. I wonder where we shall all be next Christmas?'

From then on there was no pause, no free days for Victor, just an endless round of intense activity. During the hot summer months of January and February 1973, which in most years were a period of suspended animation, the election campaign went into full swing. The opposition were doing everything in their power to obtain a two-thirds majority in the Congress in order to be able to impeach Allende. However, the most reactionary among them considered the election to be a useless exercise. 'Una meta sin destino' were the words of Onofre Jarpa, leader of the National Party – 'a blind alley'.

Opposition propaganda was directed principally towards women, to convince them to vote against Popular Unity, no doubt calculating that the problems of distribution and scarcities had affected them more than anyone else. For the first time, during this campaign, the opposition used pamphlet songs in an organised way, in an attempt to counteract the influence of the New Chilean Song Movement. It was a sign that they recognised the political power of song. However, few artists supported them and they only used song at the lowest level – as sheer propaganda – putting topical words to ready-made cumbias or other popular rhythms or, as in one television commercial, using the recognisable tune of Victor's 'El hombre es un creador' to accompany filmed scenes of street riots of their own making and their slogan 'Allende = Chaos'. In most countries it would have been actionable. There was no question of them being able to compete with the song movement as a cultural phenomenon with real roots among the people.

The work of artists in support of Popular Unity was better organised than in previous elections. Instead of everyone working rather haphazardly all over the place, individuals and groups were asked to support one particular candidate intensively so that the work was more evenly distributed. Apart from singing in all the national demonstrations, Victor campaigned for Popular Unity in the mostly working-class districts to the west of Santiago, including the neighbourhood where he was brought up. Travelling in an old bus together with Inti-Illimani, he spent the summer campaigning for a woman candidate of the Communist Party, Eliana Aranibar. They sang in factories and on building sites, in the street to people fixing the drains, in poblaciones, schools and markets, going out early in the morning and coming back at night tired out after performing a dozen times in different places.

Victor not only supported Popular Unity with his songs and in the introductions with which he interspersed them, but for the first time in his life, at Eliana's suggestion, he made campaigning political speeches. It wasn't a moment to hang back and say, 'No, I can't. I'm an artist, not a politician.' It made Victor very nervous because he wasn't used to that kind of speaking, but he was ready to do anything that was useful, and in his own informal way he explained to people why it was necessary, at all costs, to support the Popular Unity government and to prevent the reactionary opposition from overthrowing Allende before his term as President was completed. The rapid rise of fascism in Chile had to be halted.

The results of the election were awaited with the same suspense as if they had been for a new President. We knew for certain that Eliana would be successful, but when it became clear that Popular Unity had won a larger percentage of votes than when Allende was elected – an improved vote in mid-term elections was almost unprecedented in Chile – and that the women's vote had held up in spite of the propaganda directed at them, the opposition recognised that they couldn't hope to defeat Allende by democratic means. With Popular Unity taking more than 40 per cent of the vote, they had failed to reach the two-thirds majority they needed. At that rate, another three years of Allende's government would probably mean an overwhelming victory for the Popular Unity candidate in 1976. At that precise moment, the decision was taken to overthrow Allende by a military coup.

The menace was there all the time. We could see it painted on the walls: the initials 'SACO' with which Patria y Libertad announced a wave of violence – 'System of Organised Civic Action' was their euphemism – and 'Djakarta is coming', a reminder of the massacre of hundreds of thousands of communists in Indonesia in 1965.

In May, one of the first victims was a young building worker, Roberto Ahumada, whom Victor had met during the March election campaign, working for Popular Unity in the población which was his home. While marching along the Alameda in a peaceful demonstration against violence and right-wing terrorism, he was shot dead with a bullet which appeared to have been fired from the roof of the Christian Democrat Party's headquarters.

Victor was personally very affected by his death. He had seen this young man working with such enthusiasm and dedication, had met his wife and family and knew the atmosphere of his home. For Roberto Ahumada, imagining his inner thoughts, Victor wrote his song 'Cuando voy al trabajo' ('On my way to work'), a love song with a premonition of death. It also expressed Victor's own feelings.

On my way to work
I think of you,
through the streets of the city
I think of you.
When I look at the faces
through steamy windows
not knowing who they are, where they're going,
I think of you
compañera of my life
and of the future,
of the bitter hours and the happiness
of being alive,
working at the beginning of a story
without knowing the end.

When the day's work is over
and the evening comes
throwing its shadow
over the roofs we have built,
returning from our labour,
discussing among friends,
reasoning out things

of this time and destiny,
I think of you, my love,
compañera of my life and of the future.

When I come home, you are there,
and we weave our dreams together . . .
Working at the beginning of a story
without knowing the end.

On 26 May, from his home by the sea in Isla Negra where he
had retired because of his ill health, Neruda broadcast on National
Television. In his speech in the Stadium at his home-coming in
December, Neruda had reminded us all of the horrors that the people
of Spain suffered during the Civil War and warned that there were
some Chileans who wanted to drag the country into the same sort of
confrontation. 'I have the poetic, political and patriotic duty to warn
all Chile of this imminent danger,' he said.

Now his message was still more urgent and he called on all artists
and intellectuals, in Chile and abroad, to join him in an attempt to alert
people to the very real danger of a fascist takeover; to make them realise
what a civil war, so blithely talked about as 'inevitable' by some sectors
of the opposition, would really mean in terms of human suffering.

The whole cultural movement responded to Neruda's call. Exhibitions and television programmes were organised; a cultural open-air
'marathon' took place in the Plaza de la Constitución. It lasted several
days and hundreds of artists, poets, theatre and dance groups, musicians
and song groups took part. It was a great anti-fascist event to which
thousands came, and there were similar events all over the country.
Victor's contribution, apart from performing as a singer, was to direct
a series of programmes for the National Television Channel with a
common theme: a warning, relating documentary material about Nazi
Germany and the Spanish Civil War to the situation in Chile, to make
people aware of the real dangers of the same things happening here and
now. Victor had put to music one of Neruda's latest poems which had
the refrain 'I don't want my country divided . . .', and he sang it as the
opening theme for each programme. Many other artists took part with
dance, poetry, theatre and song.

As winter approached, life became more and more difficult. It
became almost a full-time job just to do the shopping, as queues

became longer, swollen by people involved in the black market who made a profession out of it. Monica and I shared the queueing between us, but Manuela also had to do her bit. Even bread became scarce, because the October transport strike had seriously affected the wheat harvest.

There were voluntary work parties every weekend, workers did voluntary overtime, skilled students helped out in the factories and mines while others joined in the harvest or the distribution of food. People of all ages took part, from primary school students to old-age pensioners. Some of Manuela's most vivid memories of Victor are from this time. Together they used to set out on expeditions to do voluntary work. In the autumn they had gone out into the country near Lonquen to help with the maize harvest, stripping the ripe cobs from the stalks in the warm sun and then resting in the shade of the fragrant eucalyptus trees at midday. Victor took out his guitar to sing a few songs and then passed it round so that everyone could play or sing something. They arrived home late, treating each other as compañeros, full of shared jokes.

When the office staff and supervisors at the El Teniente copper mine came out in a strike inspired and planned by the Christian Democrats, the students and staff of the Technical University gave intensive support to the majority of the miners who continued to work – in spite of threats and intimidation – in an attempt to maintain the copper production so vital to the national economy. Bus loads of technically skilled students made the journey south to Rancagua and then up to the mine, high in the cordillera. Victor went with them on more than one occasion. I remember driving him down to the Technical University early one morning to join the bus. As we waited for it to fill up with students, I got into conversation with two hippy-looking gringos with a guitar, who were sitting on the campus steps. They told me that they wanted to go to the mine to show their support for the miners and maybe sing a few songs to tell them that many Americans condemned the policies of the US government.

Apparently the Chilean students didn't trust them and hadn't given them permission to get on the bus. As the conversation progressed, they introduced themselves as Phil Ochs and Jerry Rubin. I took them over to where Victor was deep in conversation with the organisers of the expedition and he intervened to allow them to go with the group. They spent all day with Victor, going into the mine with him. They heard him singing and talking to the miners and were impressed with his easy relationship with them and how much they appreciated his songs. Victor gave them a chance to speak and to sing a few songs, translating for them, and then all together they sang Pete Seeger's 'If I had a hammer'. The three of them had such a good time together that in the evening, when they reached Santiago, Victor took them to the Peña, where they were warmly received.

During these months, Victor was busy with *Los Siete Estados*, working with Patricio, Celso and the National Ballet, as well as composing and recording new songs. I was involved with my teacher's course, and already seeing the first results as I went the rounds of their practice classes in primary schools, in community centres in the poblaciones, and in the larger satellite dance schools. It was a small start, but one which promised well for the future, especially as a new scheme had just been approved which would give scholarships to primary school teachers interested in specialising in dance, and new facilities for students to come from the provinces to study. If we could continue the multiplication process, within a few years dance would really be a part of the education system.

Meanwhile, revelations about the covert activities of the CIA in Chile had started to appear in the *Washington Post*, and we knew that the same conspiracy against Allende must be continuing. But there were more and more problems within Popular Unity itself – there was no unity of command in the face of powerful enemies. Different solutions were put forward by different sectors. Some, including the Communist Party, wanted to pursue the goal of a dialogue with the Christian Democrats in order to avert the threatened civil war; others wanted no compromise, were demanding an outright confrontation, although how people without weapons were to win military victories against a modern army was not clear. It seemed suicidal, and if the government were to attempt to 'arm the people', it could only precipitate a military coup.

At the same time, the idea of a dialogue seemed difficult if not impossible. It was not easy to make a distinction between the Christian Democrat leadership and the truly fascist elements within the opposition. They seemed to work together, hand in glove, and to use the same methods. Victor and I used to discuss this problem. Even on a personal level, or among our neighbours, it was almost impossible to begin to communicate with people who we knew were trying to sabotage the government and to shut the door on the progress that was being made for the deprived majority; people who would go to any lengths to hang on to their own comfort and privilege, even to the extent of conspiring with the fascists.

Although those in opposition were more and more aggressive, they did not have all the initiative. The working class was constantly mobilised to counteract violence in the streets. Committees of defence were set up in factories, universities, schools, government buildings, to prevent sabotage or occupation by the opposition. Our Faculty had to be guarded twenty-four hours a day, with teachers, ballet dancers, students and all the staff taking turns to keep night-watch, sleeping on improvised camp beds in offices and studios. As Victor was working with the National Ballet he also did his share of this, although I and other mothers would always be at home at night because of the children. It was already painfully clear to me that our different responsibilities would separate us even more as the revolutionary crisis deepened.

Victor himself had several lucky escapes from gangs of Patria y Libertad when he was out late at night. I didn't learn of these until later, as he didn't want to worry me. On one occasion, also, the paramilitary brigades of the National Party were lining up and drilling in the street outside the Faculty with no interference from the police, when a girl on one of the upper floors of the building couldn't resist the temptation to pour a bucket of water over them. As they rushed around the corner to attack the entrance, Victor was coming along in the opposite direction. 'There's Jara!' they screamed, 'Get him!' But the guards on the door opened it quickly, and as he slipped out of his attackers' reach, the doors slammed in their faces.

Once we were on our way to the centre in the citroneta when we stopped at a traffic light in Avenida Colón, beside an enormous light-blue Chevrolet. The driver, glancing sideways, recognised Victor and leaning over took an enormous knife out of the glove compartment and brandished it at us, his face distorted with hatred. As the lights changed and the cars behind began to sound their horns, he drove off with a dramatic squeal of tyres. That was in broad daylight.

On another occasion, late at night, when votes from an internal election were being counted in the foyer of the theatre on the ground floor, a group of thugs tried to break down the glass doors to beat up the small group of people inside. Only the arrival of a group of students, summoned rapidly by an emergency telephone call, saved the situation. The leader of the attackers was an elected deputy of the National Party.

This sort of incident was a daily occurrence. We worked to a background of shouting in the street, the noise of breaking glass, the crunch of tear-gas grenades exploding, and their sickly, stifling fumes seeping up even to the seventh floor. Several times a week we would have to run the gauntlet of a street riot in order to get to work, taking refuge in shops or arcades until these too became so chronically full of tear-gas that the air never cleared. The 'destabilisation' process was in full swing.

In response to the growing menace of fascism, Victor wrote another song which was to prove prophetic. One of his favourite poets was Miguel Hernandez who had been born a peasant and died in one of Franco's prisons. He kept his complete works, together with a copy of the Bible, on his bedside table and it was on a verse from one of Hernandez's poems that Victor based his song 'Vientos del pueblo'. It was arranged with Inti-Illimani, in some concentrated sessions in the workshop at home.

> Once more they want to stain
> my country with the blood of working people –
> those who talk of liberty
> but whose hands are marked with guilt;
> who want to separate
> our children from their mothers,
> and want to reconstruct
> the cross that Christ bore.
>
> They try to conceal the infamy
> they have inherited from past centuries,
> but the mark of murderers
> cannot be wiped from their faces.
> Already thousands and thousands
> have sacrificed their blood
> and its streaming rivers
> have multiplied the loaves.

Now I want to live
together with my child and brother
in the new world that all of us
are building day by day.
Your threats do not intimidate me
you masters of misery,
the star of hope
will continue to be ours.

Winds of the people are calling me,
winds of the people are bearing me,
they scatter my heart
and blow through my throat.
So the poet will be heard,
until death takes me away,
along the road of the people,
now and for ever.

When Victor came to record this song, he commented to the members
of Inti-Illimani who were in the studio with him, that the line 'until
death takes me away' was 'too depressing' and he changed it, then
and there, to 'while my heart goes on beating'.

The rehearsals of this song must have been heard all over our block,
with drums and quenas sounding through the tidy, well-kept gardens
of our neighbours, many of whom were now our mortal enemies.
Even those who we knew had all Victor's records and presumably
liked his songs, avoided us now. We were no longer dealing with
a normal political situation. For me it was difficult to adjust to that
reality, but Victor had already faced it. His song was an expression
of the time we were living in, a reflection of his own mood of
determination. It was necessary to go on working harder than ever.

Towards the end of June, Victor left Chile to visit Peru where he
was invited by the National Institute of Culture to give a series of
recitals in different parts of the country. As I came back from seeing
him off at the airport, I was rather scared at the prospect of being
alone, but at the same time almost relieved that for a couple of weeks
at least he would be safe. I knew that if any crisis developed, Victor
would be sure to be in the midst of it and in personal danger.

For Victor it was perhaps the culmination of all his journeys and

one which took him to the roots of a Latin American cultural
identity. He was at last able to visit the ruins of Macchu Picchu,
to touch the massive stones, to share the feelings of Neruda and
so many other Latin American artists. He did so in the company
of an anthropologist, a Peruvian Indian, who was working in the
excavations. Mariano Sanchez Macedo insisted on taking photos of
Victor with his guitar among the ruins, or poised high above them on
a rocky peak overlooking the Inca citadel, with the sky and the high
Andes around him. This experience was for Victor a confirmation
of so much history, so many aspirations shared, so much suffering in
common with his own people.

When he came home he wrote about two incidents that he felt
gave the essence of what this journey had meant to him. Although
he had performed in great concert halls and in television studios in
Peru, it was not these experiences that stayed with him. Two small
encounters as told by Victor sum up, I think, his whole attitude to
his work and to life:

Salazar, a worker of Lima, had heard me sing. He was different
from the other people who came round after the concert to ask
for an autograph or to see if I were real. He said to me, 'I should
like you to come and see my home, to meet my wife and children
and all the other people who live around us . . .' His invitation was
so direct and sincere that I accepted it.

We took a bus towards the outskirts of Lima. A crowded old
micro. It was a grey, overcast day . . . (just like in the old song)
. . . We came to Coimas, a new working-class district rather like
the Población José María Caro here in Santiago. Lots of children
playing football. It was about four o'clock in the afternoon.
We began to walk and meanwhile he explained to me about
all the voluntary work that was done by the community, like
installing a supply of drinking water, bringing electricity, making
a place for the children to play. We climbed up and up through
narrow streets. Suddenly I stopped and turned round and saw
in the distance the tall buildings in the centre of Lima and all
around me hills covered with the tiny dwellings which make
up the 'mushroom' communities. We passed a food store and
Salazar bought some bread and eggs. I bought some chocolate
for his children. We went on climbing. He never stopped talking,

telling me about his life. It was as though we had been friends for years.

When we arrived at his house, he introduced me to his wife. She was dark-haired and *simpática*, but she became very nervous. By coincidence she had just been listening to me singing on the radio and it seemed altogether too surprising that this Chilean should suddenly appear in her home. But over tea and fried eggs, we quickly understood one another. With the children playing all around us and showing me their homework, we talked about everything important to us: home, children, Peru, Chile, revolution, changes and so on . . . then they showed me their house. You could see the love and the hard work of a man and a woman in each centimetre of cement, in every piece of wood and in every nail of that home, humble perhaps, but with a human warmth which great mansions would envy.

Salazar confessed to me that he had known beforehand that I would go with him to his home. Otherwise he would have been too shy to ask me. He knew, 'because I was singing for them and he felt that I was part of them.'

This is not the first time that something like this has happened to me. Sometimes I feel that I am losing my way, that other sorts of interests are undermining my conscience and separating me from everyday things, from simplicity . . . but this sort of experience is a profound stimulus. It strengthens me and makes me feel that what I am doing – and how I am doing it, is valid.

Salazar came back with me. We walked down the hill together and he accompanied me all the way back to the centre of Lima.

Then, near Cuzco, I sang to a group of peasants. They sat there with their ponchos, their traditional hats and ojotas (rough sandals). They looked at me as though they were surprised. I was also surprised. So many years of history seemed to pour over me at being there together with them. Songs began to sprout, one after the other. I talked to them about Chile, about the Araucanian south, about Angelita Huenumán, about the land, the agrarian reform. I told them Chilean riddles . . . some of them smiled, but shyly. The sunlight was transparent and you could hear the rushing of the Apurimac River. There was a feeling of restraint as when tears want to flow, but we hold them back. When I had finished, one of them came up to me. He spoke to me in Quechua and began to sing. I felt as though we had clasped hands. With a mixture of exaltation and joy, I heard the Quechuan song. A song with the antiquity of the high mountain peaks and the lyricism of the rivers.

Song is like a noose with which we can either join our feelings or with which we can strangle them. There is no other alternative. Singers who laboriously pursue personal glory, who profit from innocence and purity, will never understand that song is like the water that washes the stones, the wind which cleans us, like the fire which joins us together and that it lives within us to make us better people.

Violeta said, 'The song of all of you is my own song . . .' and her words are as eternal as the mountains, as the stones of Macchu Picchu.

Only a few days after Victor left for Peru, on 29 June, there was an attempted military *coup*. I was already at work in the Dance Department that morning when we heard the news that tanks were advancing on the Moneda Palace, only a couple of blocks away from us. We shut and guarded the doors, prepared to face a siege, as we listened to gunfire and waited for news of what was happening. Radios were our only link with the outside world and the mood was one of being prepared for the worst. I remember being grateful for the presence of tough male dancers, who night after night had been guarding the building and training in self-defence – perhaps foolishly, because there was little that they could do without arms to defend us against a military attack.

We learned that the uprising was confined to a single tank regiment, led by a Colonel Roberto Souper. A much more ambitious and complex military plan had been called off at the last moment, and only Souper's regiment had not received, or possibly not obeyed, the message of cancellation.

We heard that the Palace Guard had proved loyal to the President and that, as the mutinous tank regiment neared the Palace, General Carlos Prats, in his role of Commander-in-Chief of the Armed Forces, had gone out on foot to meet them, armed only with a sub-machine gun. He had ordered the officers commanding the tanks to surrender. Seeing themselves isolated, without the support they had anticipated, they obeyed and the tanks turned round to go back to their barracks, while Souper was placed under arrest. The crisis was over and the Armed Forces as a whole had apparently shown their loyalty to the constitutional government. But twenty-two people died, among them a Swedish photographer whose cinecamera remained running as he was shot by a rebel officer. The film was retrieved and shown later all over the world.

That same morning, coming out of a block of flats in the barrio alto, Patricio had seen several Chevrolet vans being loaded with brand-new sub-machine guns, passed from hand to hand by a chain of tough-looking men. Without knowing it, he had been living for months above a secret arms store of Patria y Libertad. Only once had he noticed any sort of suspicious movement, although he had registered the frequent visits of a tall, blonde American. Later we were to learn that the *Tancazo*, as the abortive military *coup* came to be called, had been directed, if not initiated, by the fascist party in combination with their contacts in the Armed Forces. As if to underline their guilt, Pablo Rodriguez and a number of the other leaders of Patria y Libertad immediately sought asylum in the Ecuadorean Embassy.

A great rally took place that same afternoon in the Plaza de la Constitución. People came from all over Santiago, summoned by their trade unions, to hear Allende speak of the loyalty of the Armed Forces. The Palace Guards were the heroes of the day and we shouted slogans such as 'Soldier, friend, the people are with you!' It seems cruelly ironic in view of later events. Meanwhile, the news reached Peru and Victor's recital in the Municipal Theatre of Lima that evening became a fervent demonstration of solidarity with the people of Chile and of support for the Popular Unity government, which was a symbol of freedom and independence in Latin America. As the concert ended, the entire audience poured out of the theatre in an improvised march through the city centre.

Victor, nervous about our safety, managed to phone us the next day, and a couple of weeks later, when he got home, he swore that he would never leave us again. Manuela, who was not usually so demonstrative, clung to him and burst into tears of relief at having him back home with us. Victor himself was even more affectionate than usual and wanted me to accompany him as much as possible on the innumerable errands that he had to carry out after his journey: going to the National Television Channel on San Cristóbal Hill, dropping into the office of a magazine to be interviewed, taking an article he had written to a newspaper, collecting tapes at a recording studio. He wanted my company and would put his hand on my knee whenever the car stopped at the traffic lights as if to reassure himself that I was there. That Victor had premonitions of his own death, I have no doubt. If I think of his nightmares, I would say even of the manner of it. It can be felt in all his last songs, and he would even joke about it.

One day at breakfast, for some reason I was cross with him, and Manuela and Monica sided with me against him. It was a women's club against the only male in the house. I think that Victor said that it wasn't *his* job to make the toast and we all joined in telling him off for having macho attitudes. Suddenly he said, out of the blue, and only half-joking, 'You'll be sorry later. You should make the most of me while I'm here, because you'll be a long time without me! I shall never get beyond forty.' We all laughed at him, but I knew that he meant it.

Victor was prepared for whatever was in store, but he was far from sad or depressed. On the contrary, he was full of energy and even happiness. In an interview in August 1973 he was asked what sort of man he was, whether shy, bold or passionate, and he answered: 'I think I'm passionate because I am full of hope. Bold, just because I suffer from shyness. But above all, I am a man happy to exist at this moment. Happy to feel the fatigue of work. Happy because when one puts one's heart, reason and will to work at the service of the people, one feels the happiness of being reborn.'

As a symptom of his unfailing sense of humour and love of a joke – even in the situation in which we were living – Victor was at this time working on an album called *Canto por travesura*, which was a collection of funny, rather bawdy peasant songs from the south of Chile. It included 'La beata', once banned, now recognised for what it was, a typically Chilean folk-song. And there were other songs containing jokes and riddles.

Victor wanted to give people a chance to laugh – 'We Chileans are naturally a very cheerful people with a great sense of humour. We need to be reminded of it. Also, I think that in our enthusiasm for Andean music from the north, we tend to forget a whole region which is rich in folklore – the south of Chile.' *Canto por travesura* was due for publication in early September, ready for the Fiestas Patrias. Although the album was pressed, it never reached the shops.

In the wake of the Tancazo abortive coup, Allende made a final attempt to reach an agreement with the Christian Democrats. But they no longer had any real interest in negotiation, and within Popular Unity, too, there was no longer a consensus. The far right now concentrated their efforts on the military. Despite the failure of the Tancazo, they knew that they could rely upon many of the officers. But there were others, 'constitutionalists', who would have to be removed.

The first casualty was Allende's naval aide-de-camp, Commander Arturo Araya, who was assassinated by gunmen at the end of July as he stood on the balcony of his house. He had been a key figure in maintaining contact between the President and the loyal sections of the naval high command. But the most important obstacle that stood in the way of a coup was the Army Commander-in-Chief, General Prats.

Prats was a man of progressive ideas, a determined champion of the Schneider Doctrine of the neutrality of the Armed Forces and their loyalty to constitutional democracy. Now the wives of a number of the most senior army generals were pressed into action against him. They staged a demonstration outside his house, waving white feathers, insulting him, and accusing him of cowardice: for not intervening 'to save Chile from Marxism'. As Prats himself expressed it later in his diary, 'behind the skirts of their wives' were hiding the generals themselves, by this action embarking on mutiny. His own position had become untenable and he saw no alternative but to resign.

Finally, the *golpistas*, those plotting a coup, hit upon a means of bringing the Armed Forces into direct conflict with the workers. They dusted off the Arms Control Law, an almost forgotten measure passed by Congress the previous year, and began a campaign of denunciations that at particular places arms were hidden. The law gave individual armed forces and police officers *carte blanche* to carry out raids without reference to higher authority, and the most right-wing ones used the pretext to raid the nationalised industries, working-class districts, hospitals, universities – anywhere where there was strong support for Popular Unity. The caches of the landowners and Patria y Libertad went undisturbed.

Helicopters flew low over the working-class district of San Miguel, graves were dug up in the nearby Metropolitan Cemetery on the pretext that workers had stores of arms hidden in them. In Punta

Arenas, Lanera Austral, a large wool industry, was attacked in a full-scale military operation in which a man was killed.

Our Faculty also was ransacked, in spite of the almost sacred principle of university autonomy which normally prevented the police from entering university precincts without special permission. Again and again, during the month of August, sometimes during the day, sometimes at night, the police came to search the 'red' Faculty. They never found any arms, for there were none to find. But a gang of armed fascists attacked the building, smashing down the doors and plate-glass windows.

The second bosses' strike began on 26 July. As in the previous October, it started with lock-outs by the lorry- and bus-owners, but this time it was a battle to the death. The majority of workers were trying to keep the country going; the bosses, with the power and finance of the multi-nationals behind them and the technical advice and direct support of the CIA, were trying to bring the country to a complete halt, to an accompaniment of bombs, assassinations, riots, terrorist attacks of all sorts.

As a family we were told that we should make plans for a place of safety to which I could take the children, away from our own home. Victor would not be with us. He would be carrying out whatever task might be allotted him. I understood that in the case of a civil war he would have to go and fight to defend the revolution. His military training would be useful, although it was almost twenty years since he had had a gun in his hands and he neither possessed nor wanted to possess one.

A small house was offered to us in Isla Negra, a primitive house intended for a holiday by the beach, near Neruda's home. We went there once to try to prepare it. In winter it was lonely, but here I was supposed to hide with Amanda and Manuela hoping that nobody would recognise whose family we were. We took insulin for Amanda, a small store of emergency food, counting on the availability of fish or seafood and driftwood for fuel. We thought we might be safer than at home where we were undoubtedly on the blacklist of the local fascists. The only problem was that to get there we should have to travel along roads which would certainly be controlled. That little refuge remained an impractical dream, but it was the scene of Amanda's last vivid memory of her father.

She was 8 years old and on the winter afternoon that Victor brought us to Isla Negra, he suggested that they should go for a walk together along the coast. A huge red sun was slowly sinking into the Pacific Ocean as they went along the coastal path which wound above craggy rocks, with the great breakers crashing and dissolving among them. Victor walked in front with his long brown poncho, Amanda skipped along behind on the narrow path. I saw them disappearing in the distance. The path, which seemed to go on for ever, the wind and sun and the sense of space and solitude, inspired Victor to make a song. As they went along, he started to invent words and music, asking Amanda's advice. She made her own suggestions which became part of the song and she felt very proud to be helping to make it. Together they went along singing it, not wanting to turn back but to go on and on, while the sun slowly disappeared . . .

Just a few miles away in that apparently empty ocean, US warships were already nearing Valparaiso to take part in joint naval exercises with the Chilean Navy. On our way home next day, on a lonely road, we came near to being attacked by a mob of armed men who came running down a hill, clambering over fences to reach us. On the crest of the hill we saw a group of lorries lined up against the skyline: one of the camps of the bosses' strike.

The song of Isla Negra was lost because it was never recorded, but during those weeks Victor was composing one which he felt that he had to write before it was too late, to express his reason for singing. He was quiet as he worked on it, introverted and withdrawn. I could hear him singing gently in the workshop as I worked in the house. Then he came to call me to ask me to listen to it. Although it was a very beautiful song, my heart contracted as he sang it to me. I knew that Victor was writing his testament.

I don't sing for love of singing,
or because I have a good voice.
I sing because my guitar
has both feeling and reason.
It has a heart of earth
and the wings of a dove,
it is like holy water,
blessing joy and grief.
My song has found a purpose

as Violeta would say.
Hardworking guitar,
with a smell of spring.

My guitar is not for the rich
no, nothing like that.
My song is of the ladder
we are building to reach the stars.
For a song has meaning
when it beats in the veins
of a man who will die singing,
truthfully singing his song.

My song is not for fleeting praise
nor to gain foreign fame,
it is for this narrow country
to the very depths of the earth.
There, where everything comes to rest
and where everything begins,
song which has been brave song
will be forever new.

('Manifesto')

3 September 1973

Today we are celebrating the third anniversary of Allende's election,
although the more important purpose of the great march which has
been called for today is to defend the Popular Unity government
and to prevent it being overthrown by a military coup. Everyone
understands that we are fighting for our lives, but we don't seem to
know by what means, with what weapons. We only know that it is
necessary to demonstrate clearly that Popular Unity is a great force
to be reckoned with, that the people are beside their government
in spite of all the problems. In the last few weeks there have been
repeated calls from the CUT to come out on to the streets to frustrate
terrorist attacks, but today is different. Four great columns starting
from different points of Santiago will converge on the Moneda Palace
to salute Allende and the leaders of Popular Unity.

As we leave the house, we see that even in our neighbourhood, we are not the only ones – many of the families who have been working in the JAP are also starting out, packing flags and banners into their cars – but we are in a minority. The other houses are quiet and closed, only the children, playing as usual in the street, observe our departure. Earlier I have seen groups of construction workers marching down Avenida Colón towards the centre, four or five miles away. There is no public transport because of the lock-out by the bus-owners, but the workers are determined to be there in the march today, and will walk all the way if necessary.

The last month has been terrible, with the continuation of the lorry-owners' strike, which neither the sacrifice of the MOPARE drivers, risking their lives along the roads, nor the mobilisation of voluntary work – sadder, but better organised than before – has been able to break. Food is scarce, unless one is involved in the black market; paraffin and gas, too. The doctors and dentists have come out on strike now as well, although many doctors are continuing to work in the hospitals.

One night, about two weeks ago, as Allende was speaking on nation-wide television (Victor and I were watching together) there was a power cut which affected the whole central zone of Chile. As the lights went out and Allende's image flickered off the screen, we knew that something terrible had happened, that it wasn't just a local failure. Luckily the transistor radio worked and we could listen to Allende calling for calm. Some of the right-wing radio stations were urging people out on to the streets, in an effort, I suppose, to cause more confusion.

The lights went on some time later, but the impression lingered – it was such a scientifically planned attack, by terrorists who had inside information about the key points where the bombs had to be located to cause maximum effect. It could only have been planned by the military, or with military advice.

There is so much talk of civil war, but it is difficult to envisage how it will come about. I have been involved with the other women in the neighbourhood who support the government, trying to make contingency plans for what might happen . . . storing medicines, bandages, learning first aid, trying to think up safe places for the children, in general trying to prepare ourselves for whatever might come.

I was desperately anxious about Amanda. Would her insulin last

out? It was already difficult to obtain. Would there be enough food
to maintain a regular diet, would we be able to reach a doctor in
an emergency? It all seemed too horrifying to be real. If you looked
around at our quiet street, everything seemed quite normal. The pink
cherry trees had flowered as usual in the early spring, there was sun
and wind, the children played and quarrelled with one another, people
went quietly about their business. Only the shuttered shops and the
queues outside the baker's were a sign that all was not well . . . that,
and the fact that as evening fell, the 'tom-toms' would begin.

Moments of the past weeks flash through my mind . . . I am in the
garden, the winter sun is hot on my back . . . it must be the weekend
because we are all at home. Victor is in the studio – I can hear him
singing quietly . . . he has just played me the first version of 'Cuando
voy al trabajo' and I have the melody and the sense of it in my head
– 'working at the beginning of a story, without knowing the end'. I
feel the grass under my feet, the plants and the trees of the garden
all around me, with the comfort of Victor's presence, the sound of
his guitar, the knowledge that Manuela and Amanda are safe, playing
nearby and will soon come in for tea . . . I have a sudden shudder
of horror as though time froze for an instant . . . a feeling that just
because of its normality, I am going to remember this moment for
the rest of my life.

But now we are on our way to the centre, or rather to the elegant
Avenida Providencia, where our column is due to assemble. A wide
street, lined with boutiques. We are glad, when we arrive, to find a
gigantic mass of people already assembled. The march is so big that it
is quite impossible to begin to judge numbers; you can see neither
beginning nor end of this column which spreads the entire width of
the avenue. We must be marching twenty, thirty abreast . . . and this
is only one of four such columns. Such is the sense of discipline and
organisation that we feel like a great army of men, women and children
assembling, but there are no arms, only hand-painted banners which
all declare their bearers to be against fascism and terrorism and ready
to defend their government. The mood, though, is a grim one. There
can be no celebration. It is quite frightening to march between those
high buildings knowing that they are full of enemies. However, when
it is our turn to march past the now empty headquarters of Patria y
Libertad, a roar of triumphant defiance surges from the crowd.

Today everyone has turned out, even those who do not usually bother to come on marches. We are surrounded by friends, although Inti-Illimani are still in Europe and so are the original Quilapayún. But the other Quilapayún groups are here as is the entire Peña with their own banner; we see some theatre friends for the first time for months. When Amanda gets tired, one of them gives her a piggy-back . . . there are dancers, painters, poets, actors, playwrights, just in our small section of the march. It is not really a question of marching, but of shuffling along, a few paces every few minutes, such is the crush and the difficulty of advancing towards the centre . . . There is a great cheer when, from a distance, we see the column from the south of Santiago pouring into the Alameda at right-angles to us, but then we turn into a side street beside the Santa Lucía Hill and lose sight of them among the narrow streets in the heart of the city . . . here the crush is almost unbearable and we stand for hours, feeling trapped, waiting our turn to advance towards the Moneda Palace.

Victor is way ahead of us. He has been roped in to help carry the banner behind which we are marching, 'Trabajadores de la Cultura en contra el Fascismo'. It is symbolic that he is not marching with us, his family, today. Although he loves us as much, perhaps more, than ever, he has moved from beside us on to another plane, far away from the cosy domesticity that he himself has always valued so much. I understand that and I understand that he has no choice. He is making himself ready to confront fascism, hoping to take his place in a movement of resistance to it, whether in open struggle or in hiding.

To do otherwise would be to betray all the values that he lives by, including those of peace and love. He hates violence as much as ever, but is being swept by the course of events and by the strength of his own convictions to be ready to fight, by whatever means at his disposal . . . I know he is anxious about our safety, although he tries not to worry me too much. I was surprised by his enthusiasm when I told him that I had received a visit from a mustachioed English gentleman who looked as though he were a member of the Country Club – one of the local British residents, checking on his flock in case of emergencies, with instructions about what to do in case of a crisis . . . they know that something bad is about to happen.

As we emerge, at last, into Plaza de la Constitución, it is already completely dark. Little by little we edge forward until it is our turn to pass the long platform where Allende is sitting with all the leaders

of Popular Unity . . . they must have been here for hours already . . .
he looks tired . . . one by one we recognise and salute them, although
we notice that the new Commanders-in-Chief of the Armed Forces,
Merino, Leigh and Pinochet, are not among them.

Everyone is shouting 'Allende, Allende, el pueblo te defiende!' and
'El pueblo unido jamás será vencido!' We feel the great power of all
that mass of people and think that it will be impossible to kill us all
. . . more than a million of us saluted Allende that day.

At last we catch up with Victor, who is waiting for us as we get
past the platform. He takes Amanda in his arms so that she can see
and we stand there for a moment looking at the people passing in
front of the Moneda Palace . . . the same sort of people that we
had seen celebrating in the streets in 1970 . . . but what a lot has
been achieved since then, in spite of all the difficulties. Now there
is a sadder, grimmer, but just as determined mood.

The great march of 3 September 1973 turned out to be the people's
farewell to Salvador Allende.

Of the following week, I can remember little, except the struggle
to keep going, to go on working, giving classes in an atmosphere of
increasing tension, the sense of a terrible threat hanging over us for
which we were completely unprepared, especially as it never seemed
clear what form the danger would take.

Were we waiting for some sort of signal to evacuate the children
from the homes of Popular Unity supporters? Homes that would be
in danger in case of civil war? Our neighbourhood was not easy to
get out of, bounded by the cordillera to the east and the Canal San
Carlos to the west. The few routes of escape could be easily cut off.

One night, when I was on duty in the JAP, in Alberto's shop,
helping to distribute rice and tea to a queue of people, I heard the
news that the Christian Democrats were uniting with the ultra-right
in Congress to declare Allende's government illegal, even though they
didn't have the necessary two-thirds majority to impeach him. This
laid the way open for the Armed Forces to act. It was frightening
news – Popular Unity was completely isolated.

People were talking about a plebiscite; Allende was closeted in
his house in Tomas Moro, just a few blocks away, trying to get an
agreement in his Cabinet about whether to accept the idea, or not

– there seemed to be no firm policy in face of crisis . . . Rumour said that a military coup would occur before Fiestas Patrias on 18 September, because with so much subversive movement within the Armed Forces it seemed impossible for the President to review the traditional army parade.

I tried to discuss the situation with Victor, to ask him what the solution was. I asked him, 'But how can we defend ourselves if we have the Armed Forces against us?' He just smiled ruefully at me and said, 'I think that that is the crux of the problem.' A civil war implied a confrontation between two sides, but what would those two sides consist of? These questions went round and round in my head, but neither Victor, nor anyone I knew seemed to have the answer.

On Monday 10 September I went to work as usual to the Faculty building in the centre. It was a political duty to keep working normally and I knew that the students would be there, even though ugly incidents took place every day around us. That morning, as well as taking my usual classes, I was directing a seminar on movement for teachers working in the theatre school. Victor dropped me off at work and continued eastwards to the Technical University where he had to do a radio programme. He was happy, because he was taking a recently recorded tape to be played for the first time. It was a song he had made at the request of the building workers' union, a kind of trade-union hymn. He was anxious that they should hear it and tell him if they approved. Victor admired very much the militancy of the building workers who were firmly behind the Popular Unity government and had their own victims, like Roberto Ahumada.

Later, in the afternoon, Victor came back to fetch me. I had not yet finished work, so he went upstairs to talk to Quena while I tackled what was to be my last class in Chile, with a group of young men and a percussionist. I remember that it was a good class.

As soon as I could get away, I rushed upstairs to find Victor installed in the office of the Ballet with a cup of tea. Señora Marta, who cleaned the floors and made tea in a little cubby hole which she had converted into a regular kitchen, was looking after him. Whenever he came, she insisted on stuffing him with food and drink as a way of showing her respect and affection. Victor drew me to him and made me sit on his lap. I can still see his tender smile as he looked at me and, for the first time in years, called me '*mi gringuita*'. I can only think that his sub-conscious was rejoicing that I had the protection of a British passport.

We said good-bye to Quena and thanks to Marta and went home. It was fairly quiet as we drove up towards the mountains, but the evening papers had glaring headlines which announced that the pilots of the National Airline (LAN) were taking all the planes to the Air Force base of El Bosque 'for safe keeping' while the strike was on. It sounded as though the scene was set.

11

THE COUP

11 September 1973

I wake early as usual. Victor is still asleep, so I get out of bed quietly and wake Manuela who has to get to school early. I go downstairs to put the kettle on and a few minutes later Monica appears, rubbing her eyes and yawning. Everything is normal, within the abnormality in which we are living. It is a cold, cheerless, overcast morning.

We have breakfast, Manuela and I, and set out for school. It isn't far by car, but difficult to reach by public transport even if there were any. Luckily we still have some petrol. We are obviously the only people stirring. Everyone else seems to have decided to stay in bed, except of course the maids, who get up early and go to queue for bread at the bakery on the corner. Monica had come back with the news that Allende's car has already raced down Avenida Colón accompanied by his usual escort, much earlier than usual. People in the bread queue and in the newspaper kiosk were saying that something is afoot.

Manuel de Salas is full of students. There is no sign of the strike here. Only a tiny percentage of families are not supporters of Popular Unity. On the way home I switch on the car radio and the news comes through that Valparaiso has been sealed off and that unusual troop movements are taking place. The trade unions are calling for all workers to assemble in their places of work because this is an emergency, a red alert.

I hurry home to tell Victor. He is already up when I arrive and is fiddling with the transistor radio trying to get Magallanes or one of the other radio stations that support Popular Unity. 'This seems to be it,' we say to each other, 'it has really started.'

Victor was due that morning to sing at the Technical University, at the opening of a special exhibition about the horrors of civil war and fascism where Allende was going to speak. 'Well, that won't happen,' I said. 'No, but I think I should go anyway. While you go and fetch Manue from school – because it's better that you're all at home together – I'll make some phone calls to try to find out what is happening.'

As I drove out of the courtyard again, our neighbours were beginning to gather. They were talking loudly and excitedly, already beginning to celebrate. I passed them without glancing at them, but looking back in the mirror, I saw one of the 'ladies' squat down and give the most obscene gesture in Chilean sign language to my receding back.

Back at the school, I found that instructions had been given for the younger students to go home, while the teachers and older students were to stay behind. I collected Manue and, on the way home, although the reception was bad, we heard Allende on the radio. It was reassuring to hear his voice from the Moneda Palace . . . but it sounded almost like a speech of farewell.

I found Victor in the studio listening to the radio and together we heard the confusion as almost all the Popular Unity stations went off the air when their aerials were bombed or they were taken over by the military, and martial music replaced Allende's voice . . .

'This is the last time I shall be able to speak to you . . . I shall not resign . . . I will repay with my life the loyalty of the people . . . I say to you: I am certain that the seeds we have sown in the conscience of thousands and thousands of Chileans cannot be completely eradicated . . . neither crime nor force are strong enough to hold back the process of social change. History belongs to us, because it is made by the people . . .'

It was the speech of a heroic man who knew he was about to die but at that moment we heard it only in snatches. Victor was called to the phone in the middle . . . I could hardly bear to listen to it.

Victor had been waiting for me to come back in order to go out. He had decided that he had to go to his place of work, the Technical University, obeying the instructions of the CUT. Silently he poured our last can of petrol, reserved for emergencies like this, into the car and as he did so, I saw one of our neighbours, a pilot of the National Airline, look over the balcony of his house and shout something mocking at Victor, who replied with a smile.

It was impossible to say good-bye properly. If we had done so I should have held on to him and never let him go, so we were casual. 'Mamita, I'll be back as soon as I can . . . you know I have to go . . . just be calm.' 'Chao,' . . . and when I looked again, Victor had gone.

Listening to the radio, between one military march and another, I heard the announcements. '*Bando Numero Uno . . . Bando Numero Dos*' . . . military orders announcing that Allende had been given an ultimatum to surrender by the commanders of the Armed Forces led by General Augusto Pinochet . . . that unless he surrendered by midday the Moneda Palace would be bombed.

Monica was preparing the lunch, and Amanda and Carola were playing in the garden, when suddenly there was the thunder and whine of a diving jet plane and then a tremendous explosion. It was like being in the war again . . . I rushed out to bring the children indoors, closed the wooden shutters and convinced them that it was all a game. But the jets kept on diving and it seemed that the rockets they were firing were falling on the población just above us towards the mountains. I think it was at this moment that any illusions that I may have had died in me . . . if this was what we were up against, what hope could there be?

Then came the helicopters, low over the treetops of the garden. From the balcony of our bedroom I saw them, hovering like sinister insects, raking Allende's house with machine-gun fire. High above, towards the cordillera, another plane circled. We could hear the high whine of its engine for hours on end – the control plane, perhaps?

Soon after, the telephone rings. I rush to answer it and hear Victor's voice, 'Mamita, how are you? I couldn't get to the phone before . . . I'm here in the Technical University . . . You know what's happening, don't you?' I tell him about the dive bombers, but that we are all well. 'When are you coming home?' 'I'll ring you later on . . . the phone is needed now . . . chao.'

Then there is nothing to do but to listen to the radio, to the military pronouncements between one march and another. The neighbours are outside in the patio, talking excitedly, some are standing on their balconies to get a better view of the attack on Allende's house . . . they are bringing out the drinks . . . one house has even put out a flag.

We listen to the news of the Moneda Palace being bombed and set on fire . . . we wonder if Allende has survived . . . there is no announcement about it. A curfew is being imposed. Quena rings to know how we are and I tell her that Victor isn't here, that he has gone to the university. 'Oh, my God!' she exclaims and rings off.

We have to assume now that all the telephones are tapped, but Victor rings about four-thirty. 'I have to stay here . . . it will be difficult to get back because of the curfew. I'll come home first thing in the morning when the curfew is lifted . . . Mamita, I love you.'

'I love you too . . .,' but I choke as I say it and he has already hung up.

I did go to bed that night, but of course I couldn't sleep. All around the neighbourhood in the darkness you could hear sudden bursts of gunfire. I waited for morning wondering if Victor was cold, if he could sleep, wherever he was, wishing that he had taken at least a jacket with him, wondering if, as the curfew had been suddenly postponed until later in the evening, perhaps he had left the university and gone to someone's house nearby.

It was late next morning before the curfew was lifted and the maids trooped out to buy bread at the corner shop. But today the queue was controlled by soldiers who butted people with their guns and threatened them. I longed for Victor to come home, to hear the hum of the car as it drew up under the wistaria. I calculated how long it ought to take him to make the journey from the university . . . As I waited, I realised that there was no money in the house, so I set out to walk the couple of blocks to the little shop belonging to Alberto who had always co-operated with the JAP and might be able to change a cheque for me. On my way, two trucks zoomed past me. They were packed with civilians armed with rifles and machine guns. I realised that they were our local fascists coming out of their holes into the light of day.

Alberto was very scared, and with reason. In the preceding weeks he had already had a couple of bombs exploded outside his shop. But he was good enough to change a cheque for me and asked after Victor. I hurried home, and on my way, bumped into a friend, the wife of one of the members of Inti-Illimani who lived nearby. She was in a state of shock too, and all alone, because Inti were in Europe. By mutual consent she came home with me and didn't leave until several days later. She had been ill the previous day and had not gone to the government department where she worked. Now she was in agony, thinking about what might have happened there and how her colleagues had fared.

Together now we waited, but Victor didn't come. Glued to the television, although near to vomiting with what I saw, seeing the faces of the Generals, talking about 'eradicating the cancer of Marxism' from the country; hearing the official announcement that Allende was dead; seeing the film of the ruins of the Moneda Palace and of Allende's home, endlessly repeated, with shots of his bedroom, his bathroom – or what remained of them – with an 'arsenal of weapons' which seemed pathetically small considering that his detectives had had to protect him against terrorist attacks. It was only late in the afternoon that I heard that the Technical University had been *reducida* – captured – that tanks had entered the university precincts in the morning and that a large number of 'extremists' had been arrested.

My lifeline, although a dubious one because it had ears, was the telephone. I knew that Quena was trying to find out what had happened to Victor. She better than I could try to find out discreetly. I was afraid to act, afraid of identifying Victor before the military authorities. I didn't want to draw attention to him . . . perhaps anyway he had managed to get out of the university before it was attacked . . . that was my hope.

Wednesday night passed, another cold night, bitterly cold for September. The bed was large and empty and there was an agonising vacuum at my side. I slept fitfully and dreamt of Victor's touch, his warm limbs entwined with mine. I woke to empty darkness and in an agony of fear for him . . . I remembered his nightmares.

Next morning, still no news. I tried to phone different people who might know what had happened in the Technical University. Nobody was sure about anything . . . then Quena again . . . she had found out that the detainees from the UTE had been taken to the Estadio Chile, the big boxing stadium where Victor had sung so often and where the Song Festivals had taken place. She wasn't sure if Victor had been among them; the women, most of them, had been released and had given her the news . . . only they weren't absolutely sure that Victor had been arrested with the rest because they had been separated from the men.

In the afternoon the phone rang. Heart jumping, I ran to answer it. An unknown voice, very nervous, asked for Compañera Joan . . . 'Yes, yes,' then there was a message for me: 'Compañera, you don't know me, but I have a message for you from your husband. I've just been released from the Estadio Chile . . . Victor is there . . . he asked me to tell you that you should be calm and stay in the house with the children . . . that he left the car outside the Technical University in the car park, if maybe, someone can fetch it for you . . . he doesn't think that he will be released from the stadium.'

'But compañero, thank you for ringing me, but what did he mean by that?'

'That is what he told me to tell you. Good luck, compañera!' and he hung up.

When Quena rang a few minutes later, I gave her the news. She began to do everything she could to find out more, to find out what would be the best way of trying to get Victor out. She even went to see Cardinal Silva Henriquez, asking him to intervene. What immobilised me was the fear of identifying Victor, if they had not already done so, his own instructions to me, which I assumed were for the best, and my blind faith in the power and organisation of the Communist Party which would, I thought, know the best way of saving people like Victor.

Even now, at this stage, I had no real idea of the horrors that were taking place. We were deprived of news and information, although rumours were rife. A responsible political leader phoned me to tell me that General Prats was advancing from the north with an army . . . this must be the beginning of the civil war about which we had been warned. (Only later did we learn that General Prats had been imprisoned and that, during the night of 10 September, even before the coup really began, there had been a purge of all officers suspected of supporting Allende's government.)

During the short time the curfew was lifted on Friday, I decided to make the journey across Santiago to fetch the car. I thought we ought to have it in case it were necessary to leave home in a hurry. It was

my first excursion outside our neighbourhood and in the midday sun
everything looked unnaturally normal: the buses were running again,
there was food in the shops. The only abnormality was the number of
soldiers in the streets, at every corner, but there were plenty of people
about, walking hurriedly, their faces emptied of expression. As the bus
made its slow way along the Alameda, we passed the Moneda Palace –
or rather the shell of it, roped off from the square. Many people were
passing up and down in front of it, I suppose with curiosity to see the
results of the bombing and the fire, but no one showed any feelings
at all, either of rage and sadness or of satisfaction.

Central Station and the stalls outside were as busy as ever. I got off
the bus and hesitated on the corner of the side road leading to the
Estadio Chile. I stood looking at the crowd of people outside, the
guards with their machine guns at the ready. It was impossible to get
near it, but anyway, what could I do? I walked the few blocks to the
Technical University . . . the campus and the new modern building
were strangely deserted . . .

And then I realise that the great plate-glass windows and doors are all
broken, the façade of the building damaged and bullet-scarred. The
car park in front, usually full to overflowing, is empty except for our
little car looking solitary in the middle of it. There must be military
guards about, but I don't notice them. I see only an old man sitting
on a wall some distance away. I put one foot in front of the other until
I reach the car, fumbling for my keys, and I find that I am stepping in
a pool of blood which is seeping from under the car . . . that where
there should be a window there is nothing . . . the car is full of broken
glass. I think, 'This can't be ours' and begin to try the keys to see if
they fit. Then I see that the old man is walking towards me. 'Who
are you?' he shouts at me. 'This is my car,' I stutter at him. 'This is
my husband's car. He left it here.' 'That's all right then,' the old man
says. 'I was looking after it for Don Victor. Look, I found his identity
card on the ground. You'd better have it,' and he passes it to me.

'But where did all the blood come from, whose blood is it?' I ask.

'Oh, I expect someone knifed a thief who was trying to steal it. A lot
of blood has been spilt around here lately. You'd better go as quickly as
you can. It's not safe.' And he helps me clean the broken glass from
the car seats so that I can drive it and sees me on my way.

★   ★   ★

That was Friday. I don't know how I got through Saturday. People phoned me. I phoned people. Marta came to see me. Angel had been arrested and taken to the National Stadium. Bad news of other friends came to me. The Popular Unity leaders were all detained or in hiding, being hunted like criminals. Other friends had disappeared.

As I lay down on the bed on Saturday night – I can't say to sleep – staring at the ceiling through the long hours of the night, a different sort of cold hopelessness began to seep over me. Suddenly, with my heart thudding, I sat up abruptly. Victor wasn't there.

As soon as it was light I went to the wardrobe and began to get out clothes which I had not used for ages . . . respectable, Marks & Spencer clothes, which would make me look like a foreigner. I put my hair up, put dark glasses on and tried to steel myself to go to the British Embassy to ask them to help Victor. It was too early, of course. I had to wait for the curfew to end. As it was Sunday, I had to find the Ambassador's residence rather than go to the Embassy itself in the centre. It was one of those large mansions of the barrio alto with high wrought-iron gates and railings, closed and with a police guard outside. No sign of life. I rang the bell and waited until one of the servants came out. 'I am a British subject. I need help.'

I thought that he would open the gate, but no. He told me to wait. I waited. The police outside were looking me over. I wondered if I looked British enough. Then the main door of the mansion opened and a very obviously British young man approached the gates. 'Oh, sorry about all this cloak and dagger stuff. Orders from above, you know. What can I do for you?'

I told him in incoherent and stuttering English, which wouldn't come out properly, that my husband was in the Estadio Chile, that I feared desperately for his safety and could they help me. Peering at me through the firmly locked gates, he said, 'Oh, but is he a British subject? You know we can't do anything if he is not British.' 'No, he's Chilean, but I fear that he may be in special danger, because he is a well-known person. Please see if you can do anything to get him out . . . if they know that the British Embassy is concerned about him, perhaps it will be better.'

'Well, I don't think that there is very much we can do, but under the circumstances, perhaps the most appropriate thing would be for our Naval Attaché to make enquiries about him with the military authorities. I'll see what we can do . . . I can't promise anything. I'll ring you if I have any news.'

So I came home, wondering if I had done the right thing, hoping that I hadn't betrayed Victor. If he had thrown away his identity card it was because he hoped he wouldn't be recognised. *Unless he were already dead*.

Monday is a blank. I suppose I went through the motions of being alive. By military decree we must put the flags out tomorrow, to celebrate Chile's Independence Day, Fiestas Patrias.

Tuesday, 18 September

About an hour after the curfew is lifted, I hear the noise of the gate being rattled, as though someone is trying to get in. It is still locked . . . I look out of the bathroom window and see a young man standing outside. He looks harmless, so I go down. He says to me very quietly, 'I am looking for the compañera of Victor Jara. Is this the house? Please trust me – I am a friend,' and he brings out his identity card to show me. 'May I come in for a minute? I need to talk to you.' He looks nervous and worried. He whispers, 'I am a member of the Communist Youth.'

I open the gate to let him in and we sit down in the living room opposite each other. 'I'm sorry, I had to come and find you . . . I'm afraid I have to tell you that Victor is dead . . . his body has been found in the morgue. He was recognised by one of the compañeros working there. Please, be brave, you must come with me to see if it is him . . . was he wearing dark-blue underpants? You must come, because his body has already been there almost forty-eight hours and unless it is claimed they will take him away and bury him in a common grave.'

Half an hour later, I found myself driving like a zombie through the streets of Santiago, this unknown young man at my side. Hector, as he was called, had been working in the city morgue for the last week, trying to identify some of the anonymous bodies that were being brought in every day. He was a kind, sensitive young man and he was risking a great deal in coming to find me. As an employee, he had a special identity card and showing it, he ushered me into a small side entrance of the morgue, an unprepossessing building just a few yards from the gates of the General Cemetery.

Even in a state of shock, my body continues to function. Perhaps from outside I look very normal and controlled . . . my eyes continue to see, my nose to smell, my legs to walk . . .

We go down a dark passageway and emerge into a large hall. My new friend puts his hand on my elbow to steady me as I look at rows and rows of naked bodies covering the floor, stacked up into heaps in the corners, most with gaping wounds, some with their hands still tied behind their backs . . . there are young and old . . . there are hundreds of bodies . . . most of them look like working people . . . hundreds of bodies, being sorted out, being dragged by the feet and put into one pile or another, by the people who work in the morgue, strange silent figures with masks across their faces to protect them from the smell of decay. I stand in the centre of the room, looking and not wanting to look for Victor, and a great wave of rage assaults me. I know that incoherent noises of protest come from my mouth, but immediately Hector reacts. 'Ssh! You mustn't make any sign . . . otherwise we shall get into trouble . . . just stay quiet a moment. I'll go and ask where we should go. I don't think this is the right place.'

We are directed upstairs. The morgue is so full that the bodies overflow to every part of the building, including the administrative offices. A long passage, rows of doors, and on the floor a long line of bodies, these with clothes, some of them look more like students, ten, twenty, thirty, forty, fifty . . . and there in the middle of the line I find Victor.

It was Victor, although he looked thin and gaunt . . . What have they done to you to make you waste away like that in one week? His eyes were open and they seemed still to look ahead with intensity and defiance, in spite of a wound on his head and terrible bruises on his cheek. His clothes were torn, trousers round his ankles, sweater rucked up under his armpits, his blue underpants hanging in tatters round his hips as though cut by a knife or bayonet . . . his chest riddled with holes and a gaping wound in his abdomen. His hands seemed to be hanging from his arms at a strange angle as though his wrists were broken . . . but it was Victor, my husband, my lover.

Part of me died at that moment too. I felt a whole part of

me die as I stood there. Immobile and silent, unable to move, speak.

He should have disappeared. It was only because his face was recognised among hundreds of anonymous bodies that he was not buried in a common grave and I should never have known what had happened to him. I was grateful to the worker who drew attention to him, to young Hector – he was only nineteen – who decided to take the risk of coming to find me, who had searched for and found my name and address in the records of *Identificaciones*, asking co-operation of other people in the Identity Bureau. Everyone had helped.

Now it was necessary to claim Victor's body legally. The only way was to take him immediately from the morgue to the cemetery and to bury him . . . those were the regulations. They made me go home and fetch my marriage certificate. So once more, this time alone, I had to drive across Santiago, now decked with flags for the celebration of Independence Day. I could say nothing to my children yet . . . the morgue was no place for them, but my friends had been calling, students, wanting to know how we were. One insisted on accompanying me, a good friend who called himself a momio. By strange coincidence his name was also Hector.

The paper work, complying with all the regulations, took hours. At three o'clock in the afternoon I was still waiting in the courtyard leading to the basement of the morgue where I was told that Victor's body would be released. Other women were here now, scanning the useless lists that were posted outside which gave just a number, sex, 'no name', found in such and such an area. And as I waited, every few minutes, through the gate from the street came a closed military vehicle with a red cross painted on its side, driving down into the basement, obviously to unload another batch of corpses, and out again to search for more.

At last everything was ready. With the coffin on a trolley we were ready to cross the road to the cemetery. As we came to the gate we met a military vehicle coming in with more corpses – someone would have to give way. The driver hooted and made furious gestures at us but we stood there silently until he backed out and let Victor's coffin pass.

It must have taken twenty minutes or half an hour to make the long walk to the very end of the cemetery where Victor was to be buried. The trolley squeaked and rattled over the uneven ground.

We went on and on, Hector, my new friend, on one side, Hector, my old friend, on the other. Only when Victor's coffin disappeared into the niche that had been allotted to us did I almost collapse. But I was without feeling or sensation, only the thought of Manuela and Amanda at home, wondering what was happening, wondering where I was, kept me alive.

The next day, the newspaper *La Segunda* published a tiny paragraph which announced Victor's death as though he had passed away peacefully in his bed: 'The funeral was private, only relatives were present.' Then the order came through to the media not to mention Victor again. But on the television, someone risked his life to insert a few bars of 'La plegaria' over the sound-track of an American film.

12

AN UNFINISHED SONG

It took me months, even years, to piece together something of what happened to Victor during the week that for me he was 'missing'. Many people could not even speak about their experiences, were afraid to testify, could not bear to remember. Under such horrendous pressure and suffering people lost the sense of time and even of which day of the week events occurred. But gradually, by collecting evidence from Chilean refugees in exile who shared experiences with Victor, were with him at given moments, I have managed to reconstruct, roughly, what he endured while I waited for him at home.

When he reached Plaza Italia on the morning of 11 September, Victor found that the centre of Santiago had been sealed off by the military, so he turned south down Vicuña McKenna and then west again along Avenida Matta, thus making a wide detour to reach the campus of the Technical University on the far side of the city. He saw the movement of tanks and troops, heard the shooting and explosions, but managed to get through. When he arrived at the Department of Communications he learnt that the radio station of the university had been attacked and taken off the air very early that morning by a contingent of armed men from the nearby naval radio station in the Quinta Normal. He must have arrived just about the time that the Moneda Palace was being bombed. From the university buildings it was possible to see the Hawker Hunter jets, to hear the rockets explode as they landed on the Moneda Palace where Allende was holding out and to see the smoke rising from the ruins as the building was destroyed by fire. Soon afterwards, Victor managed to get his turn on an overworked telephone to tell me that he had arrived safely and to ask how we were getting on.

There were about six hundred students and teachers gathered in the Technical University that morning. At the opening ceremony, President Allende was to have made an important speech announcing his decision to hold a national plebiscite to resolve by democratic means the conflict threatening the country.

As the first military *bandos* threatened that people on the streets were in danger of being shot and killed and that a curfew was to be enforced from the early hours of the afternoon, Dr Enrique Kirberg, the Rector of the University, negotiated with the military for the people gathered there to stay put all night for their own safety, until the curfew was lifted the next day. This was agreed upon and orders were given for everyone to remain within the university buildings. It was then that Victor must have phoned me for the second time. He didn't tell me that the whole campus was surrounded by tanks and troops.

Through the long hours of the evening, listening to the explosions and heavy machine-gun fire all around the neighbourhood, they tell me that Victor tried to raise the spirits of the people around him. He sang and got them to sing with him. They had no arms to defend themselves. Then in the staff room of the old building of the Escuela de Artes y Oficios, Victor tried to get some sleep.

All night long the machine-gun fire continued. Some people who tried to get out of the university under cover of darkness were shot outright but it was not until early next morning that the assault began in earnest, with the tanks firing their heavy guns against the buildings, damaging the structure of some, shattering windows and destroying laboratories, equipment, books. There was no answering fire because there were no guns inside.

After the tanks had crashed into the university precincts, the troops proceeded to herd all the people, including the Rector, out into a large courtyard normally used for sport. Using rifle butts and boots to kick and beat people, they forced everyone to lie on the ground, hands on the back of their heads. Victor lay there with the others, perhaps it was on the way out of the building that he had got rid of his identity card in the hope that he might not be recognised.

After lying there for more than an hour, they were made to get into single file and trot, still with their hands on their heads, to the Estadio Chile, about six blocks away, subjected to insults, kicks and blows on the way. It was when they were lining up outside the stadium that Victor was first recognised by one of the non-commissioned officers. 'You're that fucking singer, aren't you?' and he hit Victor on the head, felling him, then kicking him in the stomach and ribs. Victor was separated from the others as they entered the building and put into a special gallery, reserved for 'important' or 'dangerous' prisoners. His friends saw him from afar, remember the wide smile that he flashed at them from across the horror that they were witnessing, in spite of a bloody face and a wound in his head. Later they saw him curl up across the seats, his hands tucked beneath his armpits against the penetrating cold.

Some time next morning, Victor evidently decided to try to leave his isolated position and join the other prisoners. Another witness, who was waiting in the passageway outside, saw the following scene. As Victor pushed the swing doors to come out into the passageway, he almost bumped into an army officer who seemed to be the second-in-command of the Stadium. He had been very busy shouting over the microphone, giving orders, screaming threats. He was tall, blond and rather handsome and was obviously enjoying the role he was playing as he strutted about. Some of the prisoners had already nicknamed him 'the Prince'.

As Victor came face to face with him, he gave a sign of recognition and smiled sarcastically. Mimicking playing a guitar, he giggled and then quickly drew his finger across his throat. Victor remained calm and made some gesture in reply, but then the officer shouted, 'What is this bastard doing here?' He called the guards who were following him and said, 'Don't let him move from here. This one is reserved for me!'

Later, Victor was transferred to the basement where there are glimpses of him in a passageway, there where he had so often prepared to sing, now lying, covered in blood, on a floor running with urine and excrement overflowing from the toilet.

In the evening he was brought back into the main part of the Stadium to join the other prisoners. He could scarcely walk, his head and his face were bloody and bruised, one of his ribs seemed to be broken and he was in pain where he had been kicked in the stomach. His friends wiped his face and tried to make him more comfortable. One of them had a small jar of jam and some biscuits. They shared the food between three or four of them, dipping their fingers into the jam one after the other and licking every vestige of it.

The next day, Friday 14 September, the prisoners were divided into groups of about two hundred, ready to be transferred to the National Stadium. It was then that Victor, slightly recovered, asked his friends if anyone had a pencil and paper and began to write his last poem. Some of the worst horrors of the military coup took place in the Estadio Chile in those first days before it was visited by the Red Cross, Amnesty International or any representative of a foreign embassy. (In spite of legal proceedings and inquiries by lawyers, I have never been able to discover the names of the officers who were in command of the Estadio Chile.)

Thousands of prisoners were kept for days, with virtually no food or water; glaring spotlights were focused on them constantly so that they lost all sense of time and even of day and night; machine guns were set up all around the Stadium and were fired intermittently either at the ceiling or over the heads of the prisoners; orders and threats were blared over loudspeakers; the commanding officer was a corpulent man and only his silhouette could be seen as he warned that the machine guns were nicknamed 'Hitler's saws' because they could cut a man in half . . . and would do so as necessary. Prisoners were called out one by one, made to move from one part of the Stadium to another. It was impossible to rest. People were mercilessly beaten with whips and rifle butts. One man who could no longer bear it threw himself over the balcony and plunged to his death among the prisoners below. Others had attacks of madness and were gunned down in full view of everybody.

As Victor scribbled, he was trying to record, for the world to know, something of the horror that had been let loose in Chile. He could only testify to his 'small corner of the city', where five thousand people were imprisoned, could only imagine what must be happening in the rest of his country. He must have realised the monstrous scale of the military operation, the precision with which it had been prepared.

In those last hours of his life, deep roots of his peasant childhood made him see the military as 'midwives', whose coming was the signal for screams and what had seemed to him, as a child, unbearable suffering. Now these visions became confused with the torture and the sadistic smile of the Prince. But even then, Victor still had hope for the future, confidence that people were stronger, in the end, than bombs and machine guns . . . and as he came to the last verses, for which he already had music inside him – 'How hard it is to sing, when I must sing of horror . . .' – he was interrupted. A group of guards came to fetch him, to separate him from those who were about to be transferred to the National Stadium. He quickly passed the scrap of paper to a compañero who was sitting beside him, who in turn hid it in his sock as he was taken away. His friends had tried each one of them to learn the poem by heart as it was written, so as to carry it out of the Stadium with them. They never saw Victor again.

In spite of the fact that large numbers were transferred to other prison camps, the Estadio Chile remained full because more and more prisoners were constantly arriving, both men and women. I have two more glimpses of Victor in the Stadium, two more testimonies . . . a message for me brought out by someone who was near him for some hours, down in the dressing rooms, converted now into torture chambers, a message of love for his daughters and for me . . . then once more being publicly abused and beaten, the officer nicknamed the Prince shouting at him, on the verge of hysteria, losing control of himself, 'Sing now, if you can, you bastard!' and Victor's voice raised in the Stadium after those four days of suffering to sing a verse of the hymn of Popular Unity, 'Venceremos'. Then he was beaten down and dragged away for the last phase of his agony.

The boxing stadium lies within a few yards of the main railway line to the south, which, on its way out of Santiago, passes through the working-class district of San Miguel, along the boundary wall of the Metropolitan Cemetery. It was here, early in the morning of Sunday 16 September, that the people of the población found six dead bodies, lying in an orderly row. All had terrible wounds and had been machine-gunned to death. They looked from face to face, trying to recognise the corpses and suddenly one of the women cried out, 'This is Victor Jara!' – it was a face which was both known and dear to them. One of the women even knew Victor personally because when he had visited the población to sing, she had invited him into her home to eat a plate of beans. Almost immediately, while they were wondering what to do, a covered van approached. The people of the población quickly hid behind a wall, in fear, but watched while a group of men in plain clothes began dragging the corpses by the feet and throwing them into the van. From here Victor's body must have been transferred to the city morgue, an anonymous corpse, ready to

disappear into a mass grave. But once again, he was recognised – by
one of the people who worked there.

When later the text of his last poem was brought to me, I knew that
Victor wanted to leave his testimony, his only means now of resisting
fascism, of fighting for the rights of human beings and for peace.

> There are five thousand of us here
> in this small part of the city.
> We are five thousand.
> I wonder how many we are in all
> in the cities and in the whole country?
> Here alone
> are ten thousand hands which plant seeds
> and make the factories run.
> How much humanity
> exposed to hunger, cold, panic, pain,
> moral pressure, terror and insanity?
> Six of us were lost
> as if into starry space.
> One dead, another beaten as I could never have believed
> a human being could be beaten.
> The other four wanted to end their terror –
> one jumping into nothingness,
> another beating his head against a wall,
> but all with the fixed stare of death.
> What horror the face of fascism creates!
> They carry out their plans with knife-like precision.
> Nothing matters to them.
> To them, blood equals medals,
> slaughter is an act of heroism.
> Oh God, is this the world that you created,
> for this your seven days of wonder and work?
> Within these four walls only a number exists
> which does not progress,
> which slowly will wish more and more for death.
> But suddenly my conscience awakes
> and I see that this tide has no heartbeat,
> only the pulse of machines
> and the military showing their midwives' faces

full of sweetness.
Let Mexico, Cuba and the world
cry out against this atrocity!
We are ten thousand hands
which can produce nothing.
How many of us in the whole country?
The blood of our President, our compañero,
will strike with more strength than bombs and machine guns!
So will our fist strike again!

How hard it is to sing
when I must sing of horror.
Horror which I am living,
horror which I am dying.
To see myself among so much
and so many moments of infinity
in which silence and screams
are the end of my song.
What I see, I have never seen
What I have felt and what I feel
will give birth to the moment . . .

Estadio Chile
September 1973

13

AFTERMATH

I shall never forget Amanda's scream when I had to break the news to her that *el Papi* was dead, just as I shall never forget Manuela's maturity beyond her years, her courage, and the support that she gave me, seeming to understand how much I needed it.

Quena was waiting for me when I returned home from the cemetery. She stayed with me from then on, sleeping in the house, accompanying me. She had to borrow my clothes, I remember, because she had brought none with her and she couldn't return to her own flat which was under observation.

One of the first phone calls was from the young man from the Embassy, now suddenly really shocked and concerned, surprised out of his jocular coolness. I was offered any help I might need, but for the moment I could think of nothing at all.

Soon afterwards, perhaps the next day, he phoned me again to ask if I would be willing to give an interview to David Wigg, a journalist working for *The Times*. Having accepted the idea, I had to go downtown to the Embassy building which was considered a safe place for such an interview to take place, and for the first time I was interrogated about how I had found Victor's body and what I had seen in the city morgue. The article, with the headline '*British woman found her husband's bullet-riddled body in Santiago mortuary after army coup*', appeared some days later, on 28 September.

Meanwhile I received a visit from a portly gentleman who brought me, verbally, the condolences of the Ambassador and a letter with a seal which informed whomever it might concern that I was a British subject with the right to get in touch with the Embassy in any emergency – a letter which we kept in a prominent place in the living room, in case of unwelcome visitors. Just as he was about to leave, the messenger from the Embassy conveyed to me the concern of the Ambassador about the 'indiscretion' of giving interviews to the press. No doubt the Foreign Office was anxious to give the idea that all was well in Chile, as they planned to recognise the military junta as quickly as possible.

It is not surprising, I suppose, that our friends became nervous about our safety, but I think the magic of a British passport and the fact that the Embassy had already acted on my behalf, protected us. Our house seemed a relatively safe place. This, anyway, is what we felt, when Patricio appeared one day to see Manuela and to share our grief. He was in hiding, sleeping in a different house every night, because he was on the list of 'wanted' people, together with hundreds of others, including men and women who only a week or so previously had been ministers of a legal government, elected senators, deputies and local councillors. Now they were being hunted like criminals.

Patricio had been in the Faculty on 11 September. Like other university buildings, it had come under attack and had been entered by the military – soldiers in such a state of fear and, at the same time, a kind of exaltation, that their actions were excessively violent and completely abnormal, as though they had been drugged.

Gathered in the Faculty were people who worked there, dancers, musicians, administrative and ancillary workers with not a weapon between them. In spite of repeated searches, both before and after the coup, no arms were found in the Faculty, indeed, there never had been any, but Patricio and the other people in authority in the Faculty were supposed to be responsible for a mythical store of illegal arms. In addition, the fact that the radio station on the twelfth floor had stayed on the air together with Radio Magallanes, loyal to Allende and the legal government of Chile, until it was occupied by the military, now brought accusations of 'subversion'.

On the Monday following the coup, the military decreed a general return to work. Patricio had not made his position any easier when, on that first day, as Director of the Dance Department, he addressed an assembly in the large ballet studio, condemning the military coup in the strongest terms and paying tribute to Salvador Allende. The great majority of those in the meeting supported him solidly although many were fearful of his outspokenness. But one of the dancers burst into hysterical tears and screamed at him to stop, at the same time rushing to the door, confessing that he would have to denounce Patricio. Apparently he was one of the people who were responsible for drawing up the lists of Allende supporters in the Faculty for the use of the military authorities . . . but even for him it was not easy to denounce a man whom he admired as an artist and who had been his teacher. By that time there could be no illusions about the fate of those who were arrested.

We persuaded Patricio to stay in the house instead of going out again on the streets where he was in danger of being arrested – especially as his identity card had been confiscated on the day of the coup. Meanwhile, we learnt that some of our colleagues in the ballet had been detained and were in the National Stadium – Gaston, whom we had known since he was a little boy, a member of Ballet Popular, two Uruguayan dancers, who had never become involved with Chilean politics, arrested because all Uruguayans and Brazilians were automatically assumed to be extremists – they were badly tortured; the Mexican director of the Chilean National Folk Ballet, Rodolfo Reyes, imprisoned in terrible conditions just because he had worked for a time with the ballet in Cuba. We learned that Angel was still in detention, that Dr Enrique Paris, one of the leaders of the reform movement on the Superior Council of the University of Chile, had disappeared after being arrested in the Moneda Palace – his body was never found. News came from Manuel de Salas that many of the teachers and older students had been arrested . . . and so the nightmare went on.

It seemed best that Patricio should seek asylum in one of the foreign embassies, as many of our friends and colleagues were doing. Most were full to overflowing but it was still possible to get into the Honduras Embassy. One day a fur-coated old lady in a large and luxurious car came to fetch Patricio – the only way to get about without being stopped and questioned was to appear rich and well-dressed. Another friend drove in a car in front, looking out to see that the coast was clear; I brought up the rear in our car – doing what, I wasn't really clear, but in case of any emergency. We had been given the information that at a certain time of day the Embassy was unguarded, and so it was. When Patricio was safely inside the wrought-iron gates, joining the already large group of people in refuge there, I wondered if I would ever see him again. It was as well that he had gone. Afterwards I found out, through the grape-vine of the children, that all the neighbours had known that Patricio was hiding in the house, but none of them had denounced him. Perhaps they felt that we had had enough punishment already.

Only a few days after Victor's lonely funeral, I heard the news of Pablo Neruda's death on 23 September, in a Santiago clinic where he had been brought from Isla Negra. The final crisis in his illness had been brought on by the shock and horror of the military coup. In the midst of the grotesque nightmare we were living through, his death seemed inevitable, almost fitting.

His funeral was announced for 25 September. It was important to go, although many people were afraid of being marked or arrested if they made the public gesture of paying homage to a Communist poet.

When Quena and I arrived, the coffin had already been taken out of the house under the steep slope of San Cristóbal and the cortège was forming, rather confusedly in the narrow street. Matilde, his wife, had been watching over Neruda's body all night long in a house that had been ransacked and damaged by unidentified raiders during the curfew . . . his coffin had lain amidst broken glass and a flood from broken water pipes, books and papers torn and scattered, trampled underfoot.

But hundreds of people had gathered to honour Neruda, in spite of the soldiers lining the streets, machine guns threatening, at the ready, and the secret police scanning the crowd for wanted faces. Quena and I started off fairly near the front of the procession, but gradually lagged further and further behind because I seemed incapable of walking faster; it cost me to put one foot in front of the other. As we walked through the back streets towards the cemetery, I heard Neruda's poetry being recited by one person after another in the crowd, verse after verse, defying the menace of the uniforms surrounding us; I saw the workers on a building site, standing to attention with their yellow helmets in their hands, high above us on a scaffolding; others lined the pavement with the soldiers hemming us in.

'Sube a nacer conmigo, hermano' ('Arise to be born with me, my brother'), and 'Come and see the blood in the streets . . .' Neruda's verses took on an even greater significance as voice after voice took them up, confronting the visible face of fascism. As I walked, I knew

I was not alone, I knew that this was also Victor's funeral and that of all those compañeros who had been massacred by the military, many of them flung anonymously into common graves. The presence of dozens of foreign journalists, film crews, television cameras, protected us from aggression and interference, but as the procession reached the last stage of the march at the rotunda in front of the main gates of the cemetery, a military convoy with armoured trucks rounded it in the opposite direction, looming over us. The crowd responded with cries of 'Compañero Pablo Neruda, presente, ahora y siempre!', 'Compañero Salvador Allende, presente, ahora y siempre!', 'Compañero Victor Jara, presente, ahora y siempre!' and then breaking into 'The Internationale', raggedly, nervously at first, but then with more strength as everyone started to sing. It was Popular Unity's last public demonstration in Chile, the first public demonstration of resistance to a fascist regime.

It was there on that march, among that crowd, that I became aware that although Victor was dead and I was alone, I could never be lonely. There was too strong a sense of collective identity in the face of a collective tragedy, the sense of a people mortally wounded but going on fighting. I became vitally conscious that I had a responsibility to them and to Victor. For me personally – and this was one of the most difficult things to bear – the thought of Victor, instead of being a source of joy and happiness as it always had been, became a cue for pain, for a sense of agony, of unbearable suffering. I knew I had to convert those feelings into a weapon to fight back: not a weapon of hatred, but an assertion of my right to remember Victor's life, so full and creative, rather than his horrifying death . . . and that right would only be mine when he and his songs were beyond the reach of the criminals who had tried to silence him and all that he represented.

As we stood around Neruda's temporary burial place – later his body was to be moved to the back of the cemetery near where Victor lay – listening to the speeches under a grey and overcast sky, many people came up to embrace me, people I didn't know, friends whom I never met again, although the name of at least one of them I found later on the lists of people 'disappeared'.

The Chilean Song Movement had become so identified with Popular Unity, it had been such a strong factor, emotional, cohesive, inspiring, that the military authorities found it necessary to declare 'subversive' even the indigenous instruments, whose beautiful sound had become so full of meaning and inspiration. Together with prohibiting even the mention of Victor's name, they banned all his music and the music of all the artists of the New Chilean Song Movement. They ransacked the headquarters of DICAP, destroying materials and all the master tapes found there, they ordered Odeon:EMI to erase all those in their possession. To be found with records of Victor, of the Parras, of Quilapayún, Inti-Illimani, if the military came to search the house, meant almost certain arrest. Records were thrown, together with books, on bonfires in the streets as the military ransacked blocks of flats and houses, confiscating 'Marxist propaganda'.

The media tried to give the impression that the country was calm and that 'normality' reigned, apart from a few pockets of resistance, snipers and dangerous Marxist extremists on the run. Indeed, superficially in neighbourhoods like ours, one could believe them, except for the sudden bursts of machine-gun fire during the nightly curfew and the military patrols constantly touring the streets, ransacking certain houses and making arrests. Food and other essential goods had miraculously appeared in the shops, brought out from secret stores where they had been hoarded to create artificial shortages. Once again you could buy toilet paper and washing powder. Only the price was different – double or triple the official prices that had been set before.

But in the poblaciones, tanks drove through the alleys, firing indiscriminately into the wooden houses without even bothering to open the doors or to find out if there were children inside.

Every day new corpses were found floating in the Mapocho river or dumped in the gutter in working-class neighbourhoods – perhaps deliberately, to maintain the climate of terror, but also to get rid of the bodies from the prisons and stadiums where the people had been executed.

Among the foreign journalists who contacted me, cautiously, asking for interviews, was a film crew from Swedish Television. Tall, blond men and women, they looked very conspicuous in Santiago, but they were doing work that was both dangerous and useful, filming some of the military operations in the poblaciones, interviewing relatives of the prisoners as they waited fearfully outside the National Stadium, even filming people trying to reach asylum in foreign embassies. Of all the Western European countries, the British Embassy was the only one to keep its doors hermetically sealed against refugees – while the Swedish Ambassador, Harald Edelstam, famous for his work in rescuing refugees from Nazi Germany, was once again literally risking his life to save other people's.

A television interview with me was arranged. I had to go early one morning to a large house, somewhere in the barrio alto. They warned me that it would be dangerous for me to stay in Chile once the programme had been shown. I suppose that interview marked a turning point for me, made me reach the difficult decision to leave my home in Chile. It was also the first time I heard Victor's voice singing 'La plegaria' since his death . . . a voice which accompanied me giving my testimony of his murder . . . and I realised the power of the inheritance that he had left me.

I had to find a means of getting his records and tapes safely out of the country. His last songs had not yet been published, but luckily I had a copy of the master tape of those that had already been recorded. Everyone was ready to help, to get them out by diplomatic means, but there was one frightening moment. I had all the tapes in the car taking them to the people who would take them out of Chile for me, when I was stopped by a military patrol which had blocked the road very near our home. Out of the corner of my eye I saw a group of soldiers dragging a man out of a house, along the garden path. I was asked where I lived and where I was going, but when I put on my best British accent, they let me through with my precious cargo, without further questions. I found myself crying with relief.

Once the decision to go was taken, I had to begin to 'clean' the house for whoever was going to stay there. Nobody could take responsibility for our record collection, with revolutionary songs from all over the world, nor for our books, papers and posters. The military or police were capable of digging up the garden in their search for subversive materials or evidence of Marxism – possession of a book about the Industrial Revolution had caused problems for someone – so it was necessary to embark on the soul-destroying task of burning them . . . my first experience of self-censorship.

Communication with friends was difficult because telephones were tapped, but as word got around that I was preparing to leave Chile, some of the more daring or those who were personally not in difficulties came to see me. I never returned to the Faculty where I had worked for almost twenty years.

One of the most memorable farewells was with a woman from a población whom I had known for many years. She came to say good-bye in the name of many friends of Victor's in her neighbour-hood. She told me how the military had entered the población firing indiscriminately, how they had rounded up all the men and taken them to the stadium. Nobody could find out what was happening to them or for how long they would be detained. She told me, 'What we lacked was hatred. We weren't capable of hatred. Now they have taught us what it means.'

The evening before we took the plane came a last message from Victor, passed along a chain of compañeros, coming originally from a prisoner who had been confined with him in the basement of the stadium at some time during the last hours of his life, when he knew for certain that they were going to kill him and that he would never see us again . . . to tell me that he loved me more than anything in the world and that I should be courageous and carry on his struggle.

Next day, with just a suitcase each, Manuela, Amanda and I left our home to go to the British Embassy where the Consul would be waiting to see us on the plane to London.

The garden was beautiful, the canelo and the mimosa tree were flourishing, soon the wistaria would bloom . . . Monica and Carola stood and waved to us on the doorstep. As the taxi drew out of the courtyard, a schoolfriend of Manuela's whose father had also been killed came rushing to say good-bye . . . 'Please go and tell people outside what is happening!'

EPILOGUE

March 1998

This month we have had to endure the spectacle of Augusto Pinochet, at the age of eighty-two, and on his retirement as Commander-in-Chief of the Chilean Armed Forces, being honoured with a lifelong seat in the Senate. When you consider all that has happened over the last twenty-five years it is difficult to understand, but with this, the transition to democracy is said to be complete.

When we left Chile in December 1973 we thought that within months we should return. We lived for a long time like the rest of the exiled community with our suitcases only half unpacked, anxious for every tiny scrap of news about what was happening in our country.

We were, I think, the first 'Chilean' family to reach England as refugees after the coup. We were surrounded by kindness and formed deep friendships which last to this day. We were given a place to stay, the girls were organised into local schools. By our second night in London we were staying in the house of poet Adrian Mitchell and out of that contact – my outpourings and Adrian's sensitivity – was born a beautiful poem about Victor which Adrian always included in his recitals. It was later put to music by Arlo Guthrie and sung by him and Pete Seeger. I didn't realise at the time that this was only the first of many instances of profound cultural solidarity expressed by artists all over the world in all sorts of media and many languages.

We found ourselves part of an enormous wave of condemnation of the military coup and world-wide solidarity with the people of Chile.

I think that what had happened there shocked many people very profoundly and even changed their view of the world. The coup was like an X-ray which penetrated the surface of society and showed up the real power and brutality beneath. The constant violation of human rights in Chile was an international problem for many years. At the end of 1973 the Chile Committee for Human Rights was founded in London and I became its first President.

We were intimately affected by the continual news we received of the imprisonment, torture, death or disappearance of friends or 'compañeros' of Victor. We were always afraid for Quena who had stayed on in Chile and was working clandestinely with the decimated trade union movement, and also creating a small pocket of cultural resistance with musicians and theatre people. Communication with her was indirect and difficult.

The two musical groups, Quilapayún and Inti–Illimani, had been in Europe at the time of the coup and were to spend the next fifteen years in exile, touring the world with the music of Chile.

In December 1973 the first big concert in tribute to Victor took place in Paris. Almost immediately there was another in Rome, in January one in Berlin, in May one in San Francisco, then Essen, and from then on, for the next decade, I found myself invited to speak at or simply attend events all over the world in solidarity with the people in Chile who were being persecuted as they tried to free the country from military rule. I toured in the United States many times, spent a month travelling all over Japan; I was invited more than once to Australia, New Zealand, the Soviet Union, Finland, Sweden, Denmark, Holland, Belgium, Italy, Spain and to both East and West Germany. These invitations became even more frequent after a British documentary film about Victor called *Compañero* was shown on international television.

Because of the way he died, Victor had become a symbol for so many. Through his music, his songs and his voice – which lived on – he could still communicate with people all over the world. To be instrumental in that communication gave me the strength to want to go on living. He has haunted me all my life, for better or for worse, and I have never been able to think of having another partner.

For the first year we travelled all together. We had no proper home in London and obviously the girls couldn't be left alone. We were a unit of three, sharing all too emotional experiences. For us it was a period of mourning and it was as though the funeral which had been denied to Victor in Chile had extended in both time and place.

However, towards the end of 1974, we had a family meeting and decided that, although I had to go on travelling, Manuela and Amanda would stay in London and continue their regular schooling. By now other Chilean families had arrived; they would no longer feel so lonely. They eventually settled down to complete their secondary education as British schoolgirls even though, perhaps too much, their hearts and thoughts were in Chile and they spent their spare time dancing and singing in a folk group of Chilean exiles which performed in solidarity events.

By 1980, the flood of refugees leaving Chile began to turn around. It wasn't that the situation was any better. On the contrary. But it was necessary to try to fight back. Many of those who couldn't return legally entered the country clandestinely. Some were hunted down and killed. Others with less serious prohibitions applied for passports in the local Chilean consulates and began the difficult and frightening task of trying to re-establish themselves in their own country.

By 1982, Manuela, Amanda and I had each separately taken the decision to return to Chile. Manuela had always known she would go back. Amanda needed to find out where she really belonged and I felt I could be free, after finishing this book, to try to regain something of my own identity and the profession I had always loved. Strangely enough, that meant going back to Victor's country where I was still remembered as myself, a dancer and a teacher, as I was before I became Victor's widow.

It was a period of incipient economic crisis and very heavy repression. There was still a nightly curfew, which was used by the intelligence services for their sinister activities; there were soldiers on the streets and very strict censorship. Opposition leaders or activists were frequently arrested or relegated to distant parts of the country and there were many cold-blooded assassinations. Many atrocities were committed during those years.

In a country where politics was prohibited, politics was everywhere, including in the cemetery. I was on a short-term tourist visa and had been threatened that if I took part in anything political I should be expelled from the country. However, I felt I had the right to believe that to go to a funeral was not a political action but an expression of mourning. There were many massive funerals of victims of the repression which inevitably turned into demonstrations of opposition to the dictatorship and were violently repressed by the riot police with tear gas, water cannons and batons. Blinded and choking you had to run, jumping over the graves to avoid being arrested. I remember the small processions of women, bearing flowers and bravely singing songs of freedom, *a cappella*, making pilgrimages from one grave to another accompanied and threatened by double their number of police. I remember a massive funeral where the police took the extreme measure of kidnapping the coffin on the way to the cemetery in order to disperse the funeral march.

It was a mystery to me how Victor was remembered. Since the coup his very name had been censored, his records prohibited. But in spite of that I heard his songs being sung in poor community centres, in church halls, football clubs and universities, with whole audiences of young people joining in the singing as though his songs had become part of Chilean folklore. His grave was always full of fresh flowers, scraps of paper with messages and poems tucked in among them. Some were almost illiterate, others in foreign languages. Brave singers wrote songs for him, using the indirect language that springs up under extreme censorship.

It was in 1982 that the first big organised protests began. People were still afraid but took courage from each other as they came out on to the streets and began to realise that they were so many. From what I saw, young people and women were in the forefront of these brave demonstrations.

My own first experience of a protest took place in the southern city of Concepción where Manuela was living with her husband and baby son, Victor. It was a winter evening and the buses had stopped running after a day of lighting demonstrations all over the city. Nervous groups of people were gathered on the street corners, silent except for bursts of clapping or whistling to the rhythm of '*Y va a caer*', 'He's going to fall'. In the side streets the police buses and armoured cars were waiting, while the main square was blocked off by the riot police, rows of tall figures with great masked helmets and shiny plastic shields. Then precisely at eight o'clock, as I was passing them, I heard a distant explosion and the street lamps began to flicker and go out. It was the signal that everyone had been waiting for.

There were shouts and cheers and immediately the clattering sound began. From all the surrounding buildings came the sound of saucepan-beating, tentative at first, but growing louder and louder until it was a pandemonium of railings, dustbin lids, anything that came to hand. An almost festive atmosphere began to develop as people competed with noises and rhythms. In the excitement, little Victor, ten months old, took his first tottering steps across the room. Then people started to come out on the street to build barricades to impede the access of the police vehicles. There were shouts and jeers as one tried to cross the barrier. Then a sudden silence as a white Susuki van came slowly against the traffic along the one-way street. People took shelter because from this sort of vehicle came the stray bullets that killed so many people during the protests. As it went slowly around the corner the noise gradually began again, until, perhaps half an hour later, the rumour went around that the army had been called out.

The protests became part of everyday life. They went on for many years, but later there was nothing festive about them. In those first public outbursts of rage, people beat their saucepans as loud and hard as they could, but nothing changed except that some were killed. In the *poblaciones* they began to resort to more violent forms of protest and self-defence. The left-wing parties were training paramilitary groups capable of producing black-outs which affected half of Chile, bomb attacks on banks and other symbolic buildings, assassination of torturers and other members of the security forces, a strategy which culminated in a failed attempt to kill Pinochet by attacking his military escort. If it had succeeded it might have changed the course of Chilean history. The members of the Frente Patriotico Manuel Rodriguez, named after a hero of the Independence, became heroes to many people, murderous terrorists to others.

Against this background of growing violence, combined in a very Chilean way with a severe earthquake, in March 1985 Patricio and I opened an independent, self-supporting dance centre called Espiral. Patricio had at last been allowed to enter his country again after eleven years of exile. I had already been asked by ex-pupils and a large group of young dancers to start teaching again. In a very small studio we set up this refuge for young people who were anxious to learn from us, as legends from the past, and to give free rein to their creativity as dancers or choreographers, which was impossible in the official institutions. A small dance group emerged, a second Ballet Popular, ready to perform in any place or circumstance outside the official circuit. It made its debut with a choreography to Victor's music in the first Victor Jara Festival to be organised in Chile. It gave performances in *poblaciones*, in soup kitchens, mothers' centres, churches and all those places where people were trying to maintain community organisations that enabled them to live and keep hope alive.

Our work was interrupted one Saturday morning. During the nightly curfew someone climbed up the side of the building where we worked and planted an incendiary bomb on the studio floor. Luckily the smoke alerted the night watchman, but the result was an enormous hole in the wooden floor and a fire in the office below. We never really knew if the bomb was for us in particular or for the building in general, because on the ground floor was a café famous for its 'subversive' music. The floor was patched up and within a week we were back at work as though nothing had happened. Indeed, it was a very ordinary occurrence.

It had become 'normal' for a student to arrive with her arm in a sling because she had been beaten up in a demonstration, 'normal' for another to be absent for days because she had been arrested in the university, 'normal' that the students from Población La Victoria were unable to get to class because their district had been surrounded in a concerted police and army action while homes were brutally searched and many people arrested.

There were so many victims. To give only a few examples: Quena's daughter was kidnapped and driven around Santiago in a white Susuki van, being tortured with burning cigarettes on her mouth to make her give information about her colleagues in the Teachers' Union. A young pianist was shot in the head by a police bullet during a demonstration of artists outside the Municipal Theatre. It was years before she could play again. The bodies of three members of the Communist Party, a teacher, a human rights worker and a publicity agent, were found with the throats cut after being kidnapped by the police. A young photographer who had only been in Chile for a few days – his family were exiled in the United States – went out with a friend to take photos during a protest. They were arrested in Población Nogales and intentionally burnt by the police in a barricade. They were dumped in the countryside, far from medical help. Rodrigo Rojas died a few days later. His was the funeral where the police confiscated the coffin. His friend, Carmen Gloria Quintana, survived but she was permanently disfigured. She didn't give in. With 65 per cent of her body burnt, she fought back and converted her scarred face into a living testimony of cruelty.

Living in Chile one realised the real value of international solidarity. It seemed like a protective shield that inhibited even worse atrocities, creating a space, watched over by the vigilant eyes of the world, where people could organise and go on struggling.

In these last stages of the military government the movement of cultural resistance came into its own. Persecuted and driven into marginality, it had existed since very soon after the military coup, when young musicians had used the prohibited indigenous instruments to play Johann Sebastian Bach. It had grown in small, independent theatres, in universities, in tiny *peñas*, and occasionally in increasingly massive events like that organised by Ricardo Garcia as early as 1977 or the three Victor Jara Festivals which took place in the midst of the repression.

In 1988, to legitimise the plebiscite which was supposed to confirm Pinochet as President of Chile, for the first time the government was obliged to allow the opposition a daily spot on national television. All the most important artists of Chile put themselves at the service of the campaign 'No to Pinochet'. It was such a refreshing contrast to the false and stale propaganda that people had had to swallow for so many years that it made a tremendous impact. It was a decisive time which culminated a year later in the election, as President of Chile, of Patricio Alwyn, a Christian Democrat supported by a wide range of political parties including the Socialist Party. Pinochet, according to his own constitution, stayed on as Commander-in-Chief of the Armed Forces.

Here at last was the moment we had all been working for. We were full of illusions about the new democratic government. On a personal level, once again it seemed that the world was upside-down because, if before I was *persona non grata* in Chile, now I was invited to the celebrations in the Moneda Palace. A piano version of 'Te recuerdo Amanda' was played to open the symbolic cultural event in the National Stadium where the new President and his wife, two human beings, walked hand in hand across the football pitch to take their seats on the stands. In that place which had been a concentration camp it seemed like the symbol of a new era, dominated by human values of kindness, solidarity and justice.

If that new era didn't come immediately it probably was no one's fault. It was as though, after a tremendous marathon, those who had taken part just needed to relax, to opt out and get on with their own lives. The common goal which had united everyone had apparently been reached and sectarianism began to divide the groups that had worked together. The spontaneous organisations in the *poblaciones* collapsed and there was nothing else yet to take their place.

The Rettig Commission, an official inquiry into the human rights violations that had resulted in death during Pinochet's regime, fostered hope that those responsible would be identified and punished so that it could never happen again. But although a report was published and the closest relatives of those who had been killed were awarded state pensions, nothing else happened.

The sense of disillusion had to be overcome and I had two obsessions which wouldn't leave me in peace. One was the idea of collective action which would restore the Chile Stadium as a place one could enter in peace, and as a tribute to all who had died and suffered there to cleanse it of the horror it had seen. So many people couldn't bear to enter it, least of all the survivors of those who had been imprisoned there.

There was an immediate response to the idea and after weeks of preparation this purification ceremony eventually took place on the 4th and 5th of April 1991. We called it CANTO LIBRE. Literally hundreds of artists, amateurs and professionals, of different disciplines and social classes, worked together to create it. Musicians, actors, writers, dancers, muralists, choreographers, puppet-makers and poets put themselves gladly at the service of this collective effort.

It was a great act of love and solidarity, shared between the many friends abroad who with their financial support made it possible, the artists who gave the best of themselves, and the six thousand people who crammed into the Stadium to participate with us. When Victor's last unfinished poem was recited for the first time publicly in that place it really felt that 'the moment' which was Victor's last cry of hope was being born. Perhaps we would be able to finish his song.

After CANTO LIBRE my other obsession became even more acute and seemed more possible to fulfil. It was to create a foundation bearing Victor's name. The state pension awarded to me by the Rettig Commission helped. I didn't want it as a substitute for justice, but it could be put to good use in a foundation which, after seventeen years of censorship, did justice to his memory and preserved the rich heritage of his work for future generations.

Today the Victor Jara Foundation is a reality. Symbolically it was born in a remote part of Chile among an indigenous Pehuenche community who are struggling to maintain their own cultural identity and the native forests of Araucarias which for them are sacred.

A unique archive has developed out of those two suitcases that we took with us to London in 1973. It is still growing. As well as Victor's work it contains the testimony of twenty-five years of international cultural solidarity. Young people come there to study and in this age of globalisation we like to think that it helps them to value their own cultural identity.

Chile is still bound by the constitution invented during Pinochet's dictatorship where the Senate is weighted by designated, unelected senators, among them other ex-generals who were his comrades-in-arms at the time of the military coup. This in itself makes it impossible to change the constitution. Now in March 1998, as Pinochet, who destroyed democracy in Chile, takes his place in the Senate, it is no wonder that there have been protests and marches all over the country. Apart from the ever present human rights organisations, like the relatives of the disappeared prisoners, the great majority of those taking part have been young, under thirty years old. A large percentage of this generation has not enrolled on the electoral register because it has no faith in this 'democracy' and repudiates an economic system where the gap between rich and poor is greater than ever before.

Immense fortunes were amassed during Pinochet's regime by that small group of his supporters who profited from the free-market system, untrammelled by democracy. The same group still wield the economic power, own or control the mass media and have the lifestyle of the international jet set. Of course, the benefits of these riches have not 'trickled down' to the poorest level of the population which still lives in extreme hardship and deprivation.

We have had nine years of this so-called democracy, but to this day the great majority of the disappeared prisoners have never been found, the torturers and murderers have not been punished, and an amnesty has protected even the known perpetrators of the crimes that were committed. I have never been able to find out who was directly responsible for ordering Victor's execution. The society we live in has deep wounds which cannot heal without justice being seen to be done, even though many Chileans do not wish to know what really happened or want simply to forget. There used to be much talk about pardon and reconciliation. I have been asked many times if I still bear a grudge against those responsible for Victor's death and I can only answer that although it is impossible to live with hatred, it is also impossible to forgive when no one has asked for forgiveness nor shown any sign of repentance. Chile is still a very divided country.

But in spite of everything we are still here. Manuela is living and working in Santiago. She formed a street-dance group in Concepción, but now teaches dance and has taken over the direction of the Espiral. Her partner is one of those 'subversive' musicians who sang against the military regime. She has recovered from cancer of the thyroid and has four lovely sons, five cats and a tortoise. In her 'spare' time she makes furniture.

Amanda has become a painter. She lives and works in a fishing village near Valparaiso where she has a little wooden house overlooking a rocky beach. Her partner is a fisherman. She paints the landscapes and the people around her, grows vegetables, makes quince cheese and rosehip jam, washes clothes in a wooden tub and cooks Chilean food. She has three enormous dogs, Victor's smile and a great sense of humour.

I live alone in our same 'little box' but now, instead of having a wonderful view of the Andes mountains, I am surrounded by high-rise apartment buildings and smog. Manuela hassles me to go on teaching and the Foundation gives me plenty to do.

Patricio is the Director of our University Dance Course, recognised by the Ministry of Education, and is writing a book about dance. Quena, who has always been close to us, is working for the Foundation. She should also be writing a book.

The future is up to the grandchildren now, together with all those young people out there capable of working for a better society. It's important that they know about the past so that they can learn from our misjudgements. I think that they will probably manage better than we did. For the sake of the human race I hope they will.

GLOSSARY

adobe – bricks or walls of tightly compressed mud, a common form of building in the drier parts of Latin America.

Alameda – alternative name for the Avenida Bernardo O'Higgins, which is the main street of Santiago, named after the man who liberated Chile from the Spanish.

altiplano – high plateau of the Andes, mainly in Bolivia and Peru, ranging from about 6,000 to 12,000 feet.

anticucho – a Latin American kebab.

arrollado – highly spiced, rolled cooked meat, in the south of Chile usually pork.

Barrancas – working-class district of Santiago.

barrio alto – 'high neighbourhood' – the wealthy eastern side of Santiago, rising towards the Andes foothills.

bombo – type of drum used in the north of Chile.

brasero – open brazier or iron dish for burning charcoal.

BRP – Brigada Ramona Parra, the wall-painting brigade of the Young Communist League.

canto a lo divino, canto a lo humano, canto por travesura – three categories of folk-song, 'divino' dealing with religious topics, 'humano' with earthly ones, and 'por travesura' for ribald entertainment.

charango – tiny stringed instrument with sound-box made from the shell of an armadillo, used in the music of the altiplano.

chicha – semi-fermented liquor like beer, made from apples, grapes or maize; apple chicha like cider.

chuico – five- or ten-litre bottle of wine, usually in a basket-container.

coligüilla – nickname for prostitute.

CORA – Corporación de la Reforma Agraria, the organisation responsible for implementing land reform.

corrido – type of dance.

cuatro – four-stringed small guitar from Venezuela.

cueca – national dance of Chile.

cumbia – type of dance.

curanto – traditional dish of meat and seafood, steamed slowly in a hole in the ground lined with hot stones.

CUT – Central Unica de Trabajadores de Chile, equivalent to the TUC in Britain, founded in 1953, to which the great majority of trade unions in Chile were affiliated.

DICAP – Discoteca del Cantar Popular, the recording company and label of the New Chilean Song Movement.

empanada – highly seasoned Chilean meat pasty with onion, raisins, olives and boiled egg.

FECH – Federación de Estudiantes de la Universidad de Chile, the national union of students of the University of Chile.

Fiestas Patrias – 18 and 19 September, Chile's Independence Day holiday.

fonda – temporary shelter erected in the open air, usually to make a bar or café, especially during Fiestas Patrias, and in rural districts for the local fair.

gañan – farm labourer (too poor to own a horse).

gringo – foreigner of European or North American origin, usually fair-haired.

Grupo Movil – specially trained riot squad of the Chilean police.

huaso – farmer or farm overseer on horseback.

ICTUS – independent theatre company in Santiago.

inquilino – permanent as opposed to seasonal farm labourer on landed estate, living in tied cottage.

ITUCH – Instituto de Teatro de la Universidad de Chile, Theatre Institute belonging to the University of Chile.

JAP – Junta de Abastecimiento y Precios, neighbourhood-based price control and distribution organisations formed during the Popular Unity period to combat the black market.

Jota – JJCC, the Juventudes Comunistas de Chile, the Young Communist League.

latifundio – large, landed estate.

Ley Maldita – 'The Accursed Law', nickname for a law passed by President Gabriel Gonzalez Videla at the start of the Cold War, which proscribed the Communist Party and led to the internment in a concentration camp of many hundreds of suspected communists. Finally repealed in 1957.

liebre – small fast bus seating about twenty.

machitún – pagan, religious ceremony of the Mapuche Indians, led by the *machi* or witch-doctor.

maestro chasquilla – odd-job man, jack of all trades, self-taught plumber, carpenter, electrician, ready to put his hand to anything.

mamita – 'little mother', term of endearment.

MAPU – Movimiento de Acción Popular Unificado – one of the parties of Popular Unity, founded in 1969 by former Christian Democrats.

Mapuche – name of the indigenous Indians of the centre and south of Chile (Araucanian).

mate – herb tea, drunk especially in Argentina, from a gourd.

mate con malicia – mate laced with *aguardiente*, strong spirit.

El Mercurio — old-established right-wing newspaper, *The Times* of Chile.

micro — bus, usually of the larger, slower sort.

militante — a member of a political party.

MIR — Movimiento de Izquierda Revolucionario, ultra-left party founded at the University of Concepción in 1965. MIR was not part of the Popular Unity coalition, and gave only critical support to the Allende government.

mistela — home-made liqueur made from different fruits.

La Moneda — the Presidential Palace in the centre of Santiago.

MOPARE — organisation of small lorry-owners founded in 1972 to support Popular Unity during the first bosses' strike.

ojotas — rough sandals with leather thongs and soles made from old motor tyres.

Patria y Libertad — Fatherland and Freedom, Chile's fascist party.

patrón/patrona — boss, owner, master, mistress, head of household.

pebre — hot-tasting garnish made with chopped coriander, lemon juice, oil, chili and garlic.

pelusas — nickname for stray, homeless children who sleep out in the streets. Implies that they are future delinquents.

peña — in Spain a literary gathering where poets read their work, but in Chile a place or event where folk music is performed in an informal atmosphere, with the audience sitting at tables.

pensión — a café, or often just a room in a house, where workers would pay by the week for a regular midday meal. Also a boarding house.

picoroco — edible shellfish.

pituco — a member of the oligarchy or richest class. Refers also to external appearance and is often used as a derogatory expression for someone with affected manners.

piure — edible shellfish.

Plaza de la Constitución – large square in the centre of Santiago, in front of the Presidential Palace.

población – a housing estate, working-class residential district, any village or settlement.

población callampa – shanty-town or 'mushroom' settlement on the fringes of cities. Usually established overnight by groups of homeless squatters, with tents and shacks improvised from plywood and cardboard.

Providencia – main avenue through the barrio alto, with luxurious restaurants, boutiques and tall blocks of flats.

Quechua – the language of the Incas and the Indians of Peru, Bolivia and the north of Chile.

quena – Indian pipe made from bamboo with a simple U-shaped mouthpiece, used in the music of the altiplano and the north of Chile.

Ranquil – remote village in the south of Chile that gave its name to the first, and eventually the largest, farm-workers' union.

roto – member of the poorest class. Derogatory term for appearance, manners, etc. *El roto Chileno* – object of many anthropological studies as an expression of national character, sense of humour in adversity, etc.

ruca – typical cone-shaped home of Mapuche Indians, made of branches and mud.

San Cristóbal – large hill on the north-east side of Santiago, quite close to the city centre, ascended by a rickety funicular.

Santa Lucía – smaller hill closer to the city centre, opposite the Catholic University, with a park and garden on it.

sirilla – Chilean folk-dance.

surazo – strong south wind.

Tancazo – the attempted coup against Popular Unity on 29 June 1973, led by Colonel Roberto Souper who commanded the second tank regiment (hence *Tancazo*).

tiple – twelve-stringed guitar from Colombia.

tortilla – flat, thin pancake made from maize flour.

UTE – Universidad Técnica del Estado, the State Technical University. The Santiago campus was situated on the west side of the city, towards the airport and on the opposite side to the barrio alto.

vega – a market, especially selling fruit and vegetables.

venceremos – we shall win.

villancico – Christmas carol.

zampoña – pan pipes, made from reeds, used by the Indians of the altiplano and with the peculiarity that to complete a scale you need two sets, played by different musicians.

zapateo – stamping and heel-tapping of folk-dances.

INDEX

Wolf, Egon 76; *Los Invasores* 76
women: belief in Christian Democrats 86–7; political activity 169–73, 201, 202; and song movement 190–1
workers: theatre groups 119; holiday camps 151–2; *see also* CUT; trade unions
Worthing Repertory Council 109–10

Yarur family 171
Young Communists 125, 136, 233; *Jota* 196
Yupanki, Atahualpa 46, 57, 82

zampoñas 83, 104
Zucovic, Edmundo Pérez 120, 121, 180; his son's school 122–4